THE RIGHT WAY

A practical guide to distributor models. Why some work and others don't.

AMIT VAIDYA

Grosvenor House
Publishing Limited

This book is published by
Grosvenor House Publishing Ltd
Link House
140 The Broadway, Tolworth, Surrey, KT6 7HT.
www.grosvenorhousepublishing.co.uk

A CIP record for this book
is available from the British Library

ISBN 978-1-80381-782-8
eBook ISBN 978-1-80381-783-5

Disclaimer Notice

Please note the information contained within this document is based on my experience and is for educational and information purposes only. It may serve as a reference document to help anyone tasked with improving or setting up an international scaleup for business or considering a career choice to move into international sales. The examples are drawn from my experiences in Africa, but most are applicable and transferable into any geographic territory, including "emerging markets" elsewhere. All possible effort has been made to present the reader with correct, up-to-date, dependable, and complete information. Some of the content is my personal viewpoint and understanding derived from my experience. Changes in legislation after authoring this book may have implications for what I have recorded based on my experiences before such changes. The reader should assess the suitability of the content for the markets under consideration.

No warranties of any kind are declared or implied. Readers acknowledge that the author is not engaging in rendering legal, financial, medical, or professional advice. Please take proper professional advice before trying any models or techniques outlined in this book.

By reading this document, the reader agrees that under no circumstances is the author or publisher responsible for any losses, direct or indirect, which may be incurred because of the use of the information contained in this document, including, but not limited to, errors, omissions or inaccuracies or changes in legislation that may have been implemented after this book went to publication.

Table of Contents

About the Author

Amit Vaidya is a life science graduate with a B.Sc. Biological Sciences whilst also holding joint honours in Biochemistry and Microbiology. He is a United Kingdom citizen, having been born outside the UK in India, but he has lived in the UK from a young age.

He has enjoyed a corporate life in the pharmaceutical industry for over forty years, which led to a huge accumulation of expertise and experience in the UK, Europe, and International Markets as well as global manufacturing.

He joined the British Pharmaceutical giant ICI Pharmaceuticals as a salesperson during a period where new product launches would trigger planned growth. ICI Pharmaceuticals was de-merged from ICI's diverse businesses to create a focused pharmaceutical business named Zeneca in 1993. Zeneca was then merged with Astra AB of Sweden in 1999 to create a global Premier League Pharmaceutical company called AstraZeneca.

His abilities, demonstrated through consistent and sustained results-delivery, meant that he progressed quickly through roles of increasing responsibility. These involved such varied roles as sales training, sales management, business development, international change manager in the supply chain and logistics function within manufacturing operations as well as being the Programme Manager implementing a major business change project sponsored by the company's Chief Financial Officer (CFO) across fifteen European affiliates of AstraZeneca. These affiliates collectively made up one-third of global sales revenues for the company and required the change project to be managed to time, quality and budget. With such a broad base of coalface experience and exposure to senior stakeholders, for his last seven years at AstraZeneca, he was appointed as Territory Director Africa in the Europe Middle East Africa (EMEA) Region based out of the UK.

The role was a General Management (GM) role that carried full Profit & Loss (P&L) accountability for 18 markets in Africa where he reshaped and redesigned these 'distributor markets' to exceed sales and profit targets. Each year, he consistently saw results that were above budget and he grew the business at high double-digit figures, exceeding the budget year-on-year.

He set up Samkoman Consulting Ltd in 2009, drawing on his pan-African experience to help global top 20 pharmaceutical companies with their issues and pain points in Africa.

At the time of authoring this book, his experience with distributor models or partnership markets spans over twenty years of working with senior executives on their international scale-up challenges.

Seniors had remarked openly that they found this geographic region to be a complex set of markets that eluded many of them in regard to the delivery of results. Many showed a poor grasp and understanding of 'distributor models' for scaleup and success factors. They shared how difficult it was to find strong, talented staff that had a good grasp of distributor commercial models that could demonstrate their competence and abilities through sustained results delivery.

Thus, a gap in know-how, referring to how you could succeed through using distributor models and finding talent, was identified.

After more than a decade of consulting with these clients, he decided to capture his experience and expertise in this book to help others meet the challenge of international scaleup and expansion.

How should we view that challenge? Well, in reality, it's a simple one.

The challenge is *"how to deliver and achieve a critical mass within five or ten years"* instead of the typical results experienced by so many companies with country clusters of small value businesses that barely make any impression on the market opportunities that attracted the expansion investment in the first place.

Seniors desired a magic elixir that could transform their results and deliver to expectations against the size of those opportunities.

Such an 'elixir' was the collective cognitive bandwidth gained from analyses, recommendations, and outcomes derived from helping clients with their pain points whilst noting the remarkable similarities in those clients' issues that are distilled into this book.

What clients paid in fees and the learnings that he shared with them are captured in this book at a mere fraction of those fees. The content is entirely based on experience and real life rather than textbook theories. This makes this book rather unique in its offering and content.

He currently works as a boardroom advisor advising senior executives on international scaleup and expansion. He draws on his corporate and consulting career to guide, challenge and advise seniors on their strategies and their plans; after all, he retains a strong interest in helping clients address the issues they face in Sub-Saharan Africa (SSA).

This book is dedicated to

All the many friends and colleagues I have had in the International Departments of AstraZeneca, having worked with them as Territory Director for Africa in the Europe Middle East Africa Region. There are simply too many to list individually, but I am grateful for the help, support, and expertise they have shared with me that enabled me to develop professionally with distributor or partnership markets through working with such talented colleagues.

It is often said that *"As iron sharpens iron, so one talented person sharpens another."*

This is stated in the Holy Bible in Proverbs 27:17.

My iron was sharpened by working with and through others with talent. As was their iron sharpened by working with me.

The book is also dedicated to the many and various clients who have allowed me to engage with them to help address their international businesses, and to all staff who find themselves in a role that involves developing international business in poorly understood markets that often require a new commercial model working with and through external distributor partners. Such markets are often described as *"distributor markets"* or *"partnership markets."*

The book is also dedicated to supporting and developing Business School students who will form the next generation of international scale-up experts in areas that are likely poorly (if at all) covered in the curriculum of a Business Management qualification for Undergraduate, Post-Graduate and MBA students.

I want to thank the close inner circle of contacts who have inspired me to author this book and gave me praise and motivation to share my experience for the benefit of others.

I believe that authoring this book will help anyone accountable for international sales in distributor markets to avoid the errors I have had to correct, the mistakes I have seen, even within Big Pharma Corporations, and in doing so, readers will develop a strong foundation of the export and international sales skills sadly found lacking in staff by many seniors.

There are no shortcuts to success. Especially not in 'distributor' or 'partnership' markets. as many senior executives have found out. Many found out through the painful inability to deliver their promises and their numbers to the corporate Executive Boards to whom they were ultimately accountable. Distributor or partnership markets are of varying degrees of complexity. None of them are easy markets to succeed in. What does success look like?

That is simple to answer.

Success is the ability to deliver an ambitious investment case and critical mass numbers leveraging the investments agreed within a five- or ten-year period. Such a simple statement of success. But phenomenally few seniors have or can deliver it. This is particularly the case in markets of Sub-Saharan Africa (SSA); however, it is equally applicable to many other geographies as I will explain.

The common denominator is a lack of understanding of distributor models that I have unravelled for readers in this book.

Foreword

By Jason Hanford
(Executive Search Consultant and Talent Partner)

For more than 25 years, I have been intimately involved with recruitment and executive searches for senior and middle management positions in the Middle East and Africa, as well as other Emerging Markets regions. Throughout that time, I have seen first-hand the challenges that my clients faced on several fronts.

Firstly, one sees the scarcity of talent to find within these regions. This is something that the author, Amit Vaidya, describes as regions with *"a high prevalence of candidates not having a consistent track record of delivery of results versus targets over several years supported by and demonstrated through evidence in writing of their results on company-headed letters and papers."*

Secondly, those job holders, who are ultimately responsible for international exports and international business development, struggle to understand the different options for go-to-market models with little or no appreciation of the pros and cons of those options. It is, in my opinion, little wonder then that they end up with underperformance and a continued state of flux in trying various models and routes to market.

Thirdly, many clients and companies apply models from one market to several others with no success. This then leads to successive rounds of restructuring and changes of senior crew while the business fails to move a step closer to attaining any critical mass.

Lastly, we see the inability to deliver and scale a business that can achieve a critical mass, thus highlighting to me and others that, from a purely business perspective, Africa is the promise that never quite gives. Many companies have registered products for export but failed miserably after five or more years of investment. Their Executive Boards demanded to know why the projections and forecasts on which those investment cases were based could not be delivered by those regional seniors and locals. Very few seniors could offer credible explanation for such miserable results. Executive Boards became accustomed to hearing the same set of recycled excuses each year by their staff.

I have known the author since his corporate life at AstraZeneca back in 2003 to the present day, as he exited that corporate life and set up Samkoman Consulting Ltd to focus on the international scale-up challenges in Africa. In this book, he explains all the above challenges, why they could not be met, and how to go about correcting them.

Amit Vaidya has always impressed me in both parts of his phenomenally successful journeys – as a corporate senior Director at AstraZeneca and then as Director of his own consulting company. His record of accomplishment at AstraZeneca is exemplary. His transition into consulting was equally impressive, landing high-value consulting assignments for the global top 20 pharmaceutical companies operating out of Africa.

He has amassed a wealth of experience within the UK, Europe, and Middle East Africa regions that I have always felt should not be lost. I have been one of a few people who have beckoned him to write about his experiences for the benefit of others who struggle with international business development where the go-to-market models involve working with and through distributors.

I have always found his style and tone very distinctive, as he says it as it is. His forthright and straight-talking manner has been appreciated by many, who label him as an 'expert' in international exports and scaleups. I am impressed not only by the content of his book but also by the distinctive tone and style that he uses.

Some of the content is forthright. It is for the reader to judge if they accept his remarks or reject them. But before rejection, readers would be well urged to remind themselves of the learnings he has shared – warts and all. It is through those glimpses of the problems and flaws that the readers can learn from others' mistakes and, more importantly, how to avoid them in the future.

That amply brings me back to the title of the book:

> THE RIGHT WAY: A practical guide to distributor models. Why some work and others don't.

By reading this book, readers will understand the range of distributor models, how to set up, scale up and deliver critical mass alongside their numbers, all whilst avoiding the mistakes made by so many, so often.

In short, readers will find the right way through the models that can deliver critical mass, and understand why many of the models will not work.

The author highlights that there is no magic bullet to success. As an author, he identifies the need for developing a deep understanding through a broad cognitive bandwidth, impeccable analytical and critical reasoning skills, and a razor-sharp focus on the financial side of running a business.

He goes on to highlight the need to address both the demand-creation as well as the supply-fulfilment factors in international business and he proposes several models of how that can be effectively achieved. Further to that, he openly shares his views on the profile and skills needed in candidates he believes would be strong for consideration in regard to these roles and he explains why with his impeccably reasoned logic and detail.

Having reviewed the book and been involved in the evolution of the chapters, I can recommend this book to readers who can and will become strong international sales professionals if they apply his learnings and experiences to their activities. If you can consider the models he has painted through his eyes and experiences, you will have a strong guiding light to illuminate a path to your success.

Background

Much of the literature on this subject, which I read when I did my research, proved to be generic content of little relevance to the pharmaceutical and life sciences industry. I discovered that the books and materials available largely focused on exporting left-handed widgets, hand-made jewellery, hand-woven baskets, homemade handicrafts and setting up an export business from the comfort of one's home. Other content included topics such as sole trader versus limited company, and the equipment to buy (such as a PC and software for running an export business) without setting foot in another country! From that research, I became aware that there was a gap in the literature that required specialist ability and knowledge in regulated markets gained through experience.

There is a demand for specialists in these commercial models of business.

Seniors gave me feedback during consulting assignments that there was a lack of understanding of scaleup models and distributors, an understanding that I had clearly demonstrated in my assignments with them. They highlighted a need for me to publish information to help the present and future generations undergoing study in a Business Management or MBA discipline to learn my craft of international sales and business development.

Seniors in the pharma industry shared how difficult it was to find international sales executives who could understand and put into practice these specialist models. They confirmed a strong need for a book based on my specific experience of setting up and running an international pharmaceutical business, drawing on my successful career at AstraZeneca and the knowledge gained from over a decade of consulting to global top 20 pharmaceutical companies, seeing their mistakes and proposing recommendations to correct those mistakes.

These seniors went on to state that the contents of the book must be relevant across different sectors and various geographical locations and should present broad applications concerning common challenges.

Selling pharmaceuticals is a tightly regulated industry that current books on developing an export business do not recognise. The global top 50 pharmaceutical companies are reliant on international sales outside of their country of origin or country of legal status. The same applies to many companies beyond the pharmaceutical sector.

Given that there is such a huge reliance on developing international sales, there is a remarkable absence of any books on this subject that are either specific to the pharmaceutical industry on starting up or scaling up a pharmaceutical business in new countries or that have applications across different industries.

I have filled this gap by drawing on my personal, real-life, direct experience, in contrast with other textbooks that have only generic content. This book is probably unique in its specificity, but at the same time it still offers general applicability beyond pharmaceuticals too.

Introduction

First, a big welcome to you, the reader, and thank you for buying this book. If you have been working in International Pharmaceutical Sales and Business Development, this book will strengthen your understanding and open the doors to how you can drive an enhanced sales and Profit & Loss (P&L) account that will impress seniors.

If you are already a senior director, this book will help you to drive confidence with the Executive Board as to why you should invest in international scaleup and expansion, and how you will avoid the mistakes of the past.

If you are a student or an employee who is new to or considering a move into international sales, this book will be the first step you take towards understanding what is involved and how to go about actually doing it. You will be better prepared to succeed from the outset and avoid the mistakes I have seen so often, made by so many.

This book is unique in so many ways.

Everything in this book is based on my real-life experience gained in over twenty years of international business development as Territory Director Africa for AstraZeneca and as Director of my own consulting company focused on clients' international business scaleup and delivery of their numbers.

For over a decade of consulting to global top 20 players, I was focused at one end of a scale, helping them expand and set up new businesses in new markets. At the other end of the scale, I worked with their established businesses where I helped them address their painful issues and disappointing sales performance in existing markets. I drew upon my corporate experience in the Europe Middle East Africa (EMEA) Region, with examples drawn from my time focused on Africa.

The lessons from Africa are highly relevant to so many international sales and export business challenges, both within the pharmaceutical and life science sector and the broader areas of devices and diagnostics and in sectors outside of them.

This content will be relevant anywhere and, in any market, where the commercial model involves designing, selecting, negotiating, and operating through distributor models. You could be working in the Latin American and Central American markets, the Caribbean Islands, Eastern Europe, the Middle East, or the Southeast Asia markets where the models involve distributor partners. The real-life examples and lessons from my time in Africa are largely transferable to all these regions, where I know similar mistakes and disappointments occur.

My suggestion is that you consider my examples from Africa and assume that they apply to your markets until you prove otherwise. This is the safest approach. If you assume they do not apply when they may do, you could be making a serious mistake that will ultimately reveal itself to you and your seniors.

Those readers involved with Africa may particularly benefit from the experience that I share. It may give a view of why they felt frustrated at not delivering the expected business results for their seniors while citing the same set of recycled excuses for failure many times over with the results never getting better, year after year. Or it may unlock the puzzle that frustrates seniors involved with Africa and can be a precursor to a career derailment move.

Some senior executives have quietly confided in me that *"Africa was a geography they never mastered."* They would go on to cite how they suffered much frustration at not being able to *'sort out Africa'*. They often said that if they lived their life again as P&L account holders for Africa, it would be a territory that they would want to take on and win.

But the *'how to win'* always eluded them in the past and they were never confident that they could unlock that magic box of *'how to win'*. In this book, I will unravel piece by piece why they could not 'win', what they needed to consider, and what they needed to do to succeed.

My oft-quoted mantra resonated with senior executives responsible for Africa, including recruiters, senior HR and 'Talent Acquisition' partners who saw my words come to life repeatedly in their failed attempts to succeed without my involvement:

> *"The plains of Sub-Saharan Africa are littered with the corpses of corporate heroes who bravely went in declaring them to be lands of opportunity. They were excited to meet the challenges set by them, only to find that they needed to beat a hasty retreat within two years, admitting defeat with a career that was quickly derailing and leading towards an enforced exit from the company."*

Recruiters and Head-hunters, HR, as well as Talent Succession Partners, wanted to know how to pick a candidate that could succeed in (a) export/international sales and (b) in the African geographies. This book will help them. See the chapter dedicated to how to pick winners for international business and the profile of a person who can succeed in International Sales and Scaleup, not just in Africa, but anywhere where the business go-to-market model involves finding, selecting, and negotiating commercial agreements with third-party partners that are typically described as "distributor or partner models".

This book is intended for all those working in export and international sales development roles and any seniors who have responsibility for export sales development either directly or through staff working for them. This latter group will particularly find the contents appealing as they will understand why their sales and Profit & Loss (P&L) account results do not deliver the expected figures and why export sales do not reach any sizeable critical mass despite year-on-year investment.

What is remarkable is that senior executives at the Corporate Main Board throw money year after year into a broken model in Africa, keeping staff that cannot deliver in Africa for far too long. Even more remarkable is the reluctance of seniors and Executive Boards to bring in external expertise. Instead, they want to rely on the same staff that, year in and year out, failed, and disappointed them with an inability to produce solutions. Often these senior executives do more of the same and expect a different set of results! Truly bizarre! Einstein once remarked:

"Insanity is doing more of the same thing over and over and expecting different results".

Failure to achieve a 'critical mass' despite years of investment is still the Achilles heel of so many senior executives accountable for delivering the P&L for Sub-Saharan Africa (SSA) and many other distributor markets. One of the reasons why corporate seniors at the Board level cannot achieve a critical mass is because of how they came to be investing in Africa and other emerging markets, which I will briefly elaborate on here.

In some instances, their investment is the result of a 'deep dive' commissioned through large consulting practices or following-the-herd investments made by peer and competitor companies with hugely different portfolios and segments. Where Africa and other emerging markets are involved, these investments may be based on often flawed deep-dive exercises sold for huge fees by big consulting practices and third-party partners.

Such recommendations of sales and profit projections are rarely (if ever) realisable from the outset! I can say that because I know where the method is flawed, and why.

But those presentations by big consulting practices are hugely impressive. If I did not know the markets better and deeper than those consultants, I would fail to spot the flaws.

That leads me to share my other mantra that resonates with seniors across Africa:

"They do not know what they do not know."

Is it any wonder that they believe that everything is the way it is presented?

They are unable to challenge or question the content when they do not know what to challenge or how to challenge the presenters with those fancy graphs and charts. They do not know what is missing or what is relevant to their business. They do not recognise that, quite probably, the data is irrelevant to their segment of the market.

Believe me, it happens.

Clients see impressive figures and link them with their portfolios. Those consulting practices with their impressive graphs and charts want you, the client, to make those subliminal associations. You have persuaded yourself those figures and projections are doable! You are well and truly hooked!

But so often, the figures are not relevant to the portfolio or the segment in which they are working! So, in this book, I will share with you along the way how the smoke and mirrors of big consulting firms, distributors and logistics partners are presented and how to spot them.

Another consequence when seniors *do not know what they do not know* is that they do not diagnose issues. So, the solutions are usually inappropriate and ill-defined. The solution must evolve out of a process of creating clarity on the issue.

A key weakness is that so many clients cannot define the issue. Implementing any solution because *"we think this might work,"* in the absence of understanding and defining the root cause, is merely shooting in the dark.

Shooting in the dark does not work. You can end up shooting yourself in the foot. Many do just that. I am always tempted to ask client staff in such instances:

> "Do you know what you are doing? Do you really know your business?"

Believe me, many do not know what they are doing, and their senior Executive Boards do not know either.

That is why, in my consulting assignments, I focus on defining the real issue before looking at solutions. I use a questioning technique that my seniors used with me in my corporate life that clients have always found extremely useful. Without really defining the issues, clients just do anything in the mistaken belief it might work. That is why I focus so intensely on defining and understanding the issues through skilful questioning and sprinklings of playing Devil's Advocate. I use the same techniques and processes my seniors used on me that developed my diagnostic skills. I have concluded that many clients lack diagnostic skills, and my technique can fill a skills gap.

The classic sign to me as an outsider of a company that does not know what it is doing and cannot diagnose the issue accurately is a combination of two or more of the following:

- Failure to deliver budgets for the sales and Profit & Loss account (P&L) for two or more consecutive years. Anyone can be forgiven for missing the budget for one year. But two consecutive years? It means repeatedly being a failure, unable to keep your promises, which is an undesirable habit.

- Constant meddling and dabbling with structures.

- Meddling with and changing reporting lines.

- Increasing staff for one year only to then lay them off within two years.

- Swinging from one distributor to another – swapping from the current partner to another distributor they know even less well than the current distributor!

- Swinging the model from one distributor to multiple distributors every two or three years (sometimes even more often!).

- Relinquishing staff to be put under the management of the distributor partner and achieving no improvement in the results. Consider for a moment how short-sighted this really is. If with your focus on your brands, with your insights and your experience of your brands, you still cannot deliver budgets and attain a critical mass, then tell me how an organisation outside of your boundary will do any better. They know even less than you about your brands and lack the collective skills of your organisation. In addition, they have many interests across different clients' products, resulting in even less focus on your brands than you can dedicate. So, considering all of that, tell me how a distributor will deliver the numbers with even less knowhow of your brands and their marketing and go on to attain and deliver a critical mass for you? I have seen this manoeuvre several times across different clients. It never ceases to amaze me the lack of cognitive bandwidth among such seniors.

- High staff churn within short tenures (typically less than three years in these senior roles).

When I see these signs as a consultant, I know that the seniors in that business have little or next to no idea what they are doing. And seniors like this are in greater abundance than you might imagine. Their job titles may be fancy, but that offers no guarantee in regard to their abilities in distributor markets.

Dabbling and meddling (for want of better words) are often the case in so many companies in Africa. They just make mistake after mistake, blunder after blunder. Yet their seniors in the corporate head offices are remarkably tolerant of successive years of underperformance and failure to deliver agreed budget numbers and still keep them in their jobs to continue to underperform year in, year out.

And, to crown it all, they will not take on outside expertise. Instead, they will rely on the same internal staff that created the mess to produce solutions. Of course, they have shown repeatedly they are unable to do so, as I highlighted earlier.

Bizarre as it sounds, it is true. And it is more prevalent at the Corporate Executive Board level than you might think. Some simply attempt to bury the bad performance and sweep it under the rug in the Boardroom. Some Boardroom rugs must be hiding a lot of mess.

The mistakes I have seen and witnessed have been put on paper in this book in an attempt to fill a gap; much-needed information and advice has simply not been available in any textbook that I have seen or read. To these examples, I have added my experience as an international sales leader from a *"been there, done that and got the scars to prove it"* viewpoint.

The mistakes cover the following broad but not exclusive areas:

1. Wrong model

2. Wrong partner

3. Wrong person in the role

This book should be a standard curriculum item for business studies students and MBAs as well as for export professionals and those aspiring to move into a senior export sales role. It is not intended for an export clerk whose focus is on making the shipment compliant with legal frameworks. That is an admin role, and this book is not for administrators, but it is for people with sales and P&L accountability for international business. From middle managers right through to corporate Executive Boards, including their CEO and direct reports.

This book should be essential reading for anyone working in export markets through distributors. It is a Masterclass. I would like it to be adopted as The Bible for this area of specialist business. But you, the reader, can only make that adoption after reading it.

Why Should You Read My Book and Rely on My Experience?

You may be wondering to yourself: "Why would I want to listen to his experience?" You may be wondering what credentials I have that would inspire you to sit up and listen.

Let me illustrate this for you.

I inherited Africa as an export territory that had failed to deliver for three successive years after the merger of Astra with Zeneca. The merger demanded greater velocity of operational success, an ambition that had to be delivered across business units and their functions. The business was no longer tolerant of "we try to do what we can in Africa", which was a synonym for underperformance and inability to deliver the numbers.

The brief was to assess this distributor business across 18 markets of Anglophone (English-speaking) Sub-Saharan Africa (SSA) and recommend what needed to be done, to invest for growth given that the Board passionately believed there were opportunities that we were not leveraging. I was given six months to make those recommendations.

Not surprisingly, after visiting all my key markets and spending a week in each one, my recommendation was to invest for growth.

Why?

Because what I saw were largely situations that I had the influence and power to change, namely:

- The choice and terms of commercial agreements were poorly negotiated.
- Marketing was anorexic.
- New products had failed to make an impact and their launches and post-launch activities were poor with poor sales results after significant investments.

- There was too much reliance on the business being in the hands of distributors (a bad mistake).
- The distributors had had it too good for too long.
- Distributors had no accountability for delivery.
- Distributors would continually cite that our prices were too high. Or they would say the competitors had been stronger influencers on prescribers with greater marketing spend and they had more reps, demanding that I should spend even more money on a business that was not meeting budgets!
- Distributors blamed the poor results on the company, never on the distributor.
- Performance management and accountability were absent.
- Perversely, staff received year-on-year pay raises and bonus payments for not delivering budgets!

Does this resonate with you?

Well, take consolation. You are not alone. There are more companies in this situation than you can imagine. But very few have turned it around. I am going to show you in this book how you can do that and turn it around.

Looking at the portfolio of products registered in my markets, the product mix was poor. There was too much business in old mature products. This exposed a major weakness. These mature brands were declining in worldwide volumes. This meant their cost-of-goods (COGs) – what it costs to make them – was rising year-on-year while global volumes were decreasing, which overshadowed any growth in Africa's volumes for these mature brands. This had driven the margins lower and lower. Compensatory price rises were out of the question when the prices were already considered too high for most patients. The business was suffering from a downward pressure on gross margins.

In any R&D innovator company, the pricing of the products, reflecting the development costs and risks, meant that the prices were only affordable to a narrow group of patients. In my case, this meant no more than 10% of the population in each country, and for some therapy areas, such as cancer and oncology, probably 3-5% of the population. I found that the business had been positioned as trying to be all things to all people. By this, I mean distributors wanted to operate in the high-volume low-margin segment at the base-of-the-pyramid population (the poor and vulnerable populations) as well as the wealthy middle classes who could pay more and wanted to pay more for reliable European-manufactured brands to avoid the risk of fakes and counterfeits that are prevalent across distributor and emerging markets and African countries.

Penetration into the base of the pyramid population was ridiculously small.

My personal belief is that no company can straddle two stools like this – being positioned for the poor people who drive low prices for access and simultaneously positioned as a premium price company for the wealthier middle classes.

Indeed, some company seniors straddle these two stools as corporate policy in Africa. I am unconvinced by the rationale of such seniors. It will only be a matter of time (in my view) before a change in senior leadership will bring a profound change of model to become either access-driven with low prices, as a philanthropic not-for-profit model, or a model based on premium pricing for optimising profit through a much smaller, wealthier segment of the population.

As if these situations were not enough to raise the hairs on the back of my neck, there was also an absence of any sound control mechanisms and business processes.

When I visualised what I saw in those visits to each of my major markets, the analogy appeared of a pilot getting into a plane with a throttle and stick but no gauges or dials or instruments! Some of the windows were blacked out, obscuring the pilot's vision from the cockpit!

The pilot was flying by sight at an altitude where this was simply not possible as if he were flying the aeroplane blind from several thousand miles away from a glorious office block.

For so many companies, this is how they run Africa – at arm's length from a comfortable office chair in the UK or Dubai or Turkey or South Africa, and some are even based in Singapore!

I assessed that the business I had inherited had been on its deathbed for the previous three years. However, the sickness was not terminal, but recoverable. A dramatic recovery and turn-around strategy would be required, and it needed to focus not on one area but several areas simultaneously.

These areas of focus included:

- New commercial deals.
- Repositioning the business to focus on the wealthy middle classes who can afford premium high-quality European manufactured products instead of pricing them down to an incredibly low base-of-pyramid population price. I honestly believe that you cannot ride two horses in this business. You need to be clear and focused. Either go for the wealthy population or go for the cheap pricing for the poor populace model. But you cannot target both. Having a foot in two camps is not a strategy. It is indecision. And indecision claims seniors' lives in this game – the lives of the very folk who many argue are paid to make good decisions!

  I describe such seniors as:

  "They used to be indecisive, but now they are not so sure!"

- Tighter controls and adoption of sound prospective business planning processes.
- Training in skills. This is a vital investment so long as it is done well. Otherwise, it is an absolute waste of money. I had been a Sales Training Manager at Zeneca UK before the merger with Astra, so I knew I could design the best, most productive training and development interventions that could create a step-change in productivity and results. I knew behavioural-based training very well over the often 'death by PowerPoint®' training provided by providers across Africa that did nothing to change behaviours and change the skill levels of the audience.

- Restructuring the sales teams and field forces on product mix and customer segments. The focus on the portfolio was ill-thought-out and needed dramatic restructuring and realignment.
- Creating a laser-sharp focus on planning and preparing the markets for launching new higher-margin (more profitable) products. We needed to change the shape of the portfolio and increase the percentage of business coming from the newer (high-margin) brands.
- Implementing financial and activity targets on a monthly and quarterly basis underpinned by high accountability through rigorous target setting and the necessary business review processes.

The investment paid off. Sales were transformed.

I delivered stretching P&L targets year-on-year for seven tough demanding years for an equally tough and demanding senior executive boss with high double-digit growth ahead of budget year-on-year!!

Allow me to share some figures which demonstrate why I am qualified to author this book and why readers should take heed and learn from me.

My 5-year Compound Annual Growth Rate (CAGR) at Constant Exchange Rates (CER) for sales was 18% per annum versus a Budget of 11%. At that time European markets for the pharmaceutical industry were growing at low single-digit rates as was North American (2-4%). Japan had negative growth. The MDs of many pharmaceutical companies in Japan could grow volume by low double digits but show only low single-digit value growth!

My Profit CAGR growth was 35% per annum versus a budget of 17%.

My Sales CAGR growth was 18% per annum versus a budget of 11%.

My Cost CAGR growth was 3% per annum versus a budget of 7%.

I was growing sales and profit faster than costs! Because the growth in values was at CER, this meant value growth was created through volume growth, not currency exchange rate fluctuations. In other words, for a prescription-based pharmaceuticals business, I was finding new patients for my brands. That is the only way to create volume growth, by gaining more patients for more brands. But achieving this eludes many, and my clients were testimony to this. This is 'demand creation' in action.

I got a lot of things right and demonstrated that I knew what I was doing. Cost-of-sales fell from 46% of sales at my start in the role to 18% at my exit seven years later. This means I was spending 18 cents to generate one dollar of sales whereas my predecessor handed me a business on his exit from the company that was having to spend 46 cents to generate one dollar with downward pressure on margins!

Many a senior executive would give his right hand for such metrics and performance!

I set up Samkoman Consulting back in 2009 when I took that tremendous set of lessons and achievements at AstraZeneca and combined it with my experience in other roles in that company in sales, marketing, training, business development and commercial excellence. The vital knowledge I gained in supply chain and logistics in manufacturing operations, when added to this (demand side) experience enabled a rich cocktail of solutions for the global top twenty pharmaceutical companies. That supply chain and logistics experience was a strong factor in my success in restructuring the distributor models across Africa.

Quite simply, I could work seamlessly across the demand-creation through to the supply-fulfilment axis, where other consultants could only work at one or the other end of that axis, which limited the value they could bring to their clients. Working at one end of that axis and ignoring the other end is a recipe for failure from the outset. It means a disjointed approach. Clients needed a joined-up approach they had hitherto not received from any consultants before my approach to them. It felt like a revelation to these clients when I knocked on their doors to offer my help.

I was truly an ambidextrous consultant! I could use either my left or my right hand with equal dexterity.

I came to be seen by my clients as a human equivalent in international sales of the Swiss Army Knife: versatile, well-adapted, a walking toolkit for every business issue, with intellectual capital of various shapes and sizes and able to use my cognitive bandwidth to switch between issues to be addressed. This rich blend of skills meant I was uniquely placed among the plethora of consultants out there vying for the same work as me. They were either supply-focused or demand-focused, but they were unable to 'join the dots' across the supply/demand axis in the way I was.

I could look at a client's business and whereas others might see disparate and unconnected issues, I could see a constellation of stars that gave me a picture that senior executives and their prior consultants could not. Much like gazing at the night sky, I would see the stars that made up Orion, or the Great Bear or the Plough and if a star were missing or misplaced in the constellation, it was clear to me. It stood out for me – a glaring omission or oversight by the senior executive team!

To succeed in international export sales, you must understand and address BOTH the supply AND the demand side of the equation. A serious mistake made by so many, so often, came from just looking at one or the other, but not both.

I never looked back after I left AstraZeneca and set up my own consulting company.

From speaking at global conferences on emerging markets and being invited into organisations that had issues and were inspired by my rich experience, I worked to help them – and I won repeat business. I also prospected new clients and landed fee-paying consulting assignments from those activities. I chose which work to take on and which not to get involved in. I saw businesses that had been sold inappropriate supply and go-to-market models that were never going to drive their success or address the issues they were supposed to solve.

Instead, those models lined the pockets of the third-party providers who sold them, often at great costs that would have been largely avoidable if they had considered my solutions. I highlight why they could never succeed with those models in this book.

How to Get the Most from this Book

Clients had learnt with my engagements that *"they had not known at the time what they should have known"* before accepting whatever any third-party providers and consultants say and recommend.

In this book, I share the details of what I did, how I did it, what I learned, and the mistakes I and my clients made that I urge any reader not to make when running an international sales business with ambitious scaleup aspirations set by seniors.

I share the mistakes I have seen in client organisations (appropriately and without names for confidentiality).

Read this book. Keep it as a handy reference on any international business trip or meeting with distributors. Make notes from it before a meeting with a distributor to help you prepare for negotiations and discussions.

I recommend reading this book with a notepad beside you to list actions that you need to consider. Do not worry, it might become a big list. But I will try to help you in the narrative to set some priorities in regard to what to tackle and in what order.

The best thing you the reader should take away is a call to action to take steps to change what you do and how you work. Translate my shared experience into tangible actions and commit to doing them. Ideas and my experiences in a book will not give you a distinct set of results. Your actions from reading my book will change your results. Commit yourself to action to change the results. Learn from this masterclass. As I have stated earlier, Einstein once remarked:

> *"Doing more of the same and expecting a different set of results was the first sign of lunacy!"*

If you want to change the results, do things differently. This book will highlight what you need to do differently as you read the chapters. Make a list of those actions and commit to them with a sense of the order of priorities. Then you will truly reap a better set of results; results that your seniors will be proud of.

Become a specialist through my shared experiences. The world is full of generalists. Developing international sales in pharmaceuticals calls for specialist skills. These specialist skills are lacking as more pharmaceutical companies close their centrally run export divisions and move the task to regional hubs in different continents to pick up the export activities as mere add-ons to an already heavy burden of business in that home country. They assume those hubs have export sales capabilities to a highly-specialised level.

They do not. Certainly not where Africa is concerned. Believe me, they do not! I know. I have interviewed them on client projects. I know how little and how poorly they and their staff understand the world of exports.

Their seniors blast social media with meaningless PR marketing hyperbole such as:

"Getting close to customers."
"Driving a Patient-Centric Business at the Heart of Customers."
"In Africa for Africa."
"Sustainability is us!"
"Health-for-All Screening Programmes."

None of this means anything. It is just some rubbish someone in Corporate Affairs made up to sound nice to people's ears. Possibly to satisfy questions asked by financial analysts at the quarterly briefings to indicate that we are indeed human. Besides being meaningless, these initiatives rack up costs with several hangers-on creating little value but having a meal ticket for life. I have yet to see one that adds incremental sales to a business.

Take health screening initiatives. In distributor markets, screening programmes do not identify patients for your brands. This sort of investment expands the market to the advantage of generics at your expense.

The false assumption that these hubs have export sales capabilities to the highly specialised level that I possess has been a root cause of so many underperforming distributor markets.

Become a specialist. Stand out from the herd of one-eyed men in a community of companies and recruiters clutching at the straw that regards the one-eyed man as King. There is no gender bias in this book. The term 'male', 'man' and 'he' is equally interchangeable with 'female', 'woman', 'she' and 'her.' Show them you are a King of Kings (or a Queen of Queens) with both your eyes at 20/20 vision and laser-focused, using the experiences I am going to share with you in this book.

There are no textbook theories to be found. Just real, rich, life experiences and examples. You will be high in demand. You will become an expert through this masterclass. Generalists are everywhere. Specialists and experts are rare and highly sought after.

If you do not believe me, talk to a headhunter or talent acquisition partner. They will tell you just how difficult it is to find good strong results-achievement candidates that clients demand in international sales and scaleup roles. This is especially true in Africa.

Look on social media such as LinkedIn and notice how so many of these international salespeople share one thing in common. So many of them share short tenure in the role, typically 18 – 24 months from one company to another. With maybe three or more roles in five years or six roles in less than ten years. Each company seems to discover they made a poor choice at the end of year 1 and by year 2 these members of staff are out.

It is no surprise that such folk who had many short stints over five years cannot produce any written evidence of results delivered. They talk generically about the 'growth' of the business. But that is meaningless. They were generalists, not specialists. What matters is what they delivered against the budget that was set. The answer is highly likely that they did not deliver the budgets that were set. Anyone who talks 'about growth' and not results versus budgets is a bluffer.

Do not be fooled.

Anyone with an impressive results-delivery record of achievements has a portfolio of evidence to prove their abilities through those results. They do not impress through having academic qualifications or talking gibberish about growth or boastful claims of having launched x new products. Notice that they mention nothing about how well those launches went and if they made budgets.

I have seen examples of new product launches that were disastrous! They failed to meet budgets and market share in the first year of launch and, within three years of launch, the products were not being promoted due to abysmally small sales values and poor market uptake and penetration. Cash investment was wasted preparing the market for launch and then wasted again in frantic launch activity that failed to deliver the numbers for new product launches. Imagine taking on such a person. You would be surprised at how many companies take on such a person expecting results only to then become disappointed.

Do not believe such remarks as *"I cannot share the results with you, they are confidential documents"* because you are not asking to keep the documents, you are sight-checking. The reality is that they cannot produce written evidence of success because they do not have the evidence to support successful results delivery sustained over time.

Specialists understand deeply and broadly. They have broad and high cognitive bandwidth. They can join the dots and see the full picture. They deliver results consistently. What do I mean by consistently? In my view, they need to show successful results delivery versus budgets, supported with results on company-headed paper for at least three years but ideally for five or more years.

There is a rationale for this:

In year 1, a job holder can blame the predecessor. In year two he is judged on his results because he submitted and agreed the numbers to be delivered. Many of these guys drop off the edge of the cliff at the end of year 2 or early year 3. Even someone who survives into the third year may not be strong on results delivery with a disappointing set of results in year 3 meaning year 4 cannot be delivered and they are out by the end of year 3/early year 4.

So, assuming year 1 is non-delivery blamed on the earlier guy, you need three strong years to the end of year 4. And if they have four strong years of results, they have been in the post for five years. I look for five years of solid results and documented evidence of delivery.

They are not one-year wonders. They show sustained, consistent results and delivery of the key metrics across the last three roles they have held. But such candidates are exceedingly rare! They can deliver a target to grow their business by 20% in value year-on-year for five years. It is tough. Very tough. As you grow your market share, there are fewer opportunities. But specialists and experts can deliver it.

This book will help you to become a specialist. With that qualification proven by results, you will be in high demand from other companies. Head-hunters, recruiters, and talent partners will be approaching you because word soon gets around who the strong specialists are. You will be likely asked to speak at international conferences and congresses as I was.

List of Abbreviations Used Throughout This Book

I am ever mindful of the need to avoid the use of abbreviations, acronyms, and jargon that may not be clear to readers on first reading. Throughout the book, I precede the first use of an abbreviation with its full word content then the abbreviation in brackets so that readers will then recognise the repeated use of the abbreviation.

Notwithstanding this, I have listed the abbreviations I have used in this summary for ease of reference:

SSA	Sub-Saharan Africa
P&L	Profit & Loss
COGs	Cost of Goods (what they cost to make)
CAGR	Compound Annual Growth Rate
LATAM	Latin America
APAC	Asia Pacific
MEA	Middle East Africa
MENA	Middle East North Africa
EMEA	Europe Middle East Africa
BRICM	Brazil, Russia, India, China, Mexico
NCDs	Non-Communicable Diseases
ICC	International Chamber of Commerce
INCO®	International Commercial Terms
HCR	Holder of Certificates of Registration
API	Active Pharmaceutical Ingredient
KOL	Key Opinion Leader
SOV	Share of Voice

RFP	Request for Proposal
FFM	Forecast for Manufacture (volume forecast)
JIT	Just in Time (manufacturing process)
LCs	Letters of Credit
CAD	Cash Against Documents
GM	General Manager/Management
GCP	Good Clinical Practice
CER	Constant Exchange Rate
FDI	Foreign Direct Investments
cGMP	current Good Manufacturing Practice
FDA	Food & Drugs Administration
PMPA	Pharmaceutical Manufacturing Plan for Africa
CFO	Chief Financial Officer

List of Illustrations and Figures
Throughout the Book

CHAPTER 1

The Focus on Export Sales

Part 1: Legal Frameworks to be Mindful Of

Before we go into details chapter by chapter, I should highlight three legislative areas that require general consideration and if necessary, you should seek specialist expert advice.

For any company listed in the US or working out of the UK, international sales executives need to be mindful of three pieces of legislation that may apply to them in their international expansion and scaleup models. Legislation advice is beyond the scope of this book. Readers must take skilled professional advice to follow any legislation including (but not limited to) the following:

The 2010 UK Bribery Act

This was introduced in 2011. For UK businesses working in the emerging and frontier markets, it had a big effect and they found themselves having to follow some of the toughest anti-corruption rules in the world. It created the following offences:

- Active bribery prohibits giving, promising, or offering a bribe.
- Passive bribery prohibits asking, agreeing to receive, or accepting a bribe.
- Bribing a foreign public official.
- An offence committed by a commercial organisation where a person performing services on the organisation's behalf pays a bribe to obtain or keep a business advantage for the organisation. This is commonly known as the offence of not preventing bribery.

What is a bribe?

The Bribery Act refers to "financial or other advantages" so it does not just cover the payment of money. it can include things such as:

- Gifts and hospitality.
- Employing the relatives of public officials.
- Paying for travel expenses and accommodation costs.
- Making political or charitable donations.
- Engaging the services of a company in which a public official has an interest.

The US Foreign Corrupt Practices Act (US FCPA) Wikipedia gives a broad outline:

https://en.wikipedia.org/wiki/Foreign_Corrupt_Practices_Act

The US Foreign Corrupt Practices Act is an all-encompassing act that according to the reference cited in Wikipedia above, applies to any individual who is a citizen, national, or resident of the U.S. and any business entity organised under the laws of the U.S. or one of its states, or having its principal place of business in the U.S.

Further details are available from the Department of Justice in the U.S.:

https://www.trade.gov/us-foreign-corrupt-practices-act

These URL links are no substitute for a full and proper interpretation of this act and how it applies to you the reader and your business. You are strongly recommended to take skilled professional advice to ensure compliance if the Act applies to you or your business.

Finally, one other for US firms:

The Office of Foreign Assets Control (OFAC)

This lists sanctions imposed by the US Department of Treasury. OFAC administers and enforces economic and trade sanctions based on US foreign policy and national security goals against targeted foreign countries and regimes, terrorists, international narcotics traffickers, those engaged in activities related to the proliferation of weapons of mass destruction, and other threats to the national security, foreign policy, or economy of the United States.

Reference:

https://home.treasury.gov/policy-issues/office-of-foreign-assets-control-sanctions-programs-and-information

The lists are updated periodically based on US foreign policy and other goals.

I can give one example during the time I managed Sudan to illustrate why an awareness of the OFAC legislation is so important:

At the time (2005) Sudan was on the OFAC list. Sudan had not been partitioned. That came later in 2014. There was a civil war in Sudan in 2005. The sanctions included a clause that prohibited any goods whose manufacture involved any stage in the US, irrespective of the release site, from being exported and sold in Sudan.

Based on new evidence, a new breast cancer drug was seen as a new gold class that would replace the current standard of care and was demanded by my distributor in Sudan to be registered.

To the unwary, this would seem like a good business opportunity and so they would jump in and request the dossier to be released for registration. The drug was made and released from a UK manufacturing site. But wait! Your company is listed on the US stock exchange on Wall Street. So, both the FCPA and the OFAC legislation apply to you – even though you are a UK citizen resident in the UK, running an international sales business for your company and your company is a UK listed company with a final release site of goods from the UK.

I was aware that Sudan was on the OFAC list. You may recall the civil war in the Darfur region that the US was opposed to and imposed sanctions on Sudan. So, being known as 'a safe pair of hands', I contacted the Vice President of Manufacturing Operations to confirm that no stage of the manufacturing process for this new drug involved its manufacture or transit in or through the US.

The answer came that, at one stage, the drug was processed in part within the US, before arriving in the UK for the final stages of

Quality Testing and release. I then referred this to my Legal Counsel for their advice and interpretation of how to follow the OFAC sanctions.

The answer was a game changer.

1. We could not register and export this product to Sudan without obtaining an OFAC licence which was a costly and time-consuming paper exercise that could take months (possibly a year or more) before we could be allowed to submit the dossiers to start the registration process. The regulatory process for registering the product was likely to last around two years.
2. The cost of an OFAC licence (if it was granted) outweighed the business opportunity size (I was asked to forecast the business opportunity post-registration in Sudan).
3. OFAC rules stipulated that instead of a commercial arrangement, the company could make cost-free donations if the product were a breakthrough or in high need by the people of Sudan. Such donations were open-ended as they stipulated that there would be no expiration time.
4. I started discussions with Medical Affairs. They reminded me that, if we started a donation programme, we could have ended up donating an expensive new medicine for many years that needs costly pharmacovigilance surveillance whose costs would be charged to my cost-centre budget. Once a donation program starts, it is challenging to withdraw it. There is a huge reputational damage risk in denying the continuity of drugs to patients already started on them. More so in sensitive areas such as cancer.
5. Medical Affairs informed me that an in-class competitor had already submitted for registration in Sudan. I wrote to the distributor explaining why we could not register our drug and suggested that they contact the manufacturer of another in-class treatment to become their distributor.

So, I resolved it exactly like that. The distributor was told why he could not register the drug. He was told another drug in the same class/category was already undergoing registration, it would be first to market, and that he might like to approach that manufacturer to be their distributor.

The message is that as an International Sales Senior Executive, you need to have inclusive matrix relationships within your organisation and seek skilled advice – be it legal, financial, regulatory, medical, or marketing support – to ensure that you are not about to step foot onto an Improvised Explosive Device and blow your legs off.

Forewarned is forearmed!

Take responsibility. If you do not know from this checklist of considerations, then ask somebody who does. Ensure that the advice is captured on a paper trail, as in the example of Sudan that I used to illustrate to you how there may be pitfalls of which you are not aware.

The key thing is to tap into that broad cognitive bandwidth and ask questions.

Over time, it becomes second nature and the mention of something triggers an association with your market or business. In the section on finding people who succeed in this environment of distributor models, the lack of cognitive bandwidth is another key reason for failure.

Company recruiters, HR, and talent acquisition partners, whatever their titles, in my experience, show they have little idea or clue on how to find candidates with the cognitive bandwidth as a key ingredient that leads to success. For these folk, I will elaborate further in another chapter as you read on.

For you the reader, before you decide to move forward with a plan for country entry, ensure you check these aspects before you commit the time, money, and activities of the company.

Part 2: Growth – The Holy Grail?

The Appeal of International Business Development

In the last two decades, one major change has been seen in the pharmaceutical industry and other business sectors. The major markets of North America, Europe, and Japan have drastically reduced growth rates for their pharmaceutical industry. From their heyday of high single to low double-digit growth rates, many of these geographies have growth rates in low single digits.

If you were the CEO of a publicly listed company, you could no longer go along to investor and City Analyst meetings with the year-on-year growth you had enjoyed in the past. There was a risk that, without a strategy on growth, investors and City Analysts were unlikely to have confidence in your ability to deliver shareholder returns and dividends. Thin pipelines of new assets under development have further made delivering sustained growth through new products challenging, to say the least. Finding new better treatments is getting increasingly difficult due to the exacting standards of current treatments that are approaching end-of-life maturity and patent expiry.

As one senior Vice President of R&D once said to me, "How do you find a treatment that is better than the current 'gold' standard of care?"

The answer?

"With great difficulty, frustration, and treading a risk-laden path."

A further pain point was that payors in these reimbursed markets began to drive down prices. The cost of government/insurance-backed healthcare was struggling to be funded through taxation and subscriptions. Payors even refused to reimburse new treatments they believed to be expensive on the basis they considered them to be not good value-for-money or cost-effective or both. Clinical efficacy, safety, and tolerability were not enough to secure reimbursement.

A fourth hurdle was introduced – cost-effectiveness and outcomes. Payors take a longer-term view of new products. They consider if these new products can change the trajectory of the condition or, do they simply "wallpaper over the cracks" of a given condition and represent an expensive process modifying and masking symptoms.

Faced with this backdrop, a CEO must have wondered how he/she is going to steer the company in increasingly turbulent waters where the focus was, and still is, on growth.

Investors want to see growth. Citing 2% growth on a $50bn business when they were used to seeing 10-15% seemed lack-lustre to investors. However, raising the growth rate is only possible through one route.

That route?

International expansion into new 'emerging' markets. This can drive a company's growth prospects. Why? Because many of these 'emerging' markets are characterised by (relatively) higher growth rates than the economies of developed markets, such as North America, the EU, and Japan. They are, however, high growths from a smaller baseline of sales. A concerted scaleup expansion into these 'emerging markets' could improve the company's overall headline growth figures to appeal to investors and City Analysts.

What are these 'emerging' markets? Quite simply all the markets outside of North America, Western Europe, and Japan. They include:

- Latin America (LATAM).
- Central America & Caribbean.
- Eastern Europe including the Baltics and Balkans.
- Russia.
- Middle East & Africa (MEA).
- Asia Pacific (APAC) including SE Asia, India, and China.

The major 'emerging' markets were named BRICM – Brazil, Russia, India, China, and Mexico.

Unfortunately, for a whole host of reasons, Brazil and Russia fell out of favour.

Some of the reasons include prominent levels of corruption, a drive towards local manufacturing investment, and downward pricing pressure. The recent war between Russia and Ukraine, which has resulted in the West creating sanctions against Russia, has also led to a de-investment model in Russia. There is still a strong focus on India and China, driven by population size, a growing segment of (wealthy) middle classes, and having low labour costs that reduce cost-of-goods and improve margin.

India and China represent around 2.5 billion population of the global 8 billion. That is over 30% of the world's population in just two markets! They both have a rising prevalence of Non-Communicable Diseases (NCDs), such as Diabetes, Hypertension, and Cancers, driving a demand for innovative higher-price/higher-margin products.

Within a cluster, some sub-divisions have bigger opportunities than other countries in the cluster. It is key to focus your market entry by country, not by cluster.

For example, in the Middle East Africa Region (MEA) the major markets are Saudi, Gulf, Qatar, and Egypt. While in North Africa, the major markets are Algeria, Tunisia, and Morocco. These tend to be managed out of a UAE hub or Egypt or Turkey. Middle East markets share a common religion (Islam) and language (Arabic). However, North Africa is bilingual in French/Arabic, and business is conducted mainly in French. This sub-cluster is often termed the Middle East and North Africa (MENA) Region. The rest of Africa is divided into South Africa and Sub-Saharan Africa (SSA).

South Africa often forms a hub within a hub of the Middle East Africa region managing SSA. These South Africa-based seniors typically report to a regional hub based in Turkey, Egypt, Dubai, or Singapore. There are some companies where the MEA and the South Africa/SSA business reports to an 'International Hub' based out of China. Such an International Hub is usually responsible for the Rest of the World outside of North America, Europe, and Japan. Exceptionally, South Africa as a hub-within-a-hub running SSA may report directly to a corporate senior Board member based in the US Europe or Japan. That senior Board member may have a title such as Executive President International or similar.

Readers may at once recognise that, with so many markets and segments, there is considerable complexity in trying to choose which markets to focus on. So how does a company decide?

The choice is dependent on a complex matrix of considerations, including but not limited to the following:

- Macroeconomic data.
- Population opportunity size.
- Product fit.
- Healthcare and sector-specific market data.
- Regulatory and approval processes and their timings to approval.
- Regulatory labelling requirements that demand the creation of a unique market-specific pack that cannot be exported into any other country because of the labelling.
- Current level and presence of competitors.
- An assessment of pricing. Can the company meet the pricing needed to succeed?
- Defining the key market forces and the drivers for their segment.
- Product portfolio mix. Many emerging markets still enjoy products growing year-on-year that have reached the maturity stage of the life cycle in the rest of the world. This means global volumes are shrinking despite higher demand in emerging markets. Will the company keep a portfolio of products where the global volumes are shrinking?
- What is the implication on cost-of-goods for such mature products on margin and selling price for emerging markets?
- Can the distribution and logistics models deliver products cost-effectively into the patients' hands in the market at the right price?
- The likely investment needed to generate brand share and ultimately dominance through attaining a critical mass within a medium/long-term – typically over a 5 to 10-year period of investment.

For a late-entrant with many competitor players already present, the investment is considerably greater than an early or first-entrant to market.

My observation is that, so often, Seniors and Executive Board members fail to convince me that they have assessed one or more of these factors for Sub-Saharan Africa (SSA). As a result, they cannot realise a critical mass from such a deficit in understanding. To succeed in Sub-Saharan Africa, seniors need a high, wide, cognitive bandwidth. And very importantly, they must not try to take a model from another market (such as South Africa) and implement it in SSA.

The same may be the case for taking a model in one large country in a cluster and implementing it in other markets. An example might be Brazil, which is a large market, and implementing the model in other markets in Central and Latin America.

The same can apply when a team appoints someone with 'distributor experience' in one region, such as SE Asia (for example, distributor markets of Laos, Cambodia, Vietnam and similar), and expects them to succeed in Sub-Saharan Africa by the incumbent trying to implement their SE Asia experience into SSA. I have seen this in one instance and the incumbent had a short tenure in Africa.

Distributor experience alone is insufficient to succeed. Essential? Possibly yes. Consider however that on my appointment, I had no prior experience of distributors, but I had a combination of other factors that collectively led to my success. High, broad cognitive bandwidth is required. Such cognitive bandwidth extends beyond 'the distributor experience', as I will develop in this book.

Sadly, my consulting experience is that many incumbents try to take a model from elsewhere (typically South Africa in the case of SSA), but also possibly from a market in the Middle East region (such as Egypt, Jordan, or Lebanon) or a market model in SE Asia and shoehorn it into markets in SSA on the flawed understanding and belief that "they are all distributor markets anyway".

The result?

Catastrophic failure.

The models of South Africa when implemented into distributor markets in SSA do not work. Fact! I will cover why as you read this book. It will become stark and clear because South Africa is not a distributor market! The same may be the case for SE Asia or other emerging markets.

It is why I say that South Africa does not understand distributor markets.

South Africa is not "a distributor market". A corporate decision to run SSA distributor markets out of South Africa has been disastrous for so many pharmaceutical companies who considered South Africa as *"the gateway to Africa"* – something which, in my experience, it most certainly is not.

So, a clear lesson to avoid failure in Sub-Saharan Africa is not to try to take a model from elsewhere and implement it. You will be guaranteed to fail from the very outset.

For any emerging market, you the reader must work on a market-by-market basis to fully understand the drivers in each market and learn how to succeed through carefully considered and constructed market entry models. The greater your understanding, the greater the likelihood you will be able to design the best-fit commercial distributor model that has the best chance of success.

There is one remarkable omission to this list. That omission is that, very often, so many companies do not assess their internal skills and capabilities for scaleup and international expansion. They overlook the fact that perhaps they have gaps in skills and understanding that could be a serious obstacle to their chance of success in these distributor markets.

Put bluntly, they believe *"they know it all"* when in fact they do not. They know their 'home turf' exceedingly well. They may be recognised as leaders in the home market and be a strong brand. But venturing beyond the home turf is different. The markets that you target may not know you or recognise you as a strong brand. You do not know the key players; they do not know you. You are often treated as a nobody. The markets have different processes and stages of approval that your 'home turf' staff may not understand. This is common in Africa.

Staff sitting in South Africa responsible for SSA may struggle to understand the regulatory requirements and the fact that their home market is in one regulatory zone (temperate, Zone II) while all the export markets in SSA are in a different regulatory zone, namely Tropical, Zone IV (a) and Zone IV (b) – sometimes this Zone is described as high heat with high humidity.

A key market in SSA (Nigeria) requires local clinical trials to be conducted as part of the registration process. This raises a significant barrier to entry for smaller companies due to the costs and lack of skills to design, conduct, monitor progress and interpret the results for the authorities.

The Regulatory body in Nigeria deals by exception with a corporate senior clinician in your head office. They demand a local Nigerian clinician who can collaborate not only with the corporate head office clinician but who will also collaborate with them in Nigeria. This requirement means having a local medically qualified staff member on the ground with full registration with the Nigerian Medical Authority. A doctor is a high-cost headcount. Add to that considerable payroll expense the fact that he may need training in clinical trial design and delivery and be accredited to run clinical trials in compliance with Good Clinical Practice guidelines (GCP). Nigeria is not a centre for global clinical studies. So, you are likely facing high investment costs to train a Nigerian clinician to the standards required for designing, conducting, and monitoring trials to international standards. All this is expensive and adds extra costs. And in addition to the headcount cost, that doctor needs a big budget for clinical trials!

As if this was not enough, owing to a high degree of counterfeit medicines in Nigeria, the regulatory authority requires products to have complex labelling requirements, such as holograms and a registration number printed on the pack. Such packs are small volumes compared to the rest of Anglophone SSA and so their cost of goods will be higher. This impacts the margin because there is little elasticity in pricing to raise the selling prices to reflect the higher COGs of what we commonly describe as a market-specific pack.

Across much of Anglophone SSA, no such market-specific labelling is required, and companies can export much larger volumes across pan-Anglophone SSA termed Standard English Export Packs. The higher volumes make for lower COGs. A similar Standard (French or Spanish) Export Pack can be used for French and Spanish-speaking markets respectively.

Do consider, though, that this could change across markets, and the reader should always check the labelling requirement in the market-entry considerations. I have seen company seniors having registered products for sale in Nigeria or other countries that do not break even to cover the registration and regulatory costs in 5 years! I am always amazed at how many registrations are made 'blind' in the absence of five-year forecasts post-registration to assess the product's potential. And where these activities are carried out, there is remarkable failure to achieve those forecasted sales that had formed the business case for investment.

It seems that seniors on the Executive Board of a considerable number of companies appear never to go back to the investment case and the forecasted five-year sales and ask, "*Were they actually realised?*" How else can one explain why there are seniors responsible for international markets that fail to deliver the investment case for sales and profits but consume all the investment cash, repeatedly, year after year?

Readers should take note:

> Always form a forward view of sales and costs <u>before</u> you embark on costly registration processes and activities. Base it on your price model, sales and marketing budget, and

headcount costs, and declare your assumptions. But that is not all. Having established minimum sales projections post-registration, you should go back and assess the sales performance and assess if ongoing regulatory support should continue at renewal or whether the registrations should lapse and not be renewed.

Sounds crazy, doesn't it? But I can tell you, some clients went ahead with regulatory submissions without any view of potential five-year sales post-registration or any idea of pricing sensitivity! Is it any wonder then that so many fail to achieve a critical mass in such markets?

Alternatively, they ask a distributor to do the forecast for them. Little do they know that the distributor's forecasts are riddled with holes and a complete absence of assumptions, upsides/downsides, and sensitivity analysis. You may have experts inside your business in forecasting. Distributors have no such talent. Be warned!

Why would a distributor, a person who does not know you, do a significant piece of work such as this business potential assessment for you free of charge and on the basis that you may (or you may not) appoint him to be your distributor? Think about it for a minute. What is in it for the distributor?

One client brought me in on a fee-paying basis to assess a priority market.

This is by far the most reliable way – bringing in an expert who is well-connected with reliable distributors, going into the market, and working with and through those distributors on behalf of clients to give a calculated and reasoned view of the opportunities.

Armed with proposed prices based on the client's lowest acceptable margin (base case) and a desired higher margin (base case plus), I built up five-year forecasted sales and costs with two distributor potential partners, both of whom I knew well and who trusted me. I worked on the projections with them and helped and supported them, using my corporate experience in business planning. I defined the data we needed and the data collection method. I devised the focus group sessions with key clinical experts. I led the focus group sessions, not the distributors. Neither the distributor nor I alone could deliver sound forecasts to a good method that could withstand scrutiny by seniors by working alone. We needed to work together because the distributor had the contacts and connections to get the data I wanted. I had the business planning and forecasting experience aligned to pricing models and investment costs required to deliver those forecasts.

The product projections that I presented back to the client were below their lowest acceptable sales and profit over a five-year investment if they invested in the market. The client was unwilling to move on prices. They paid my fee and congratulated me.

Because they had been so keen to enter that market, I asked them, "Why?"

They replied that what they spent on my ability and experience was a small drop in the ocean compared to the money they would have thrown away in registrations to deliver sales below their five-year minimum expectations. No distributor would do that exercise if that client had made their approach directly to a distributor that they did not know. They went on to state that they had saved a fortune. The senior executive told me that I had saved him and his senior colleagues' careers by stopping them from making a blindfolded, flawed venture into an international market through considerable investment in a territory they did not understand!

They made a wise decision to engage me <u>before</u> investing in the expansion into that market. Many did not. Do not fall into this trap as so many have done. Understanding the market opportunity and risks is key before deciding on market entry and incurring significant costs over the next five to ten-year period. The cost of an expert consultant is negligible in this assessment of opportunities.

Remember, setting up a business in new markets is not your main challenge. The main challenge is to establish an ambition for a critical mass to be achieved in (say) five years AND then to go on to deliver it each successive year! It is the attainment of achieving and delivering a critical mass in new markets that eludes so many senior executives that causes their career derailment and early exit from the company.

The company ends up with a liberal sprinkling of country markets with a few hundred thousand dollars of sales here, a few hundred thousand there, or maybe even the odd few million dollars. But their common feature is that the values they attain are small versus the opportunity size, the projections that were made to seniors, and the investments that were committed that led to their business case to invest for growth! Such disappointing sales will drain central support staff costs and probably consume costs in the markets also. In such cases, the senior team decides to consolidate by getting rid of the export sales executive as they cannot justify a dedicated headcount with such low sales.

Consider bringing someone with first-hand experience to help you develop a better view of the business potential and opportunity. Someone who can highlight risks and assess your own company's capabilities in new markets and highlight the financial stamina required before generating revenue.

Many corporate manufacturing sites are in temperate zones. To prove that your products are stable and bioequivalent in a Tropical setting, companies need to show this data is captured over two years (or, under an accelerated programme, in exceptional conditions, of one-year data subject to full submission of data at two years) at different heat and humidity settings. This data takes time and costs money. Getting the data might be a two-year journey of costs. And, even then, the products may not meet the standards needed for registration in a different temperature and humidity zone. In short, this is high costs and high risks!

I was engaged in a piece of work for a client in Zone II regulatory for exports into Africa and South Africa. For South Africa, being in Zone II, you would think the products for that client would be registered easily in South Africa.

No.

The regulatory dossiers were weak and could not stand up to the scrutiny of the South African regulatory authority, which has well-defined standards. As for Sub-Saharan Africa, the client was told that these markets require stability and bioequivalence studies for Zone IV – hot and humid – and that this is a two-year wait. Two years of costs but no sales!

Prior expectations, built from bad advice, had been set with the CEO based on ignorance, and the CEO had been informed that they could quickly get into Africa and make money there. There is no quick entry or a quick way to make money in Africa or any emerging market that operates through distributor models as I will develop and demonstrate. Do not be fooled.

Another area of flawed thinking is not recognising that the distribution and supply models in SSA require a different approach than the models of those operating out of South Africa.

So many companies have chosen to replicate "the South African Model", which as I mentioned earlier, is not a distributor market. Bringing a model, that you know from South Africa (or anywhere else) to SSA is to qualify to be a kamikaze pilot on a suicide mission. That is the best-fit analogy of which I can think. South Africa's distribution, delivery, and supply models do not work effectively in SSA and are inappropriate when applied to SSA.

These South African models are costly and risk-laden. The models work well in South Africa, which tends to operate as a developed market with a different market model and have larger sales value. In my experience of reviewing such models for clients, these models often labelled *pre-wholesale consignment models* help the service provider, not the client. An alternative term for these models is that of an *Intermediary model* and can be conveniently disguised by confusing terminology which I will explain in more detail as you progress through the book.

They do not address the situation for which they are being implemented. That situation centres around pharmaceutical companies running out of stocks and the ensuing inability to fulfil prescriptions as a result. So, these pre-wholesale service model guys sell a costly, risk-laden model to the pharma companies in SSA whereby they present holding stocks locally in regional depots acting as an intermediary between you and your customers as the solution to running out of stocks. But my experience has reviewed this model for client work and the pre-wholesale consignment model or indeed any intermediary model does not address the issue of running out of stocks!

These companies fail to understand the root cause of running out of stock lies in a different area. I will develop my reasons for saying why these models do not work and why they are wholly inappropriate to solve the situations they are claimed to solve (but do not) as you read the book, in further chapters covering distributors and go-to-market models with a dedicated section illustrating the pre-wholesale consignment model.

Not recognising your lack of core skills, capabilities, and understanding of the export markets, not being able to design the best-fit distributor model that can achieve a critical mass within a five or ten-year window of investments and not bringing in outside ability and experience are probably the most common contributors that link all those senior corporate kamikaze heroes that ended up as corpses on the plains of SSA.

"They did not know what they did not know."

I would add: *"Neither did their staff on whom they relied!"*

There are four magic words that seniors cannot bring themselves to utter from their lips. If they could, they would stand a chance of success by bringing in outside abilities.

Those words?

"I do not know." Followed by *"I need help."*

For SSA, the regulatory process is never as simple as either any distributor partner claims or each country's regulatory authority claims. Distributors are the biggest bluffers when it comes to sales projections and getting you set up in the market. South Africa takes around three years to register a product with a strong dossier – that's three years of costs with no sales! You will need premises and your own employed registered pharmacist for this. Alternatively, you could do it with a distributor as your "Holder of Certificates of Registration" (HCR), but there are downsides to this (that can be mitigated in the legal agreement) as I will explain further in the book.

In Sub-Saharan Africa, depending on the market, the timeline for approval with a strong dossier compliant with their submission requirements can take between two and three years – up to four years in exceptional circumstances. Site inspections are mandatory across all the major markets of SSA, and no timelines are given for inspection. With registration formalities completed, a company could be waiting for two years for the authorities to inspect and audit their manufacturing sites. Until the inspection is completed, and the site passes with no advisories to be corrected, the registration and permission to import will not be granted to the distributor or the company. That is a long time of costs with zero sales.

Products cannot be sold without regulatory approval and without the country authority issuing an importation permit. The exception might be products for the Government considered to be emergency supplies. Setting expectations with the Senior Executive Board is key but seldom done. Too many international business development folk over-promise and under-deliver when they should under-promise and over-deliver.

Despite these challenges and difficulties, export markets and scaleups internationally in the 'emerging' markets are a good opportunity to drive enhanced growth at modest levels of investment in the medium-to-long term. But there needs to be a considered choice based on sound analysis and reasoning with a high, broad, cognitive bandwidth that helps to set realistic expectations and maximises the chance of success.

In common with other emerging markets, SSA tends to be brand-loyal but *'slow-burn'*, meaning they take time and effort to be established but give sustained yield in the medium to long term.

The metaphorical 'fire' takes a while to get started, but once alight, it lasts longer, giving off heat and light for a considerably longer time than a flash fire 'bang'. A company can see benefits from having a combination of high-burn/fast-burn markets as well as slow-burn/longer-burn markets. The latter supports the fires going out in the fast-burn markets.

In the next part of this chapter, I will share how I conducted analyses to find the focus markets for my scaleup and expansion.

Part 3: Basic Analysis to Define Target Markets

In my view, companies either go overboard with data (paralysis by analysis) or make only a very superficial analysis based on a single feature of a market that proves to be a big catastrophic mistake.

Neither approach is good.

When I had to help clients name the top four or five markets in Sub-Saharan Africa, I could not tell them "My experience is that you focus on x, y, and z."

I had to show how I arrived at my recommendations through logic, analysis, and assumptions. It was instilled in me in my corporate life that seniors demand logic, rationale, and data through considered risk assessment versus the benefits that form the foundations of recommendations. All these elements need to be blended into a high cognitive bandwidth.

The most powerful tool I recommend is Microsoft's Excel® for a quantitative assessment and then combining that quantitative assessment with the often-missing ingredients:

- Qualitative factors.
- An expert's view and assessment of company capabilities.
- The company's appetite for risk and the level of patience needed before sales can be generated.

Excel® enables data to be manipulated easily. Data can be ranked, and the use of formulae makes the task so much simpler than using paper and a calculator. I recommend developing your skills in Excel® for anyone in a business or sales role. Relying on either quantitative or qualitative measures alone is a surefire way of making a mistake in the chosen market(s). Very few make a qualitative assessment. They may cobble together some numbers and miss the qualitative step altogether, driven by the fact that *"they do not know what they do not know."*

For qualitative assessment, they often will substitute *'gut feel'* and blind faith in what a third-party distributor or distribution company has told them. They are mesmerised and in a seductive trance. Remember my mantra?

"They do not know what they do not know."

"Neither did their staff on whom they relied!"

The source of data I recommend on the quantitative side is the CIA's World Fact Book©. https://www.cia.gov/the-world-factbook/

There are several reasons I recommend this:

1. It is updated regularly and available on the Internet.
2. It is free to use.
3. Much of it is copyright-free. Unless a copyright is declared, information on their website is in the public domain and may be reproduced, published, or otherwise used without their permission. They do ask that their Agency be cited as the source of the information and that any photos, or similar, be credited to the photographer or the author or the Agency. However, if copyright is shown on a photo, graphic, or any other material, permission to copy these materials must be obtained from the source.
4. It gives at-a-glance summaries and useful maps that I used to use with distributor discussions when discussing how many reps and where we locate those reps. Their map of population density helps give an idea of where placing staff is cost-effective and perhaps where it will not be cost-effective.

Other data is also available (at a price) from third-party suppliers that a company may consider.

If it is any help, I never bought third-party data in my seven years of running SSA. I am of the view that much of it is inaccurate, of questionable relevance to the client's portfolio and market segment and so often, it relies on small sample sizes with high 'projection' factors. Some clients in my opinion foolishly try to purchase prescription data in the market. There are only two metrics that matter:

1. What you can invoice out of the factory gates to your distributor (cash collected).

2. And this reflects the stock sales out from the distributor (demand in the market).

There is a message there to consider before parting with your cash to purchase third-party data.

Let me illustrate my approach to analysis using Sub-Saharan Africa as an example. A reader can repeat this for any cluster of 'emerging' markets, be they Eastern Europe, Asia Pacific (APAC), SE Asia, LATAM, Central America, the Caribbean, or the Middle East.

Let us start at the beginning with how I go about it. You will be surprised just how often this level of analysis has not been carried out!

Sub-Saharan Africa is a cluster of countries. The UN Development Programme applies the "Sub-Saharan" classification to 46 of Africa's 54 countries, excluding Djibouti, Somalia, and Sudan.

That is a large cluster to get your head around.

The first task is to break it down into its constituent parts. I did this based on language and colonial ties. You could use common trade groups or any other first-cut parameters you choose as being relevant.

My breakdown of language and colonial ties gives us three clusters in Sub-Saharan Africa:

1. Anglophone SSA (English-speaking) former UK colonies as the last occupiers.
2. Francophone SSA (French-speaking) former French colonies.
3. Lusophone SSA (Portuguese-speaking) former Portuguese colonies.

My corporate experience was in Anglophone SSA – the largest cluster and the biggest commercial opportunity, spread across East, West, and Southern Africa. The next cluster size is Francophone SSA, which is much smaller than the Anglophone SSA opportunity and is spread across West and Central Africa. Finally, the Lusophone cluster is made up mainly of two markets – Angola and Mozambique with the addition of Principe and Sao Tome which are small islands.

Readers can analyse all forty-six countries, and the figures will identify the top few markets below as per my analysis.

From my analysis (attached), to succeed in SSA, a company needs to succeed in Anglophone SSA. The Portuguese-speaking SSA is almost the same size as the Francophone but is excluded here because it requires Portuguese as a business language and is strongly connected and related to Portugal for both the regulatory process as well as export sales.

I never advise any client to run Portuguese SSA out of South Africa. They should be managed as export territories from the Portugal affiliate office due to the interaction with Portuguese regulatory authorities and having to deal with exporters out of Portugal into Lusophone SSA.

The Southern Africa cluster is negligible compared to the opportunity size of West and East Africa. The Southern cluster is usually regarded as South Africa's export markets (Namibia and Botswana), but they are small in opportunity size.

North Africa and South Africa are included for completeness.

Country Detailed Breakdown

Country Detailed Breakdown	CIA Factbook (2020 estimates) Population (m's)
Nigeria	214
Ghana	29
Anglophone Focus Markets West Africa	243
Kenya	54
Tanzania	59
Uganda	43
Ethiopia	108
Anglophone Focus Markets East Africa	264
Zambia	17
Zimbabwe	15
Namibia	2.6
Botswana	2.3
Anglophone Southern Africa (SA Exports)	37
Total Anglophone SSA	544
Cameroon	28
Cote d'Ivoire	27
Senegal	16
Gabon	2
Typical French SSA Focus Markets	73
Guinea-Bissau	2
Chad	17
Niger	23
Mali	20
Mauritania	4
Central African Republic	6
Republic of Congo	5
DRC	101
Other French West & Central SSA	178
Angola	32
Mozambique	30

Country Detailed Breakdown	CIA Factbook (2020 estimates) Population (m's)
Portuguese Sub Saharan Africa	62
Algeria	43
Tunisia	11
Morocco	35
Maghreb	89
South Africa	56
Total Africa	1002

Regional Summary

CIA Factbook 2020 estimates	Population (m's)	% of Total Africa
West Africa (Anglophone)	243	24%
East Africa (Anglophone)	264	26%
Typical English SSA Focus Markets	507	51%
Southern Africa Typical SA Export Markets	37	4%
Total Anglophone SSA	544	54%
South Africa	56	6%
Maghreb	89	9%
Typical French SSA Focus Markets	73	7%
Other French SSA Markets	178	18%
Total French SSA Markets	251	25%
Portuguese Sub Saharan Africa	62	6%
Total Population Opportunity By Cluster	1002	100%

Typical English SSA Focus Markets opportunity is:

7 x bigger than Typical French SSA Markets with similar GDP/capita

8 x bigger than Portuguese SSA but Angola has the larger GDP/capita

9 x bigger than South Africa but South Africa has the larger GDP/capita

The first sift is to focus on the top five markets in English-speaking SSA. Companies sell products that customers buy. The top markets in Anglophone West and East SSA have a population size of 507m out of 543m. Compared to French-speaking SSA which has its focus markets at 73m out of 178m in French-speaking SSA.

Anglophone SSA focus markets are almost a seven times bigger opportunity compared to French-speaking SSA focus markets (507m versus 73m respectively).

The larger the population size, the larger the number of customers assuming access is no barrier. East and West Anglophone Africa is over 50% of the total African population!

For Pharmaceuticals, with very few exceptions, R&D Innovator companies have a pricing model that can only be met by a small (wealthy middle-class) percentage of the population.

If that is 5%, then clearly 5% of the Anglophone population (507m = >25m) in the chart above is much more than 5% of the population in the Francophone Focus markets (73m = <4m).

A company then needs to reduce this list further using macroeconomics, such as GDP per Capita and GDP based on Purchasing Power Parity as well as possibly GDP % Spent on Healthcare. But this last metric reflects Government spending on healthcare. If the company is working in the private or out-of-pocket market, it is not relevant.

Choose the metrics carefully, keeping them relevant to your business. Too many and you get paralysis by analysis. Too few metrics? Equally meaningless.

Ensure you understand each metric being used by you, or presented by a consulting firm, or a third-party distributor or a logistics partner, and sense-check it for relevance and accuracy to your business. There is no value in using a metric that has little or no relevance to your business segment and portfolio appeal.

Choose (say) 4-6 metrics for each country after a first sift on population size. Buy the data if you believe the data is dependable and correct.

And here is the step that so many clients omit:

Split each metric into aliquots and assign a score for each aliquot. I have assigned five aliquots in the example below. Splitting the scores by aliquots enables consistency in scoring the country against the metric and reduces discrepancy in subjective scoring by different individuals.

Here is an example of:

Scoring Metrics by Aliquots

Chosen Metrics					
Population Size	Up to 20m	21–40m	41–60m	61–100m	>100m
Score	1	2	3	4	5
GDP Per Capita ($)	Less than $1000	$1001–$2000	$2001–$3000	$3001–$4000	More than $4001
Score	1	2	3	4	5
% GDP Spend on Healthcare	Less Than 2%	Up to 4%	Up to 6%	Up to 8%	More than 10%
Score	1	2	3	4	5

For each metric, assign a % weighting from 0-100 for each that defines how important those metrics are in influencing your considerations for the business opportunity.

The sum of all the weightings across the metrics equals 100% for that market.

Now, for each market, assign a score from one to five, using the aliquots above as a reference. Multiply the score x weight for each market. The market with the highest total score becomes your #1 focus market to consider seriously.

The next page gives an example to illustrate with a summary highlighting markets for further evaluation:

Scoring Summary & Identifying Markets for Further Evaluation

Market	Population Size (millions) 2m eligible patients				GDP per Capita				% Spend on Healthcare				Total (Max 5)
	Actual	Weight	Score	Score x Weight	Actual	Weight	Score	Score x Weight	Actual	Weight	Score	Score x Weight	
A	100	50.0%	4	2	2200	25.0%	3	0.75	3.80%	25.0%	3	0.75	3.5
B	62	50.0%	4	2	3400	25.0%	4	1	4%	25.0%	4.0	1	4
C	18	50.0%	1	0.5	2900	25.0%	3	0.75	4.20%	25.0%	5	1.25	2.5

Summary	Total Score Max 5	Priority	Comments
Market A	3.5	#2	Take forward for evaluation
Market B	4	#1	Take forward for evaluation
Market C	2.5		Hold - Evaluate Market A and B
Threshold for Evaluation = 3			

Large consulting firms may use metrics and other macroeconomic data that have little or no relevance to an R&D-based Innovator company. For example, a large R&D Innovator company may have products whose prices will only be affordable to a small percentage of patients in the private sector who are 'out-of-pocket' payors. Using metrics for Government spending on healthcare may not be relevant to assess the opportunity for such a company.

So far, I have used an illustrative quantitative assessment.

The qualitative assessment needs to be added. Without the qualitative assessment, big mistakes can happen. Let me give you an example of how I build a qualitative assessment.

Qualitative Assessment

The data for the top markets in Anglophone areas, based on population size, shows Nigeria to be the biggest opportunity, with its 200m population size, followed by Ethiopia.

In our example above, Nigeria might be market B and Ethiopia might be market A.

When *you do not know what you do not know*, you will head straight to market B – it is the biggest opportunity after all. You will propose priority investment should be on Market B (Nigeria).

That is based on quantitative assessment. Let me illustrate the value of the qualitative assessment – an assessment that many omit or are unable to conduct because they lack the knowledge and an appreciation of the risks and hurdles involved when looking only at the quantitative dimensions.

The qualitative input from me as an expert can tell you that the barriers to entry are remarkably high for Nigeria. Lack of awareness and lack of cognitive bandwidth means that you will only discover such high barriers to entry once you commit to entry procedures and sink money into the registrations and entry activities by which time you will be at a point of no return.

These barriers to entry for Nigeria include:

1. The high regulatory burden with a need to conduct clinical trials locally. There are exceptions where this may not be needed, but most companies will not be aware of how to go about being granted an exemption. And an exemption is never guaranteed. Their regulatory procedure does not even mention the possibility of granting an exemption to the requirement for clinical trials in the country!

2. Nigeria is a huge country that poses significant challenges in distribution and supply chain that affect a product's price, making an expensive product even more expensive. There are lots of intermediaries in Nigeria that result in price mark-ups at each stage to be borne by your payors – the patients.

3. A sizeable chunk of Nigeria's large population is 'out of bounds' in remote areas. For example, the North is unsafe due to Islamist activity from Boko Haram. The accessible eligible population is in the south, so around 50% of Nigeria's total is now your population, not that 200m that you considered as the opportunity size. I usually define a 'magic triangle' of opportunities in Nigeria to clients to make them aware of where they have the greatest likelihood of success and, within which, how many reps to place and where. These are usually much lower than distributor recommendations which want you to place too many reps all across the country.

4. With the most often used go-to-market model for Nigeria, all the products will be registered in a third party's name and that third party (your distributor) will become an exclusive importer of your products. You will not be allowed to appoint another importer without the consent and agreement of the current importer (which he will not give).

5. If you need to change distributor because of poor sales, it will be extremely expensive to end the agreement unless you are a skilled specialist negotiator. This feature is also quite common outside of SSA, and you must check to understand the implication of your go-to-market model. More of this is in the next chapter. Be warned. Do not discover this after it is too late.

6. The currency is unstable, putting any Nigerian importer at substantial risk of defaulting on payment if offered credit terms

(which he will demand). It means continuous revisions in the importer's selling price to his customers, due to the devaluation and fluctuations of the currency. The last thing your customers want is an unstable in-market price. That would be difficult to control, but it has to be considered in your entry model.

7. Nigeria demands specific labelling requirements on all packs of finished goods imported into Nigeria. As a company, you end up with a market-specific pack that cannot be exported to any other country. If those packs are not bought by your distributor, they cannot be exported to any other English-speaking SSA market. In such instances, they will have to be destroyed at a cost to you!

   These market-specific pack volumes are minor compared to a Standard English Export or Standard French or Standard Spanish Export pack applicable for export to those countries that use those languages and do not specify market-specific labelling.

8. The consequence of this is that those market-specific packs with high labelling burdens will increase the manufacturing costs to make them (their COGs will be higher), making them more expensive when landed into the market because you will apply a margin on the invoiced price to a more expensive COG's price.

9. If dealing with cash in advance, there may be other dangers. He may offer to use an offshore or overseas bank account to pay you. This creates a serious breach of Governance rules for you. If he pays from within Nigeria, he can only pay you with lesser amounts of 'white' money that has been declared to the tax authorities. His 'black' money that was not shown cannot be used to pay you. Many emerging markets have 'black' money (not shown to the tax authorities) as well as 'white' money that has been shown to the tax authorities. Black money is held as cash or in overseas accounts.

Be warned: if anyone asks or demands that they pay you from an overseas bank account, check with your Sarbanes-Oxley (SOX) regulations and fiscal controls compliance teams.

Your business can never get to a critical mass if your distributor cannot buy enough of your products. It can never get to a critical mass if he cannot afford to pay you what your sales projection is saying.

Getting a view of a Nigerian distributor's liquidity is nigh on impossible. And whatever he tells you, is almost impossible to confirm or substantiate. Even a letter from his bank may be forged, counterfeit, or obtained by deception and the payment of a bribe. Assume this to be the case until proven otherwise.

These nine points give you qualitative views around Nigeria that need to be factored into a decision to enter Nigeria.

Nigeria is one of the most complex and challenging markets to enter. It is not an easy market for the first entry to Africa. But it looks seductively attractive for a new entrant. It is a good opportunity for those who know how it works and understand the best-fit go-to-market model and how to use it.

Many senior executives have stumbled trying to enter and succeed in Nigeria. It is perhaps the story of Adam and Eve in the Garden of Eden. Too many seniors took a bite of the forbidden fruit only to be banished from this existence.

The key message with analysis is to make it relevant, and quick, and do not get into paralysis by analysis. Use a professional expert with experience in the markets that you want to shortlist for entry to guide you and put missing information on the table that you may not even know about any one market or cluster of markets.

Always use a mix of factors to decide.

Part 4: Understanding the Language of Exports

There is a generalist area around exports that I believe benefits those working in this key area. Your company will likely have departments with experts in this subject matter, but to hold a meaningful conversation with colleagues, you should familiarise yourself with a basic understanding of this language.

An export business involves you (the seller) making goods in one country and selling them to an importer (buyer) in another country. You transport these goods from your premises to the country of the buyer by air, sea, waterways, or land.

The relationship that defines who pays for what, and the obligations and responsibilities of each of you and when those responsibilities shift from one to the other, is captured in a set of terms defined by the International Chamber of Commerce (ICC).

These are called Incoterms®.

Incoterms®

The Incoterms® rules give guidance to individuals taking part in the import and export of global trade. They were devised by the International Chamber of Commerce in 1936. "Incoterms®" is an acronym standing for international commercial terms. "Incoterms®" is a trademark of the International Chamber of Commerce, registered in several countries.

The Incoterms® rules feature abbreviations for terms of carriage, like FOB ("Free on Board"), DAP ("Delivered at Place"), EXW ("Ex Works"), CIP ("Carriage and Insurance Paid To"), which all have very precise meanings for the sale of goods around the world. These terms hold universal meaning for buyers and sellers around the world.

The latest edition of the Incoterms® rules at the time of publication of this book is Incoterms® 2020 and I recommend that anyone responsible for exports should buy a copy of this publication.

https://2go.iccwbo.org/incoterms-2020-eng-config+book_version-Book/

You will find yourself referring to it many times in your international sales role.

I am a generalist in this subject matter and always recommend you speak with experts in your export department and trade finance for a full understanding. But I will try to give you a brief overview because I believe that any export professional should be a generalist around the edges but a specialist at the core of the business.

There are 11 Incoterms. Seven of these terms cover any mode of transport and four cover sea and waterway transport.

The seven that cover any mode of transport are:

EXW – Ex Works (insert place of delivery)
FCA – Free Carrier (Insert named place of delivery)
CPT – Carriage Paid to (insert place of destination)
CIP – Carriage and Insurance Paid To (insert place of destination)
DAP – Delivered at Place (insert named place of destination)
DPU – Delivered at Place Unloaded (insert the place of destination)
DDP – Delivered Duty Paid (Insert place of destination).

The four that are specific to sea or waterway transport are:

FAS – Free Alongside Ship (insert name of the port of loading)
FOB – Free on Board (insert named port of loading)
CFR – Cost and Freight (insert named port of destination)
CIF – Cost Insurance and Freight (insert named port of destination).

In practice, I used FCA, CPT, and CIP for my export business. Many in international sales often use FCA and FOB interchangeably but remember the former applies to air and any mode of transport and the latter only to sea shipments. Even I used them interchangeably, despite not using sea shipments for any of my markets!

Why is it key to understanding Incoterms? They will be discussed in the negotiations between you (the seller) and the importer (the distributor or buyer).

When you are negotiating a contract with a buyer, you will need to discuss and agree:

- Where the goods will be delivered.
- Who arranges transport.
- Who manages and pays for insurance.
- Who manages customs procedures.
- Who pays any duties and taxes in transit (if relevant) and at arrival at the destination?

For example, you might agree to deliver goods, at your expense, to a port in the customer's country. That could be a shipping port or an airport. The customer might then take over responsibility, arranging and paying for customs clearance and delivery to their premises.

You might take responsibility for insurance for the goods until they reach the port but pass this cost on to the customer by building this cost into your product price or as a pre-arranged payment. The basis for this is that a large exporting company can usually buy freight and shipping at a better price through a freight provider as a global freight and logistics contract than an importer in that one country.

As an example, an exporter may buy freight to the importer's destination at 3% of the invoice plus a factor for weight and cubic metres ('cube') of pallet consignment. The importer of that country may have to pay 8% of the invoice plus weight and cube for the same consignment. That 8% of the invoice price to cover freight will be added to the importer's selling price in the market making your products dearer than if you supplied the products and paid for carriage.

Incoterms are used to ensure these responsibilities and handovers are clearly defined and agreed upon.

The other aspect of export trade that I recommend you familiarise yourself with is trade finance, which includes letters of credit (LCs), guarantees, or insurance and is usually provided by intermediaries. In some terms, 'trade finance' can include short-term loans to purchase goods by an importer or for an exporter to meet the costs of exports. I use trade finance specifically to refer to payment terms of Letters of Credit and other guarantees of payment from your importer customer.

You should also understand and familiarise yourself with credit limits, how to set them, and the methods available to you for securing payment.

If you want to grow your business to a critical mass, you will need to find a distributor partner that has liquidity and can pay you. I will cover this in a separate section in more detail. Typically, you want to limit your shipments to four quarterly shipments or a maximum of six shipments that align with your manufacturing model of (usually) make-to-order. Small orders are expensive for you to process, hence the four quarterly or the six bi-monthly orders.

In the days of old, pharmaceutical companies used to make products and store them in warehouses until they were sold. That is a bit of an oversimplification. The manufactured volumes were related to global forecasts for sales volumes. Manufacturing uses Forecasts for Manufacture (FFM) which are always volumes, not value. You will read later why forecasting in volume is as important as forecasting in value. I always started with volume forecasts.

The downside to this make-and-store-until-sold model was:

(a) Cash tied up in inventory (high working capital)

AND

(b) Stock write-off through being held in storage too long before being sold. This usually erodes shelf life to the point that it is not acceptable to a buyer and must be destroyed.

Those write-off costs are borne by you as manufacturer/seller, and such write-off costs can be a heavy expense on a business, even though they are at cost-of-goods prices rather than at invoiced prices. Because they are not sold, the write-off value is always at the cost-of-goods price – in other words, what it costs you (the manufacturer) to make them.

The current model for manufacturing in many sectors to avoid the above issues is called "Just-in-Time" Manufacturing (JIT) whereby goods are only made-to-order. This has involved reengineering how manufacturing processes work internally. It has also changed the way that buyers interact with the seller in the placing and receiving of goods for delivery.

Buyers (your distributors) need to plan for in-market demand and place orders in a forecasted delivery time so that their products can be made and shipped to order. This gives the distributor fresh stock with the highest shelf life.

Many small (and bigger) companies still trade on 'cash in advance' and wonder why their business is still woefully small in value. The relationship in such an arrangement is one of mistrust. The buyer pays upfront, not knowing if the goods will be despatched. The seller does not trust the buyer to pay after despatch. No wonder a long trusting relationship cannot be built.

I can understand at first, for a new customer, you may trade cash in advance. But a point comes when you need to consider credit terms – at say 30, 60 or 90 days – and set a suitable credit limit. For that, I recommend that you sit with your credit management team to set the proper level of credit based on four factors:

1. The expected total annual value of sales to that distributor.
2. The number of orders to be delivered in the year – four ideally and not more than six. It is extremely expensive and inefficient for your manufacturing site to be shipping small orders every week, fortnightly or monthly to your importer in the destination country.
3. The proposed credit period being offered.
4. The lead time from receipt of forecasted order to shipment. For a strong manufacturing company, this might be anything

between 10 to 12 weeks with un-forecasted orders being around 16 weeks or more.

These factors decide the proper level of credit limits to be applied, given that each quarterly order is sent 10-12 weeks in advance and cannot be despatched if the prior quarter's invoice has not been paid (hence factor three is important in the mix of setting credit terms).

If you do not want to apply credit terms and want the security of payment, there are two other means at your disposal – Letters of Credit and Cash Against Documents (CAD).

Letters of Credit (LCs) are complex and challenging to understand. I know the basics, so I will not try to convince you, the reader, that I am a specialist on these terms. Simply described, they are agreements between the seller and the distributor's bank to honour payment for goods despatched by you to the distributor.

Letters of Credit can be 'Confirmed Irrevocable Letter of Credit at Sight' or over specified days, such as 30 days or 60 days. Or they can be 'Confirmed Revocable Letter of Credit' with several other variations. If you consider Letters of Credit, my recommendation is to only consider Confirmed Irrevocable Letters of Credit at Sight or 60 days (at sight usually equates to almost 30 days in any case).

LCs are costly to set up for both the distributor (the buyer) and you as the seller. The implication is that if the distributor incurs these extra costs, he will add them to his selling price in the market to his customers. This may adversely impact your products' in-market selling prices, making them more expensive due to the costs incurred in setting LCs as the form of payment.

Remember the Rule of Reciprocity:

"Anything that you do that makes your products more expensive to buy for the distributor means he will reciprocate by passing on those costs in the market to his customers."

LCs are dependent on compliant documentation throughout all the stages of the transportation process – otherwise, the buyer's bank will reject the payment to you.

Your Trade Finance resource in the company is best placed to guide you. I had one market where I traded on Confirmed Irrevocable Letter of Credit at Sight, set up for me by an incredibly talented Trade Finance expert. She explained all the intricacies, and how it was to be set up and consulted with the export customer team to double-check documents before despatch and check documents on collection by the buyer's freight forwarder before loading onto the plane. Trivial things such as the weight of the pallet leaving the factory had to match the weight of the pallet after inspection before being loaded onto the plane. She would follow the entire shipment and documentation and present the documents for the cash collection and confirm to me when it was received. I just left it to her to manage and she did it exceptionally well.

If you do not have a Trade Finance expert dedicated to this function, you can liaise and involve your Finance Director and Financial Controller or turn to your business bank. Your Trade Finance or Finance Director will likely work with and through your bank in any case. It is a bank-to-bank assurance for which banks take payment.

There is a much simpler, easier, and less expensive way to assure payment that may be suitable for both you as a seller and your importer (buyer).

This is Cash Against Documents (CAD).

Cash Against Documents

Cash Against Documents can be thought of as cash on delivery. It may be likened also to real estate transactions, where funds are held in escrow by a neutral third party (the correspondent bank) until the transfer of titles (payment for the release of shipping documents) is complete.

Once the funds are received, the buyer's correspondent bank releases the payment to the seller's remitting bank (minus a fee), and the remitting bank transfers funds to the buyer (minus a fee).

The fee is usually a fixed fee rather than a % of the invoice value. For this reason, Cash Against Documents is less costly and simpler than Letters of Credit.

This description is brief. But setting up Cash Against Documents (CAD) requires meticulous diligence by your export clerk. I have summarised it in outline in the schematic diagram.

Cash Against Documents is used to protect both parties in the event the seller does not ship the goods, or the buyer does not pay. It overcomes the catch-22 dilemma of your importer sending cash in advance where he does not know if the seller will despatch the goods once his payment has been made.

In CAD, the buyer knows the goods have been despatched and the documents are available to release the goods from the airport. The seller can ensure that the document of title (bill of lading) is only transferred to the buyer once the full payment has been made.

The CAD arrangements are suitable in several circumstances:

- The buyer (distributor) does not have a long history with you, the seller.
- The buyer has a poor credit history. The buyer has a history of overdue payments or where a transaction did not follow through.
- The buyer is a new company and so is a new customer with an unknown history and requires time to show credibility that may lead to credit terms being offered.
- Larger orders where there is an increased risk of defaulting on payment and guaranteeing the release of the documents and cargo if the buyer has made the full payments.

There are downsides also. The main one is the buyer refuses the payment and does not clear the goods that the seller has despatched. This risk can be mitigated by specifying in the arrangement that in this instance, the buyer must pay the returned shipment costs and charges.

Cash Against Documents Schematic

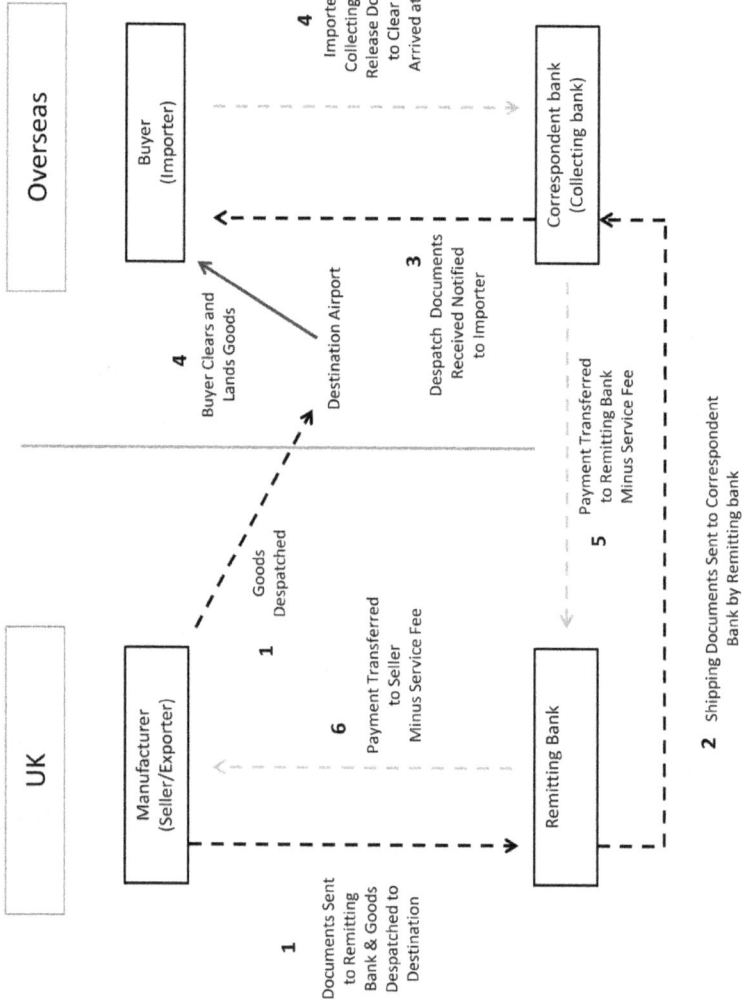

UK		Overseas

Manufacturer (Seller/Exporter)

1 Documents Sent to Remitting Bank & Goods Despatched to Destination

1 Goods Despatched

Destination Airport

4 Buyer Clears and Lands Goods

Buyer (Importer)

4 Importer Pays Collecting Bank to Release Documents to Clear Goods Arrived at Airport

3 Despatch Documents Received Notified to Importer

6 Payment Transferred to Seller Minus Service Fee

Remitting Bank

5 Payment Transferred to Remitting Bank Minus Service Fee

2 Shipping Documents Sent to Correspondent Bank by Remitting bank

Correspondent bank (Collecting bank)

The black dotted arrows define activities in numbered sequence between the manufacturer (you) and your buyer (distributor). The grey dotted arrows stand for the activities in numbered sequence between the distributor back to you.

Note the involvement of an intermediary in each country – in the UK, your bank (called the Remitting Bank) and in your export market, the distributor's nominated bank (called the collecting or Correspondent Bank).

Goods go to the destination airport. The documents needed by the distributor to clear the goods through customs on arrival in the country do not go to the distributor. They go via your remitting bank to the collecting bank. The collecting bank releases the documents to the distributor when he pays the invoice to the collecting bank, and with the documents, the distributor can then clear and land the goods at the destination of arrival.

Both the Remitting Bank and the Correspondent or Collecting Bank take payment for acting as intermediaries. So, you either build those payments into your invoice to arrive at the net invoiced value of goods (which you negotiate into your commercial distribution agreement), or you lose the value of the invoice in charges by these intermediaries.

Remember, if you invoiced goods at $100k and the charges were 10% of invoice value by each bank, you would receive a net payment of $80k after charges. That gives you a $20k shortfall value against your invoiced value that you would have to make up within your sales targets.

If you had a fixed fee, it might be a smaller shortfall. So, if it were $3k by each bank, you would receive a net payment of $94k. A shortfall nevertheless that you will have to make up.

I negotiated the fees to be added to the invoice value – distributors did not like it. But we both had to share the pain as we both had our respective business interests.

And there is a point in this about negotiations. Very few seniors negotiate a commercial deal with distributors in my experience. Many simply discuss a distributor being appointed for their products and hand it to a legal team that issues a standard legal contract.

Do not do it.

Your legal team is not a negotiator. You are the negotiator. You design the model, and you negotiate it. You tell your legal guy what you have negotiated, and the legal guy translates the negotiation of the model into a contract and removes any red-line aspects of the deal – which may require further re-negotiation before a legal contract can be issued.

I used to draw out the model between me and the distributor, who is responsible for what, the payment terms, in-market pricing markups etc. I then handed that to my Legal Counsel who drafted a first-cut template of the legal agreement adapted from a master standard template that could satisfy what I submitted. Only after we agreed on the cut did I send it to the distributor, followed up with an in-market visit to seek the distributor's views and assurances that he was happy to proceed. If not, we would explain and re-negotiate where needed.

The legal guy never came with me. There is a logic and a sound reason for this.

I have seen clients sending their legal teams into the country to address distributors. It is not appropriate and conveys the wrong messages. Bringing in your legal guys is heavy-handed and means the distributor will bring in his legal guy and it will be lawyer to lawyer instead of you and the distributor. Once it is handed to lawyers you have lost! Additionally, bringing in your legal team at this stage conveys the message to the distributor that you have truly little clout, independence of negotiating ability or decision-making authority. That undermines your role and your position.

44

Remember, you are dealing with the owner of the business, and he is the decision-maker. Never waste your time talking to anyone else who is not a decision-maker. If he is not the owner, you need him to produce a letter from the owner stating that the person you are dealing with has a mandate to negotiate the deal on his behalf.

If it was required, I could produce a letter when I was in the markets signed off by a senior director confirming that I had the mandate to negotiate and set terms and conditions for all commercial aspects of deals. But I never needed it. Distributors knew that I was the decision-maker and did not waste time writing to my boss. Always negotiate as equals – as decision-makers with a mandate on behalf of each of your businesses. Gravitas, maturity, and seniority should ooze out in your interactions with distributors. This is a man's job. Not for a young boy to manage (substitute woman/girl where applicable).

Another reason I do not send lawyers to the distributor's team is that lawyers are extremely risk-averse. They do not want to have any risk to themselves or the company. If both your legal team and the distributor's team adopt that position, you are in a risk-averse stalemate. By all means, bring in a lawyer to explain things if the distributor needs clarity on anything after at least two or three discussions between you and him. If I had a legal member present, he would stay silent throughout the discussions in the room. It was I who was in the boxing ring going the full rounds with Mike Tyson and doing the serious task of negotiating.

If you cringe at negotiating and driving a deal with the best outcomes – often described as where neither of you quite obtain what you individually want – then re-think doing this role.

There is always a need to be constantly negotiating, re-negotiating, and challenging distributors who may not stick to the agreement and a constant need for you to have 'uncomfortable' discussions. It goes with the job. You will have to face difficult discussions with a distributor over sales and operations, random stock checks and forensic examination of his debit note expense claims.

Distributors will renegotiate with you on many fronts after the deal is concluded:

- Wanting to charge fees for admin of your staff expenses and administering the payroll.
- Renegotiating prices based on currency devaluations etc.

There is a significant chunk of negotiation abilities in the job of an international sales executive. Sending someone into that role without prior negotiation experience is almost always doomed to be disastrous from the outset. You will recall that I had no prior distributor experience when I was appointed into my Territory Director Africa role. But I had a lot of negotiating experience in high value deals with the UK's National Health Service with our specialist high-price products and negotiating different types of contracts from straightforward discounts to tiered discounts based on price and volume – and demanding cash rebates if the customers did not fulfil their volume agreements at those prices.

We will revisit this when we talk about finding good candidates for these types of roles.

This has been a brief introduction to the language of exports. It is a specialist area.

But that does not mean that, as an International Sales and Export specialist or as a General Manager with P&L responsibility, you rely solely on specialists in the subject matter. You will be a stronger specialist by understanding these areas of generality to engage in meaningful dialogue with your specialists in these areas.

Their job is to ship goods from your country to a buyer.

It is your responsibility to achieve your sales targets. That is achieved by (a) collecting the cash and (b) understanding that shipping fees, bank charges and letters of credit fees may adversely affect your results.

In many instances, these costs are transferred directly to you as the P&L holder. The support staff payroll costs are usually borne as central operating costs. The shipping of orders and transactions are usually charged to your budget as costs that come out of your margin and therefore reduce your gross profit. In another model, shipping costs are met centrally by Manufacturing Operations with funds created by top-slicing each international sales executives cost budgets. There is no Money Tree unfortunately. In this model, each international P&L executive will actually only receive cost budgets net after top-slicing and allocated to Manufacturing Operations. This might be 5%, meaning the P&L holder only receives 95% of the agreed cost budget, and that 95% is the figure held in the system.

Before you yell in frustration with a distributor who does not pay you on time and tell your export clerk to move to Letters of Credit, you need to understand in outline how they work and what adverse impact they can have on your sales performance.

My most common terms of carriage were FCA, CPT, CIP, and CAD. By exception, I had one market where I traded on Confirmed Irrevocable Letters of Credit at Sight.

But I had an exceptionally talented Trade Finance Manager at AstraZeneca (who taught me all I know in this area) and a superbly talented team of export executives that got the documentation right every time and got my orders out on time every time, so I never missed a delivery and did not, therefore, have to explain why sales were down against my projection for the month because of a missed shipment. Remember, the sales invoice is raised at shipment, not upon collecting the cash. You cannot afford to miss a shipping deadline for the month.

It pays to be a well-rounded executive. I highly recommend it.

In the next chapter, I will begin the real essence of the International Managers' remit. That remit is the accountability and responsibility to design and deliver bespoke, go-to-market models, which can deliver ambitious scale-ups and go on to achieve a critical mass agreed with the Executive Board for your markets within five years.

If you have a business that struggles to get to (say) $10m in five years, which the Executive Board expects as a minimum with an investment over five years, they may cut investment and that could lead to making you superfluous to requirements. That may make your role redundant.

Much of my consulting assignments with big pharmaceuticals found a major flaw.

That flaw?

Poor go-to-market models with no hope of delivering the results agreed between the Senior International Sales Manager and his/her Executive Board. Big gaffs and blunders. But you will avoid their gaffs and blunders by reading the next chapter.

CHAPTER 2

Go-to-Market Models

Part 1: The Range of Options Available

I was often asked, *"Who is your agent in Country X?"*

I would reply, *"I do not have an agent in that country. I do not have an agent anywhere in my markets."*

Puzzled, they would ask: *"But I know your products are available in country x."*

I would reply: *"Yes, that is true. But not through an agent. I do not have any agents."*

This illustrates the shortfall and lack of cognitive bandwidth of people, even in international sales, not knowing what they are talking about. Do not fall into that trap and look a fool if you meet me or my equivalent in an interview and open yourself to unsustainable questioning about your understanding of an 'agent' model to enter new markets.

So let me begin first by clarifying what the model options are for entering new markets:

1. Agent (Agency Agreement)
2. Distributor (Distribution Agreement)
3. Wholesaler
4. Legal affiliate
5. Local Production and Manufacturing

Agency Agreement

An agency agreement is formed when one person in a market, called the agent, is authorised by you, the principal, to act on your behalf. When you as principal assign agency to an agent, you are creating a legal relationship with the agent. Thus, legal professional advice is needed.

An agent acts on behalf of his principal and can either:

- introduce a customer to you, the principal or
- create a contract between the principal (you) and the customer.

An agent is not a party to the contract between you, the exporter (the principal)) and the end customer. The end customers are <u>your</u> customers, <u>not</u> the agent's customers.

Where the agent is promoting the sale of your goods, the title to the goods will normally pass directly from you (the principal) to the end user (your customer) in that market.

So, an agent (loosely) finds you customers for your products for which he receives a success fee.

The customer is not a customer of the Agent but a customer of you, the principal. The agent usually receives a commission as a success fee agreed between the parties on all sales orders he places with you, the principal.

An Agent may be likened to taking orders for your products from customers in the markets, but those orders are fulfilled and invoiced by you, the principal, directly to the customer.

As principal, you take responsibility for invoicing and collecting the cash. At no point does the title to the goods ever pass to the Agent.

Your legal department will be far more knowledgeable about Agency Agreements and their pros and cons and your company's position on offering such an arrangement.

I did not have any Agency Agreements under my stewardship of International Markets, and you can understand how those not knowledgeable might use the terms Agent and Distributor interchangeably.

But they are not interchangeable and are completely different go-to-market options. Stand out from the crowd in telling people the difference between the two.

Distribution Agreement

A distribution agreement is used when you, the supplier, have no presence or representation in a particular market or country. You appoint a distributor rather than an agent and enter into a Distribution Agreement.

The main key difference between an Agent and a Distributor is that a distributor purchases goods from you, the supplier or manufacturer, to sell them to his customers in the geographic territory you agree, adding a margin to cover his costs and generate a profit. Some people call it a distributorship agreement.

Title to the goods transfers to the distributor either on being loaded onto his freight forwarder at your manufacturing release site (FCA) or on arrival at the destination (CPT or CIP).

Until that title transfer, you the manufacturer own the title and the risks and responsibility for the goods. Once the title is transferred to your distributor, the responsibility, and risks pass to the distributor, and he owns the goods.

To summarise, the main difference between an Agent and a Distributor is that:

The Agent finds you customers, for which he receives a success fee. At no point is the customer a customer of the Agent. As a supplier, you fulfil the order and manage the cash collection.

In contrast, a distributor enters a contract of sale with his end-users (customers) on his behalf. You, the manufacturer, are not involved, except by way of the manufacturer's guarantee or warranty and product liability. The customers he sells to in the market are his customers, they are not your customers. He is responsible for collecting cash from his customers.

This has significance when negotiating distribution agreements. To plan and forecast for your business, you need to know who the (distributor's) customers are for your products in the market and what data you need to capture. I will cover this in the next chapter.

The goods are the property of the distributor once he has bought them from you. The distributor, therefore, takes the risks for selling the goods, covers his storage, distribution, and invoicing his customers' costs as well as collecting payments in the market from his customers.

Importantly, he also takes the risk the goods may not sell and have to be destroyed due to shelf-life issues. Understand that in a negotiation, he will want you to accept the risk if goods do not sell and become short-dated or expire by negotiating credit for such goods or free-of-charge replacement stocks.

Do not fall for it and give in. But leave room for flexibility to offer discretion in individual circumstances.

All my distributor agreements stated explicitly that we (the manufacturer and supplier) will not be responsible for goods that expire or cannot be sold by the distributor for whatever reason unless the goods on arrival did not meet the specifications agreed in our contract.

But I was flexible in overriding that clause and exchanging a percentage of the goods that became short-dated or expired on an ad hoc exceptional basis. In this gesture, I offered to carry some of the risk – but not all the risk.

The distributor's obligation to you financially is to pay for the goods in his agreement at the prices agreed, for the minimum quantities specified for each product and to the quality specifications (for example, the minimum shelf life on dispatch from the manufacturer's release site) and according to the terms and frequency of orders to the volumes agreed in the Distribution Agreement. Many products came packed in an outer packaging of 12 or 24 packs (sometimes more). Such outer packaging formed the minimum order quantity. A distributor could not order split packs as it was wasteful because another customer was unlikely to accept split packs with possibly different batch numbers and expiry dates.

There are three main types of distribution agreements:

- Exclusive
- Non-Exclusive, and
- Sole distribution agreements.

Exclusive rights prevent you, the manufacturer as the supplier, from actively developing sales in the distributors' agreed territory and from appointing other distributors in the territory. Sales are developed through the Exclusive distributor. Enquiries from third parties for the availability of your products in the market are referred to your distributor for follow-up.

If you deal directly by supplying those third-party enquiries, your distributor may litigate for breach of contract. Do you think the distributor will not find out?

Believe me, they can, and they often do find out. They are well connected. Here is a real example that happened with a client on a project:

Unknown to you, a $100k order you sent as a third-party enquiry that came directly into your mailbox is being sold to the distributor's customers. They ring up the distributor saying they have just been offered your products from another source at lower prices. They obtain confirmation of the supplier and prices and pass it to the distributor.

The next you hear; the distributor has written a complaint and grievance letter to the CEO alleging a breach of contract and you are summoned to your Executive Board and Senior Legal Counsel to explain.

Trust is key. Such actions break the trust between you and your distributor.

Do not do this. Be warned.

Some companies have a rigid policy never to offer Exclusivity and they will only offer Non-Exclusive agreements. Non-exclusive rights give you, the supplier, the possibility of appointing other distributors in the same territory to develop your business. Good distributors will usually walk away on such insistence. They have too often seen companies relying on a distributor to set up a business and then having the rug pulled from under them by appointing several distributors to share that business with the guy who set it up for them.

Insisting on Non-Exclusivity may prompt distributors not to collaborate with you. You are starting a long-term relationship with a distributor to enter and grow your sales in the market. You are looking to him to work hard to help you get established. A non-exclusive agreement means you are keeping the door open to appointing other distributors to share the fruits of your joint labour. Can you see how this might be a red line for the distributor? It does not instil a sense of trust between you.

There are ways of making a Non-Exclusive agreement, in practical terms, an Exclusive Agreement that a distributor will (or should) be prepared to accept. I used this when a client insisted that they only wished to issue Non-Exclusive agreements. It is a secret that I share with fee-paying clients, but I will share it with you in this book.

To create exclusivity within a non-exclusive agreement, I built an exclusivity period for products for three years tied to achieving the budget value and volume of purchases after post-regulatory approval for three consecutive years, *"duration and terms extendable thereafter by agreement between the parties"*. The agreement was Non-Exclusive, but this clause gave Exclusivity to the distributor.

If he could not or did not deliver three years of budget delivery, the agreement's core non-exclusivity allowed me to appoint additional distributors. It had to be three consecutive years of delivering budgets. Missing one period made the exclusivity clause void and open to me appointing additional distributors. This would be a test to see if the distributor was confident to deliver the budget figures during our sparring and negotiations.

Read further and you will learn my secrets that can drive success.

Sometimes, you need to be aware that markets only allow Exclusivity of Distributor Agreements by their regulatory authorities and drug safety monitoring policies.

This is in place so that the Drug Authority knows the source of the supply from a single (exclusive) distributor rather than trying to work out through batch numbers of the stock from the manufacturer or supplier as to which distributor purchased and sold the item of stock in the country.

This might be a risk that you need to be prepared to take if the market is sufficiently attractive to you. I had such an arrangement in Sudan. I had two distributors, but each had exclusive agreements on various products based on their different reach into the market. One was the exclusive distributor for products released from Sweden (Distributor A) and the other for products released from England (Distributor B).

When the manufacturing site for a product was moved out of Sweden to England, distributor B did not get the rights to the product from the new release site, even though it was transferred to be released out of England. I had already built that possibility into the legal agreement because companies can move sites for the release of products for operational and other reasons.

Distributor B had the disadvantage that the Sudan customers for that product were with distributor A for Sweden products. The regulatory authority also had Distributor A as the importer of the product – not based on the release site but on product lists covered in Distributor A's distribution agreement.

It would be suicide to take that product off distributor A and give it to distributor B simply because B was the importer of products released from England. He did not have customers for that product and did not know the market and the competitor dynamics!

Distributor A had set up that product from ground zero. To take it off him and give it to the other guy would have been suicide and he would have ended our agreement out of protest. This is a situation with a risk of high reputation damage. Word gets around fast! Trying to appoint a good replacement distributor would be made exceedingly difficult when the others in the market get to know what happened.

Remember what I said? High broad cognitive bandwidth is needed. Trust is also needed.

Do not risk breaking trust. You will pay a heavy price. It can and likely will lead to your downfall and failure. You are sitting away from the market. The distributor is in your market. He is your eyes and ears. Suddenly you can lose those eyes and ears and become blind and deaf in that country in an instant.

Sole Rights

Sole Rights prevent you, the supplier, from appointing another distributor in the territory, but will not prevent you from developing sales there. An example of this might be that in a sole agreement, you can still deal directly with Government tenders without having to go through your distributor.

But this means, specifically in this example, having an insight into a competitive price to quote, filling in all the paperwork, and if awarded, supplying in tight timescales. However, most importantly you need to get paid, which is never easy when dealing with any Government buying pharmaceuticals and medicines.

I never issued any sole agreements. I did work on selected tenders, but always through my appointed distributor – be it an Exclusive or a Non-Exclusive Agreement. They had an inside track on competitive prices if we were to have any chance of success. Often, they had contacts and connections inside the procuring organisation and were able to obtain competitive intelligence (without bribes or any payments or favours).

They understood the paperwork, which is always considerable.

There are also competition issues to be considered with exclusive and sole distribution agreements. I had a mixture of Exclusive and Non-Exclusive Distribution Agreements. There are pros and cons for each of them.

Do not get too hung up on them. Everything is negotiable, irrespective of whether it is a Non-Exclusive or Exclusive Agreement. That is why I say that negotiation skills are critical to the success of a job holder for this international sales business through distributors.

If your company insists it will only issue Non-Exclusive Agreements, there is a way around negotiating a Non-Exclusive Agreement into what is in practice an Exclusive Agreement. This is a way to keep your seniors and legal guys happy that I used and was very acceptable to distributors confident on being able to deliver the numbers and work with me.

Exclusive and Non-Exclusive Agreements can be with or without commission payments that are tiered against sales targets to be achieved. Commissions are a sensitive topic. The distributor already makes a nice margin selling your products to his customers. To then pay him a commission on top of all purchases means those payments must come from somewhere. Companies do not have a money tree as I stated earlier. Where are commissions paid from?

You guessed it! Commissions are paid directly out of your margin, and therefore impact on your gross profit!

High, broad cognitive bandwidth is always needed. Distributors will ask for it. Be prepared with your response.

Wholesaler

The term wholesaler causes great confusion.

As an International Sales and business development professional, unless you have a Legal Affiliate in a market (where you become the importer in many instances), you should banish this term from your vocabulary.

When I presented my SSA markets to the South Africa affiliate that was going to take over my SSA markets, the GM of South Africa and his senior executive team wanted to understand these new export markets across Anglophone SSA, which they knew nothing about. They were exporting to Namibia and Botswana from South Africa – as so many affiliates in South Africa do.

Therein lies a massive mismatch in their export capabilities. They believe that by selling to Namibia and Botswana, they are experts at export trade. Namibia and Botswana are linked to South Africa's regulatory authority and have easy export modalities from South Africa. Hence so often, the guys in South Africa are not experts and have a poor understanding of export sales models! They are also tiny markets with populations around two and a half million each. Sales to these from South Africa are usually small against the size of the South Africa business. It is questionable how much effort goes into developing these two export markets out of South Africa and questions the export understanding and capabilities in South Africa.

Back to my presentation to this senior executive team of the South Africa affiliate pharma company. South Africa loves fancy titles. They call this local senior leadership group the Executive Committee, often abbreviated to "EXCO". I got my presentation underway to these EXCO members.

I noticed that every time I mentioned the word 'distributor', and the name of the distributor in each country, collectively all these senior executives in the Boardroom looked at each other with confused frowns. I continued uninterrupted.

But after a while, I was interrupted.

One executive member of that senior leadership team spoke out: *"The GM and I were confused a little by the terminology. You kept saying 'distributor' throughout. Here, in South Africa, we have wholesalers."*

He went on: *"So, do you mean wholesaler when you say, distributor?"*

I replied: *"No. I mean distributor. If I were to mean wholesaler, I would use the term wholesaler."*

He then asked: *"So, what is the difference between a wholesaler and a distributor?"*

I replied: *"If I must explain to you the difference between a wholesaler and a distributor, you really should re-think if you want to take over running these SSA markets. It might be premature for you before understanding such differences."*

I never explained the difference to them and highlighted my concerns to the senior corporate team back at HQ. After I set up as a consultant, I discovered this to be a great advantage of being a consultant. You deliver projects with locals, but the sponsors were always the big guns at corporate HQ. These corporate seniors invariably ask me questions about the calibre of the staff I worked with and for my assessment and view of their capabilities. It is all off-the-record and purely verbal. I loved those discussions with seniors. I still miss those interactions.

Back to these local South Africa affiliate seniors:

South Africa is a wholesaler model, <u>it is not a distributor model</u>. Understand that basic tenet!

Implementing a South African wholesaler model in Sub-Saharan Africa does not work.

These guys found out the hard way taking over SSA. They just could not get their head around distributors versus wholesalers. And they paid the price with their careers for their ignorance. The South African export model most commonly in use is termed a "Pre-Wholesale Consignment Model." I will cover this separately for readers, highlighting how it works and the pros and cons.

By now, you must be wondering: *"So, what is a wholesaler? How is it different from a distributor?"*

You the reader are going to kick yourself when I tell you the answer. The answer those unfortunate souls did not know. So here goes. Put simply in the context of international sales:

"All distributors are wholesalers, but all wholesalers are not distributors."

The distributor works directly alongside (you) the manufacturer as an importer and re-seller of your products to his customers.

Your distributor represents you in the market. The legal agreement defines the geographical territory and the terms and conditions for that representation. This can be either on an Exclusive (no other distributor can be appointed by you) or a Non-Exclusive Agreement (you may appoint more than one distributor) for a given geographic territory.

Wholesalers are a distributor's customers. The distributor is <u>your</u> customer.

VERY BIG DIFFERENCE!

Get that fact clear in your head. Wholesalers are NOT distributors. But all distributors are wholesalers. Wholesalers buy goods from distributors. The distributors buy and import goods from you, the manufacturer, from your manufacturing site(s).

Distributors pay you for those goods and sell them in their country to wholesalers, hospitals, clinics and selected large-account retailers. Distributors carry many risks.

Examples of risks carried by distributors include credit/non-payment risks from customers in the market; the risk of stock not selling, and shelf-life being eroded, making it unsaleable and having to be written off as well as currency exchange rate risks between their buying price from you and the selling price to customers in the market. They are usually required to carry and pay, for a minimum of 12 weeks of stocks on their shelf at any time, ordering your brands in minimum order quantities. This means they are carrying risks of inventory and working capital (money tied-up in your stock).

Wholesalers by contrast carry extraordinarily little or no risk.

A wholesaler sells to many retailers (probably several hundred in number). They buy small quantities (sometimes just one or two packs to supply on a pre-order). Wholesalers can be a high credit risk and often do not pay on time. Distributors also function as wholesalers supplying (usually) large volume-usage clients and retailers.

Wholesalers sell to retailers and are exposed to significant credit risks and defaulting on payment to them by retailers. That is why wholesalers order smaller quantities (frequently) from a distributor compared to what the distributor orders from you as the manufacturer.

A wholesaler might order just a few packs from a distributor that may only amount to $100 in local currency value.

A distributor cannot order $100 of goods from you on demand from your factory. They need to order typically four quarterly orders of your sales budget, which will be several thousand dollars in value, at least three or four months in advance – and that is in addition to the stocks (working capital) held on their shelf, which can be typically 12 weeks' shelf stocks plus 12-16 weeks stock on order. That is considerable inventory and working capital tied up on a distributor's shelves.

Wholesalers will not and they cannot do that. They only order what they have in their hands as firm requests from retailers and what they can sell. They are effectively market-stall traders and peddlers.

Wholesalers can deal directly with a manufacturer when the manufacturer is present as a legal affiliate in the country – and I will explain how they do this using a pre-wholesale consignment model in a separate section.

In the next section, I will explain distributors in general before going on to detail the four basic distributor trading models.

Legal Affiliate

This is a complex area with legal definitions and interpretations. I will keep this quite simple and practical for readers and address it from a direction exploring the challenges facing a company wanting to scale up internationally that cannot do what it does at Headquarters in the markets.

A company wants to enter a new market 'x'. For its commercial model, it needs to hire staff and pay them locally in local currency. It needs to purchase vehicles and spend money on promotional and regulatory costs. It needs a bank account into which it transfers funds to pay for these things.

Unless a company is legally registered in that country, it cannot do any of these activities directly. It can only achieve these by hiring a distributor that employs its staff, manages its payroll, buys the cars, or takes out the lease on cars, and takes out a lease on premises for the staff to work out of.

All this will have to be done for you in the name of the distributor, who will be reimbursed for the costs by you, the supplier, wanting to set up in country 'x'.

The distributor is legally registered as a company in country 'x' and can contract for the sale and purchase of goods. The distributor is liable to send tax returns to his country 'x'. He can be sued by the authorities or creditors in country 'x'. The supplier (you), for whom they are acting, is not legally registered and cannot be sued in that country (at least not easily) and is not obliged to send tax returns. You are working at arm's length through the distributor in the country.

Sometimes, pharmaceutical companies decide to set up their own company as an offshoot of the parent company in country 'x'. This 'offshoot' of the parent company is called a legal entity or formally a 'legal affiliate'. Having a legal affiliate gives the company the flexibility to employ staff under the company name, buy or lease cars and premises and conduct business, and the ability to enter contracts with vendors and suppliers as well as have a bank account in that country to facilitate these transactions.

Some argue that a legal affiliate or legal entity is the only model that can 'move the needle' to prove a scaleup business capable of achieving a critical mass in international markets. This is pure humbug in my experience. The only people who say this are people who do not know what they are talking about for emerging markets, and they reveal their ignorance with such nonsense.

I urge companies to think carefully if they are considering a first-entry market model as a legal entity.

I have two simple rules to be answered if you want to create a legal entity:

1. Creating a legal entity must confer a significant advantage over a distributor model. In other words, it must give you something commercially for your P&L that a good distributor model does not give you. Define that advantage and articulate it in two sentences.

2. Alternatively, creating a legal entity must remove a restrictive element present in a distributor model. Define that and articulate it in two sentences.

If you can define either or both, a legal entity is the preferred mode of market entry.

I will develop the options with a legal affiliate in more detail further in Chapter 3.

Local Production & Manufacturing

A company desiring to set up in a new international market may decide to go in with a model that involves local manufacturing of their products. Many reasons underpin this model for consideration, but high on the list is market access that may be achieved by lowering prices enabled by lower cost-of-goods (COGs). Local manufacturing as a go-to-market option is not standalone. It requires creating a legal affiliate alongside the local manufacturing model. I am not aware of the possibility of doing this without a legal affiliate. If this is to be considered, readers should take skilled advice before proceeding.

Too often, consultants and their firms author articles about the need to change models in international markets to improve access through local manufacturing. They will cite company x made a local manufacturing deal with partner y in country z and suggest that more principals should consider this. They go on to explain how they can 'help' make the transition (and charge you a lot of money by doing so). These articles (often badged as "thought leadership"), from authors that I do not recognise as outstandingly qualified leaders in this sphere, are just marketing hooks trying to attract the fish (clients) to bite on the baited hook.

The articles tend to be one-sided and promote claimed advantages without really drawing attention and caution to the downsides of these and other models.

Another feature is that these articles are devoid of any audit of whether the local manufacturing deal had improved access through lowered cost-of-goods. This is extremely difficult to know. So, we have little idea if these models did deliver what they were supposed to deliver.

Even I do not know if those principals that pursued local manufacturing models found if this delivered the investment case for this approach. It will be a closely guarded secret. But one thing I can probably guess is that many of these local manufacturing models did little to deliver the investment cases. Many of these shortcomings will remain buried in the annals and bowels of the Executive Boards that went down this route. And you would need to be Hiram Abiff to know the pass grip and the password to the entrance to King Solomon's temple to access the information!

We should just clarify what "Local Manufacturing" can mean.

At the most comprehensive interpretation, it can be full-scale local production with Active Pharmaceutical Ingredient (API), formulation (into tablets or liquid dose forms), fill and finish and packaging, through to distribution and logistics. This is the most expensive option.

Owing to a high degree of Quality Assurance required at each step to avoid a quality breach, the principal must have a high degree of control along each step of the manufacturing process. This is very costly. Control is costly. Giving up control is also costly because it may result in a breach of quality along any part of the process that could damage your reputation.

A breach of quality standards is costly. And to avoid a breach is costly too! But a company's reputation hinges on the quality of its products and the high standards of manufacture. Can you afford to expose yourself and your company to the risk of a quality breach?

At the other end of the scale, local manufacturing can simply package bulk quantities into primary packs (blisters or cartons or bottles) and secondary packaging (blisters into cartons) into outer, which is comprised of minimum sales packs such as a box of 24 cartons of tablets containing blister strips of tablets.

In this simplified local manufacturing model, the cost is much lower because the quality standards have been carried out by the principal's main manufacturing site in Europe or the US with the highest-grade API, and tightest controls on formulation and fill and finish. These are quality assured and signed off as drums of bulk loose tablets and five-litre drums of liquid formulations sent to the local manufacturing site in Africa.

On receipt in Africa, the local manufacturing site places tablets into blister foil strips that are then inserted into cartons that have been supplied flat packed, pre-labelled to be assembled locally or labelled and assembled locally to comply with labelling requirements. Examples of local labelling requirements specific to a market might be:

• Bar codes.
• Retail price to be printed on the carton.
• Anti-counterfeit measures, such as holograms.
• Tamper-proof packaging, whereby if the seal is broken the pack has been tampered with and may be rejected by a customer.

The liquid formulations are filled into empty plastic bottles, supplied by the principal, or made and labelled locally with the same labelling conditions as above.

A special mention must be made for injectables. The manufacture of injectables is extremely expensive and requires the highest standard of quality controls to avoid cross-contamination from micro-aerosols in the air as well as sterility issues. Some injectables require 'sterile fill', meaning the contents are sterile before they are filled into the ampoules or syringes for injection. Temperature and humidity controls may also be required. Imagine an injection ampoule with contents that are not sterile. Even water for reconstitution in an ampoule for injection must be guaranteed sterility.

For any principal where any step in the process from manufacturing to distribution and logistics is not carried out at its manufacturing site, there is the risk of a breach of quality and compliance.

A few companies have publicly exited local manufacturing, but there will be many who are ashamed to admit defeat.

There are two options available:

1. Build a manufacturing asset on the ground.
2. Partner with an existing manufacturing company in the market.

Examples of both exist. Be clear from the very outset of their respective risks.

Building a Manufacturing Asset on the Ground

Building a manufacturing asset on the ground is a very costly and time-consuming affair.

Modern pharmaceuticals' asset strategy hinges on consolidating and reducing global manufacturing sites. Creating a new site in a new market may create political tensions within the Manufacturing Operations Board opposed to your heroic plans. The trend for major pharma and other large manufacturers is to consolidate their manufacturing assets, not increase them. As companies undergo more and more mergers and acquisitions, the name of the game is to strip out costs and assets, not increase them!

Your idea for market entry with local manufacturing may not be welcomed by Manufacturing Operations. It creates more work, and in these times, they have to do more with fewer resources and now you are demanding even more from their reduced capacity.

It probably takes ten years or more from its inception, and great cost, to have a fully functioning manufacturing facility that meets current Good Manufacturing Practice (cGMP) and FDA standards.

At today's prices in 2024, I would estimate it will not be less than a $50 million investment! That may make the break-even point a decade or more down the road! And that break-even point would be if it were running to full capacity. In reality, some of these run at less than 50% capacity because demand is nowhere near that which was predicted when the business case was made. This can push that break-even point even further down the road!

Partner with an Existing Manufacturer in the Country

If local manufacturing is desired or required as a condition of market entry, the more practical choice is to partner with an existing manufacturer that is present and fully compliant with cGMP and

FDA standards. If you intend to deal in tenders, your partner will need to have World Health Organisation (WHO) Pre-Qualification. Some partners may promote themselves on quality standards other than cGMP, FDA and WHO Prequalification.

These are the only three standards that matter. Do not be misled by local partners pushing that they are ISO 9001. ISO 9001 is defined as the internationally recognised standard for Quality Management Systems (QMS). It does not equate to being FDA standard.

If you still want to jump into this new market with the complexity that local manufacturing presents, and you are prepared to stake your career on it, let me tell you that, in my honest experience, the odds of you succeeding with this model are stacked very heavily against you.

The dead body count for something simple, such as an export model of finished goods to a partner or distributor in a distributor model is remarkably high. And those models are easy and remarkably simple. Yet far too many fail with such simple models.

Imagine then trying to succeed with the complexity of local manufacturing in compliance with local laws in the country of production.

Much of the drive to local manufacturing is from the Governments of these countries to create an increased flow of foreign direct investment (FDI), create local jobs, and strengthen the local economy for a given industry, or sector. Governments put a biased slant to attract that investment. Ethiopia did that several years ago, with a generous rent-free period with low-cost offices.

Imagine a company created a legal entity and signed a local manufacturing agreement. All was well for a few years. However, they did not carefully evaluate the risks of forex and changing fiscal controls in the local manufacturing operations. Within five years they were almost busted with debt. How? Because they could not get their debtors to pay them. Let me illustrate with an example based on Ethiopia:

In August 2013, the exchange rate was €1 = 25 Ethiopian Birr (ETB).

By August 2023. That exchange rate had devalued such that 1€ = 60 Birr.

The government have imposed a strict fiscal control policy on the banks. People start to bid for forex. You are trading in local currency (Birr) but struggle to convert it to your reporting currency and repatriate it back to corporate HQ to consolidate into the global financial reporting results. Imagine also the soaring inflationary prices for your products in Ethiopia with such devaluation. This is a real possibility, and such risks should never be underestimated. Local manufacturing means dealing in local currency and meeting all fiscal reporting in that country including paying local rates of taxation.

Local manufacturing remains a small percentage of total consumed products. In Africa, for example, over 90% of drugs and pharmaceutical medicines are imported as finished dose-forms manufactured outside of Africa and exported to different countries in an international scaleup and expansion model.

Furthermore, in Africa, Governments have been talking of a "Pharmaceutical Manufacturing Plan for Africa" (PMPA) for over two decades to reduce dependency on importing finished dose forms. At the start of those early discussions over two decades ago, less than 10% of drugs by volume were fulfilled by local manufacturing. Two decades on, it is still less than 10%! That is not much progress in over two decades! And that small 10% by volume is mainly in North Africa (Algeria), South Africa and Egypt.

So do not believe everything you read, or whatever some consultant tries to sell you as a strategy for access through a local manufacturing model. They might tell you it is the way to go. It is not. And there are plenty who went down that road and lost money, failed to get market share, and had low utilisation capacity of local manufacturing (one example ran at 30-40% of capacity for several years) with very few wins being documented or announced.

Local manufacturing presents many risks. In most cases, you move from trading at arm's length through a distributor, invoicing that distributor in your reporting currency and collecting payment in that reporting currency, to directly trading yourself in the market, selling goods to customers at prices set in local currency and collecting payments in local currency. This exposes you to currency risks, such as the example I illustrated earlier in this section.

These risks warrant serious consideration before embarking on this journey. It will also involve having to create a legal affiliate and I elaborate on that model in the next chapter. I do not recommend a local manufacturing model for anyone but the most senior experienced international sales expert capable of making an accurate investment case and confident in being able to deliver it.

It is better to look at other 'low-hanging fruit' countries with simpler, less risky models. Local manufacturing is extremely high-hanging fruit that you may never reach in ten years. If you are not a commercial giraffe able to stretch to such heights, then look for lower-hanging fruit! Your career might just thank you and reward you for that decision to stay away.

In some markets, entry can only be made either as:

1. Local manufacturing at the outset. For example, in Nigeria, the regulatory authority specifies some drugs that cannot be registered as they already have a number of those drugs registered. In such situations, the regulatory authority will allow a principal to set up local manufacturing. I have yet to see a compelling business case in this situation. The numbers do not add up when I have examined them. There is also the option to enter this market with newly registered products with a local manufacturing model. I can see no benefits but only risks with such a market entry model. The risks rarely justify local manufacturing, in my opinion.

2. In some markets, a principal may enter initially with a distributor with a condition of entry being to set up a local manufacturing facility within a defined period. This could be as short as five years or less (up to the renewal of the product registrations). Because initial entry is being made with a distributor, he is under no obligation to disclose to you that you will need to set up a local manufacturing facility at huge risk and cost to you. This is why your initial assessment of the environment is so important, alongside flushing out such surprises that hit you well into the market entry registration. I know of instances where a principal was not aware of this requirement at the first renewal of registrations.

Key Tasks Before Submission of Dossiers

Irrespective of whichever Go-to-Market model you decide, in simple terms, never submit dossiers for registration until the following are completed and agreed upon by the senior Executive Board:

1. A full quantitative and qualitative analysis of the market has to be completed and no aspect of the analysis can present a red line for your company and Executive Board. Examples of red lines may be currency volatility; the number of players already present that present challenging competitive forces and price sensitivity versus your proposed ex-factory price. This analysis is sometimes referred to as "a deep dive exercise" and should include the below points.

2. A full and accurate appraisal of the regulatory requirements and timelines and your company's ability to meet those requirements, or whether extra data needs to be generated. Involve your regulatory senior manager in this evaluation, estimate the timeline for approval as well as calculate regulatory costs payable to the regulatory authority in the market and confirm that you can comply.

3. A full business case investment appraisal is prepared to show:

   a. Pre-regulatory authorisation costs – both external costs payable to the authority as well as internal costs charged to your cost centre for regulatory approval. Companies do not have a money tree. As a regulatory service, the costs are borne centrally and usually supported by charges against each market P&L holder. Make sure you know what both those costs are.

b. Any market-specific peculiarities, such as market-specific labelling requirements that make for a high cost of goods for small market volumes with a potential for destruction costs if not sold to that market.

c. A requirement for manufacturing site inspection at the outset and thereafter at renewal with costs of such inspections highlighted.

d. If there is a requirement for local manufacturing downstream of initial registration. This may have a huge impact on your decision to enter.

e. Business case five-year forecasts post-regulatory approval based on volume and value of sales. They should include staff costs, selling and marketing expenses, capital equipment and if charged to your cost centre, you must add-in the costs of regulatory resources and support because those regulatory costs have to be recouped in the five-year sales forecasts. There is no free regulatory service internally. Either the company takes it as a central cost or shares the cost with each P&L holder.

f. The business case should also include currency volatility and availability of forex in your reporting currency (USD, GBP, or Euro) and repatriation ease or risks for consolidation into the group financial reporting function. Be aware of issues with trading in non-convertible currencies.

g. Summary of year 1 through to year 5 of sales, sales margin, costs, and gross profit. This summary is what you will be measured on to deliver each year.

Only after gaining approval and sign-off to this investment case by the senior Executive Board should you proceed.

No senior Executive Board should venture into new markets and international expansion without a thorough appraisal of risks and benefits. In reality, many do – on flawed and superficial business cases from staff that *"do not know what they do not know"* and staff *"that do not know what they are doing"* in a blind leading the blind scenario. It happens.

Any market that requires local manufacturing, or where you choose to deploy a local manufacturing model where it is not mandatory, carries a great many risks. A major multinational created a strategy in Africa to lower the price of their products through local manufacturing hubs that lowered the cost of goods (COGs). But with a lower price in Africa, it lowered its operating margins considerably declaring the cost of those products would be less than 50% of those in developed markets.

The trade-off to maintain profitability if you lower prices and lower margins has to be in increased volumes. Increasing volumes means finding new patients. And finding new patients is a challenge for all players in Africa. Indeed, anywhere, finding new patients and new customers is one of the biggest challenges facing any business. In the above example, where the company lowered its margins, it struggled to increase volumes and numerous other challenges. After more than a decade, it withdrew from the market, reversed the local manufacturing model and went back to exporting finished goods direct to distributors in Africa! What does that tell you about the local manufacturing model? You can guess.

Careful consideration is required based on the risk appetite of the Executive Board and the financial stamina of the company to sink monies into local manufacturing when such a move contradicts a manufacturing asset strategy of consolidating global assets rather than creating more manufacturing sites. Wherever there is local manufacturing under consideration, you must involve your main board Operations Director to assess and evaluate your proposed market-entry model. You are going to need his expertise and support.

In short, you might be the senior International Business Development Director, but you should not have sole authority to take the company down a path of sinking costs into high-risk investments. Therefore, you must deploy a joined-up approach involving different functions for that functional expertise into your proposed strategies. Involving others commits them to your plans. They are with you whether you sink, or you swim. It is just that they have someone to throw them a safety buoy if it all goes wrong. They will not drown in the water with you if it that happens. You cannot blame them, since, like the captain of the ship, you alone are responsible if the ship goes down. You took their advice, and you made your decision to move ahead with the plan.

You are in the water alone at sea because the final ultimate decision was yours. There is no responsibility without accountability. Always remember that. It is you who is accountable for delivering the numbers, for delivering the critical mass, and for delivering the investment case.

This makes the job quite lonely. You are on your own in the markets as the ambassador for the company and negotiating for the company's interests against distributors who may be shrewder and sharper than you at the negotiation table and who are selective with what information they feed you. They know that *"you don't know what you don't know."*

Part 2: Distributors

Distributors vary in size and scale and territorial presence. Let us remind ourselves of what I mean by a distributor.

A distributor is a trading company in an export market in which you wish to establish a trading business. The distributor is legally registered in that country and therefore able to offer employment to your staff, buy cars and other assets for your staff's use and offer premises. This is all on a reimbursable basis. He pays them and you pay him.

As a trader re-selling goods in the market, he should have a good idea of the market size and opportunities for your brand. And finally, the most important feature:

A distributor buys goods directly supplied by you from your manufacturing site, imports and clears the goods at customs, and sells them to <u>his</u> customers (who you consider to be your customers for your products supplied by the distributor). He creates demand collaboratively with you for your products (more on the distributor models later).

He pays you in your reporting or nominated currency, not in his local currency – for which he carries an exchange rate risk to buy foreign currency to pay you.

Furthermore, he typically purchases four large quarterly orders based on the sales forecast/sales budget. If that budget is $2m for the year, he buys approximately $500,000 of your goods per quarter.

A distributor holds stock of your product based on the legal agreement between you. He does not order products when a customer demands a product but holds his stock of your products in the market.

There are instances (such as with medical devices) where the distributor pays for products that he sells based on you placing consignment stock (belonging to you, until sold). With single-use devices, such as sharps and syringes, he will buy them from you. For more expensive devices, such as coronary stents or hip joint prostheses, you may operate a consignment model placing stocks into the distributor, paying for all the landed costs, and then invoicing him only for those he sells.

In my legal agreements, a distributor typically held three months' stock on his shelves at any time PLUS the goods on order. It is not three months of stock being the sum of goods on order and goods on the shelf. At least it should not be, and you are a poor negotiator if you succumb to this definition of stockholding. You run the risk of running out of stock and becoming unable to fulfil patient demand due to lead times from his order being received, making the goods to order and the shipment of goods.

In short, a distributor buys goods directly from you and sells them in the market. Keep this firmly fixed in your mind. We are going to revisit this later in the book.

The following schematic shows the relationship between the distributor, you as the manufacturer and the distributor's customers in the market. Note your distributor's customers include wholesalers, some of whom are distributors of other companies' products. I have also illustrated the impact of mark-ups. This is why designing the in-market distribution model is critical to success and attaining a critical mass.

Impact of Price Markups on Product
Flow from Manufacturer to Patients

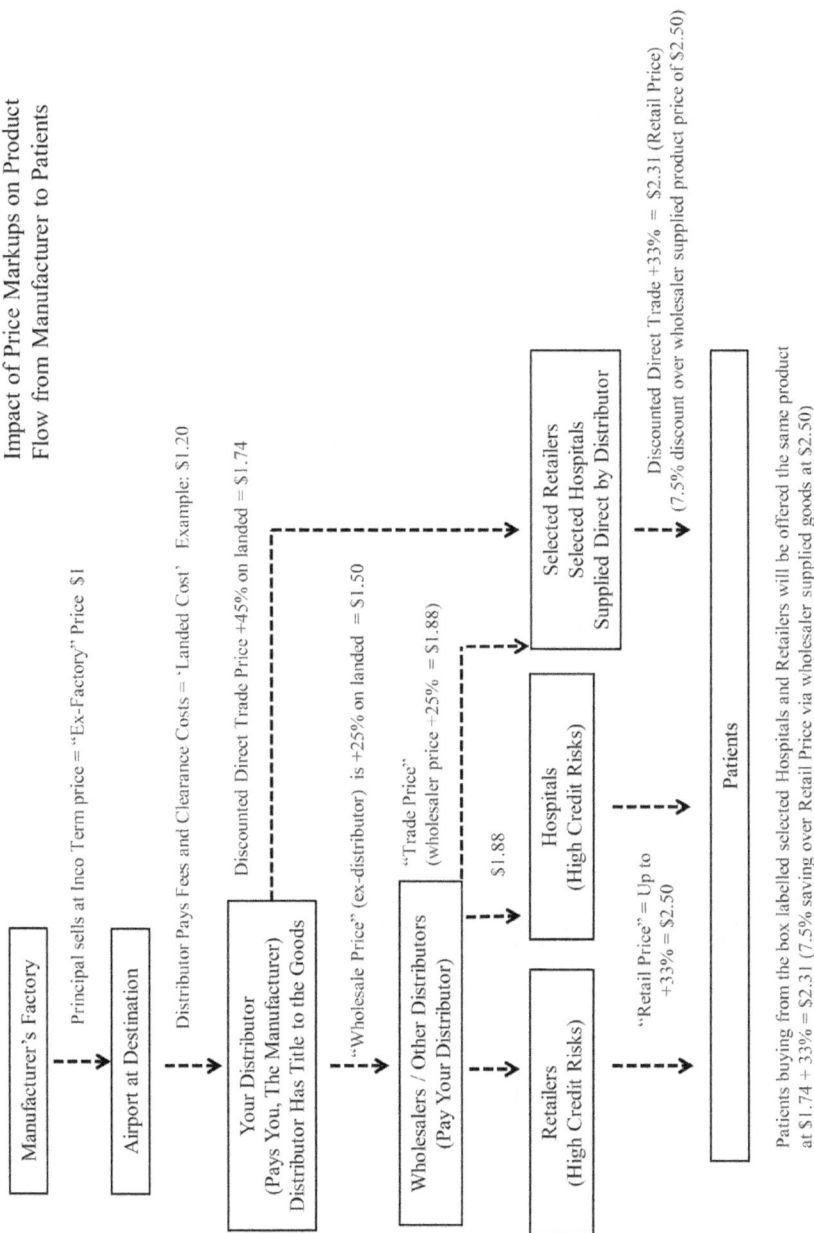

Principal sells at Inco Term price = "Ex-Factory" Price $1

Distributor Pays Fees and Clearance Costs = 'Landed Cost'   Example: $1.20

Discounted Direct Trade Price +45% on landed = $1.74

"Wholesale Price" (ex-distributor) is +25% on landed = $1.50

"Trade Price"
(wholesaler price +25% = $1.88)

$1.88

"Retail Price" = Up to
+33% = $2.50

Discounted Direct Trade +33% = $2.31 (Retail Price)
(7.5% discount over wholesaler supplied product price of $2.50)

| Manufacturer's Factory |

| Airport at Destination |

| Your Distributor
(Pays You, The Manufacturer)
Distributor Has Title to the Goods |

| Wholesalers / Other Distributors
(Pay Your Distributor) |

| Selected Retailers
Selected Hospitals
Supplied Direct by Distributor |

| Hospitals
(High Credit Risks) |

| Retailers
(High Credit Risks) |

| Patients |

Patients buying from the box labelled selected Hospitals and Retailers will be offered the same product
at $1.74 + 33% = $2.31 (7.5% saving over Retail Price via wholesaler supplied goods at $2.50)

77

This schematic illustrates the relationship between you as the manufacturer and your distributor. Notice the impact of channel markups in the destination market.

The distributor buys goods from you to sell in the market. He acts as a wholesaler supplying selected hospitals and retailers and he also sells your goods to wholesalers in the market. Note the wholesalers are his customers, not yours. The difference is that the distributor is the importer and re-seller, not the wholesaler. You have no direct relationship with the wholesalers.

Note also in this example the impact of markups for a product that you sell at $1 ex-factory. The price to the patient can become equivalent in local currency of $2.50 in this example. In other markets, this price to the patient can be even higher!

Note: Some of the wholesalers your distributor supplies may be distributors/importers of other companies' products. But they can only obtain your products by being supplied by your distributor. Therefore, they are wholesalers of your products. There is an important but subtle distinction to be aware of in this matter.

It supports what I stated earlier:

"All distributors are wholesalers, but all wholesalers are not distributors."

You may be thinking that your distributor sells to a few wholesalers and makes a nice margin for clearing goods, holding them in his warehouse, and selling to wholesalers.

So, you start to think....

Why not appoint one of those wholesalers at the current selling price to your distributor plus a smaller margin than the distributor is applying, and improve my margin?

Let me kill that idea straight away.

It is how so many seniors have derailed their careers in Africa.

The reasons why such a move will not work are many:

- Many wholesalers lack an import permit granted by the regulatory authorities for the importation, storage, and distribution of pharmaceutical products.
- Wholesalers may not be able to meet storage conditions for temperature and humidity or cold-chain facility for any sustained period.
- Most wholesalers do not have the liquidity to buy your committed annual volumes in four or six orders in a year. They may say they do, but trust me, they do not. They prefer to buy a few units daily or weekly to meet local demand.
- Wholesalers work with low inventory, low working capital, and high stock turn. Stock turn refers to how often the stock moves out to be completely replenished. In other words, they do not like goods tied up on the shelf that cost them money. Any goods they buy, they want them to come in and go out quickly, collect their cash and replenish as needed from the distributor – even single packs, rather than minimum order sizes of multiple dozens.
- Wholesalers are not involved in the promotion and marketing of your products or in the continuous regulatory activity that is required for registrations.
- Wholesalers deal mainly with only their local retail customers. They struggle to give you a country view of demand across different channels that a distributor can give you. The distributor works across channels. Therefore, he is better placed to discuss forecasting demand based on what he buys and sells across the country through a network of wholesalers and key accounts, such as hospitals. He may also have intelligence on Government purchases and opportunities for tenders.
- Wholesalers are extremely risk-averse. More so than distributors who are often acting as distributors for several principals. Imagine the value of stock tied up at a distributor's warehouse premises collectively across all his principals.
- Wholesalers are like market stall traders. They are transactional. They sell a pack here, and they sell a pack there, but only in that locality. They collect cash and that is it. The distributor has (or should have) national reach.

Distributors promise the Earth and deliver none of their promises!

Wholesalers promise to deliver nothing except line their pockets at your risk!

In a country where the affiliate's sales run into several hundred million dollars of sales, the manufacturing site can supply the affiliate directly for distribution and supply to the affiliate's customers through a third-party warehousing, logistics and distribution service provider that is erroneously labelled as a 'distributor'. I call such a service provider a 'box-shifter' because they just supply your products to your customers and charge you for the service. I will explain and elaborate on this model later in the book.

In practice, very few pharmaceutical companies will adopt this model in emerging markets because their business in those export emerging markets fails to achieve scale and critical mass to justify creating a legal affiliate. Setting up and running trucks, drivers, warehousing and distribution, invoicing and collecting the cash is simply too costly for an affiliate to justify versus the small size of the business.

However, in the home territory of the affiliate with many millions of dollars of sales, there is some rationale and logic to use a third party for warehousing and distribution on the grounds of cost-effectiveness and convenience. In such a case, the manufacturer supplies the affiliate. In this setup, the affiliate is a *de facto* importer AND distributor. The third party is NOT a distributor. It is a logistics and distribution company that charges the affiliate to provide these distribution and logistics services. The costs can be considerable for such services. This model using a third-party logistics provider carries considerable risks. This is the Pre-Wholesale Consignment Model that is operated through a third-party 'Intermediary' partner.

When the affiliate extends its home model of direct importation exporting to these emerging markets, with this pre-wholesale consignment distribution model that is operated on its behalf by a third-party logistics and warehousing provider to export products into emerging markets, the model has serious flaws. It is a model I do not recommend.

I mentioned that global manufacturing has moved away from making and storing stock locally to a process called 'Just-in-Time manufacturing' to forecasted orders. The forward visibility of forecasted demand means less wastage of materials. Making to order ensures the highest shelf life at the point of export and removes warehousing costs, inventory and working capital. Not holding goods in a warehouse and waiting for their sale means there is no shelf-life erosion. Shelf-life erosion can result in having to destroy the stocks because it has become short-dated or out of date.

This pre-wholesale consignment model for importing stock and storing it at a third-party service provider's premises takes an affiliate back almost thirty years on the manufacturing axis! It creates local stockholding in third-party warehousing and logistics service providers. These providers are not distributors.

Distributors buy and pay for goods from you, the manufacturer, to sell to wholesalers and hospitals, large accounts, selected retailers, and Government tenders.

Distributors take part in promotional activity and ideally should collaborate with you to grow your business. They should share some of the risks with you if you are a good negotiator.

A key role for distributors in your go-to-market strategy is drug registration and interacting with the market's regulatory authority through their in-house registered Nominee Signatory Pharmacist.

Wholesalers are not involved in collaborating with you as the manufacturer or interacting with the regulatory authorities to get your products registered. Wholesalers exist to sell to retail customers and are simply transactional in this respect.

When wholesalers do not pay distributors on time, they can upset the distributor's cash flow, which may affect the distributor's ability to pay for the next order. However, the distributor manages his cash collection through wholesalers.

I hope this has given you a good perspective on the options available:

- Agency Agreement
- Distributor Agreement
  - o Exclusive Agreement
  - o Non-Exclusive Agreement
  - o Sole Agreement
- Wholesaler
- Legal entity / affiliate
- Local Manufacturing / Local Production
  - o Build new assets on the ground in the market.
  - o Partner with an existing local manufacturer.

CHAPTER 3

Understanding Distributor Models

Part 1: The Four Distributor Models Explained

The term 'distributor markets' creates an impression that there is a simple one-size-fits-all model that companies use.

This is incorrect. It is not a binary choice – distributor or something else. There are several shades of grey within distributor models. These shades of grey are right for different companies with different appetites for risk and costs, different levels of ambitions and indeed with consideration of the portfolio and the segment in which you want to work.

These 'shades of grey' distributor models also define your likelihood of success at achieving scaleup and achieving critical mass. As I see it, there are four basic distributor models with three legal affiliate models. I will cover the legal affiliate models in a separate part.

So, there are a total of seven models to consider for your international scaleup and expansion!

The four distributor models are:

1. The Hamburger Model
2. Hamburger Plus
3. Basic Scientific (or Representative) Office
4. The Premium Scientific (or Representative) Office

These are summarised on the next page.

The Four Distribution Models Outlined

At a Glance Parameters by Model	Distributor Option 1	Distributor Option 2	Distributor Option 3	Distributor Option 4
	Hamburger Model	Hamburger Plus Model	Scientific or Rep Office (Basic)	Scientific Office (Premium)
Degree of Control	None	Very Low	Low	Very High
Costs to the Principal	Very Low	Low	High	High
Likelihood of Achieving Scale & Critical Mass	Zero	Very Low	Very Low	Very High
How Commonly Adopted	Very Common	Very Common	Very Common	Not Very Often

Option 2 and Option 3 are the most prevalent across the pharmaceutical industry that I have seen. Option 4 is the only distributor model that can attain a critical mass in my experience for reasons that I will explain. The costs are the same, or almost the same, as Option 3 but there is remarkably high control over the staff, and it gives a remarkably high likelihood of being able to achieve a critical mass for that very reason.

As a consultant, I see the greatest mismatches between client's go-to-market models and client expectations. Clients never convinced me that they had taken time to think through the models of best fit to realise a critical mass within five or ten years.

Too often, clients want both costs and risks to be low. But they want high control, and a high likelihood of scaleup to achieve critical mass! Control increases as the client spends more on the go-to-market model. If a client has a low budget, it will result in a low degree of control.

If achieving scaleup and critical mass to catalyse the business performance is the top reason for expansion internationally, then companies must recognise there are risks of failure. Such risks can be managed/mitigated if approached correctly. The ability to achieve critical mass can only happen by spending money and taking control of the staff and the market.

People with deep pockets but short arms cannot achieve scale and critical mass. They must spend on the best-fit model and seek the best professional advice when *"They don't know what they don't know."*

First, understand the distributor and his principal activities. I can outline these as:

Distributor Activities and Levels of Engagement

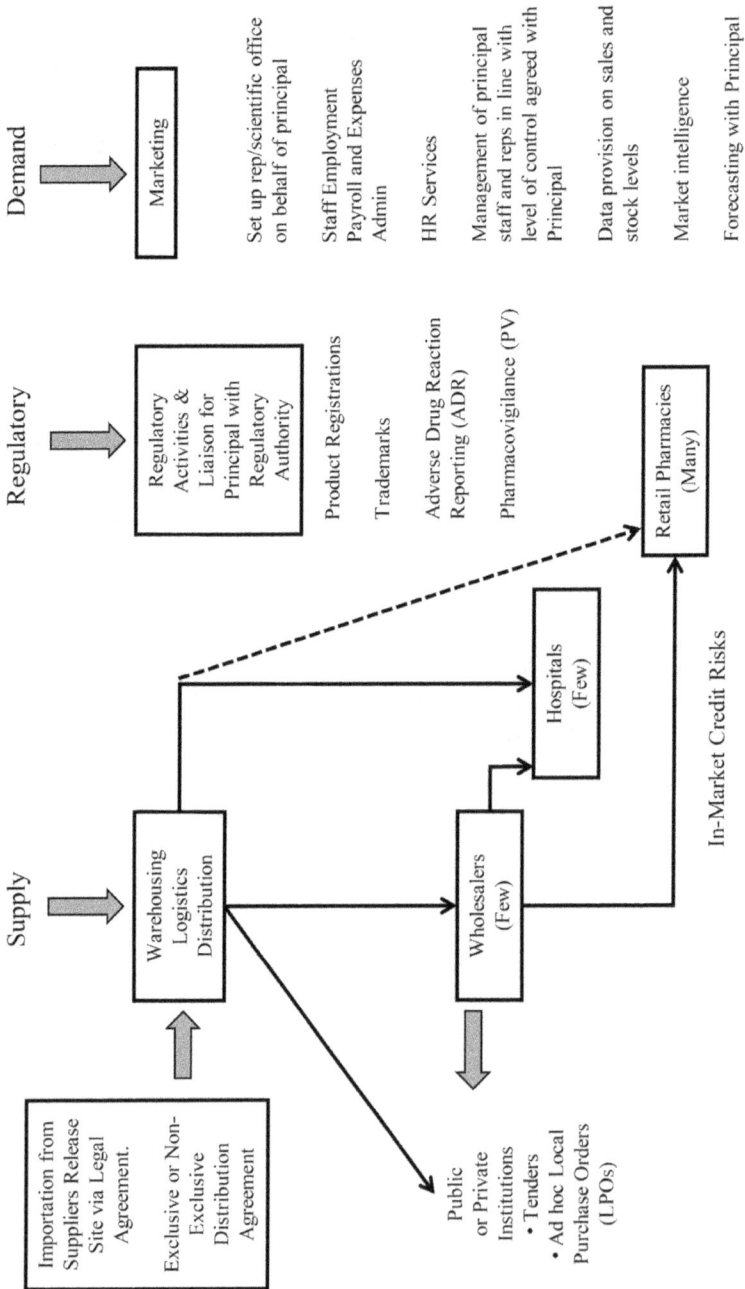

In designing and negotiating the distribution agreement, you need to decide what involvement you want to have for the distributor across those activity areas (Supply, Regulatory and Demand).

Letting the distributor manage everything is appropriate at some stage, and for some markets for some companies. As we describe the different models for distributors, you will see what is controlled by you, the principal, and what is controlled by the distributor.

Let me explain each of these distributor model options for distributor markets.

The Hamburger Model

So-called because I liken this to a hamburger maker who appoints a distributor to sell their hamburgers in another market. The manufacturer works on the basis: *"Tell me how many burgers you want to buy in the next 12 months, and we will ship to you in 12 monthly orders of equal volumes at the prices quoted. You pay for shipping and customs duties, and you are liable for any spoilage and unsaleable burgers. For any stock that expires, we will not be responsible. You take the write-off costs and are committed to the full 12 months' volumes under your contract with us."*

Imagine if anyone would order your hamburgers on such a basis. And paying cash-in-advance!

This model is described as: *"We have no risks; you have all the risks. Not our problem. The problem is entirely yours."*

The distributor only has the cost of regulatory submissions paid by the supplier. And that is usually because the supplier (you) wants the licenses in the manufacturer's name and are paying the regulatory costs for that reason.

The importer must fund the cost of promotion and create demand from customers from his selling margin. Occasionally, the supplier may agree to part-fund the cost of training a rep or sending promotional leaflets on a CD for local printing for reps to use.

Schematically, we can depict this Hamburger Model thus:

Hamburger Model

"tell us which of our range of hamburgers we should register with the agency, how much effort you will put into selling them and how many you will sell. We will supply them to you to your forecast"

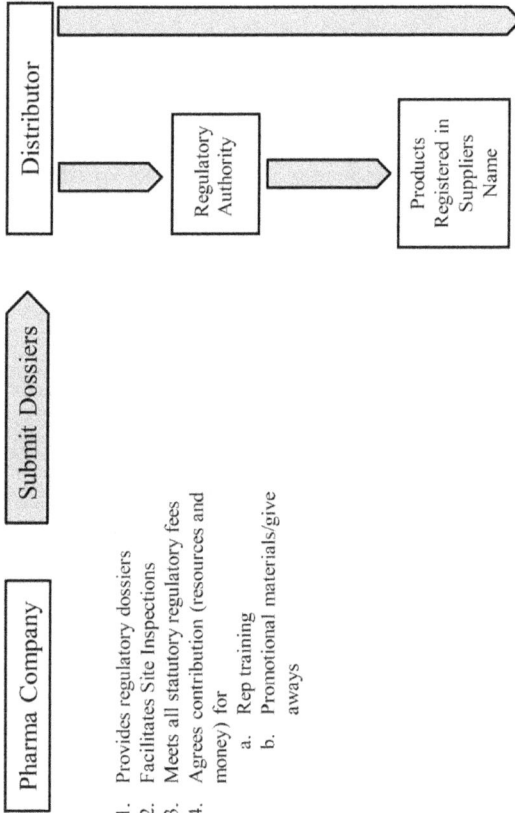

Pharma Company

1. Provides regulatory dossiers
2. Facilitates Site Inspections
3. Meets all statutory regulatory fees
4. Agrees contribution (resources and money) for
   a. Rep training
   b. Promotional materials/give aways

Submit Dossiers

Distributor

Regulatory Authority

Products Registered in Suppliers Name

1. Imports, Markets and Distributes Products (Supply).
2. Generates Demand to Deliver Forecast Volumes and Values
3. Cost of sales funded through margin on selling price and includes marketing expenses, KOL development, promotional material, reps and cars, training

Hamburger Model	
Pros	Cons
• Rock-bottom minimum cost • Minimal risk to the supplier • Guaranteed sales by volume and value within the contract terms and conditions	• The distributor will only commit to small volumes guaranteed to sell. • The distributor will put minimal effort into promotion as these activities are being funded from his pocket, from his selling margin or both. • Will never be able to achieve a critical mass whilst all the risks are on the distributor. • The supplier has no control over promotion once burgers are sold to the distributor. • Distributors are unlikely to have strong sales and marketing experience for your products to be a success.
Too many disadvantages to consider adopting this model. It is a model considered by high volume/low margin commodity suppliers, where products have little differentiation and so are unable to command any high price or high sales margin to the supplier. It relies on volume sales by the supplier in what might be described as "sell it cheap; pile it high." Not a serious model for any company that wants to scale up and achieve a critical mass.	

Hamburger Plus Model

This is essentially the same as the Hamburger model, with the addition that the manufacturer meets some of the costs of promotion. Despite the manufacturer bearing added costs compared to the Hamburger model, the Plus model confers no control over the sales activities in the market and the model has no chance of attaining scaleup and critical mass for the manufacturer.

Schematically, it can be represented thus:

Hamburger Plus Model

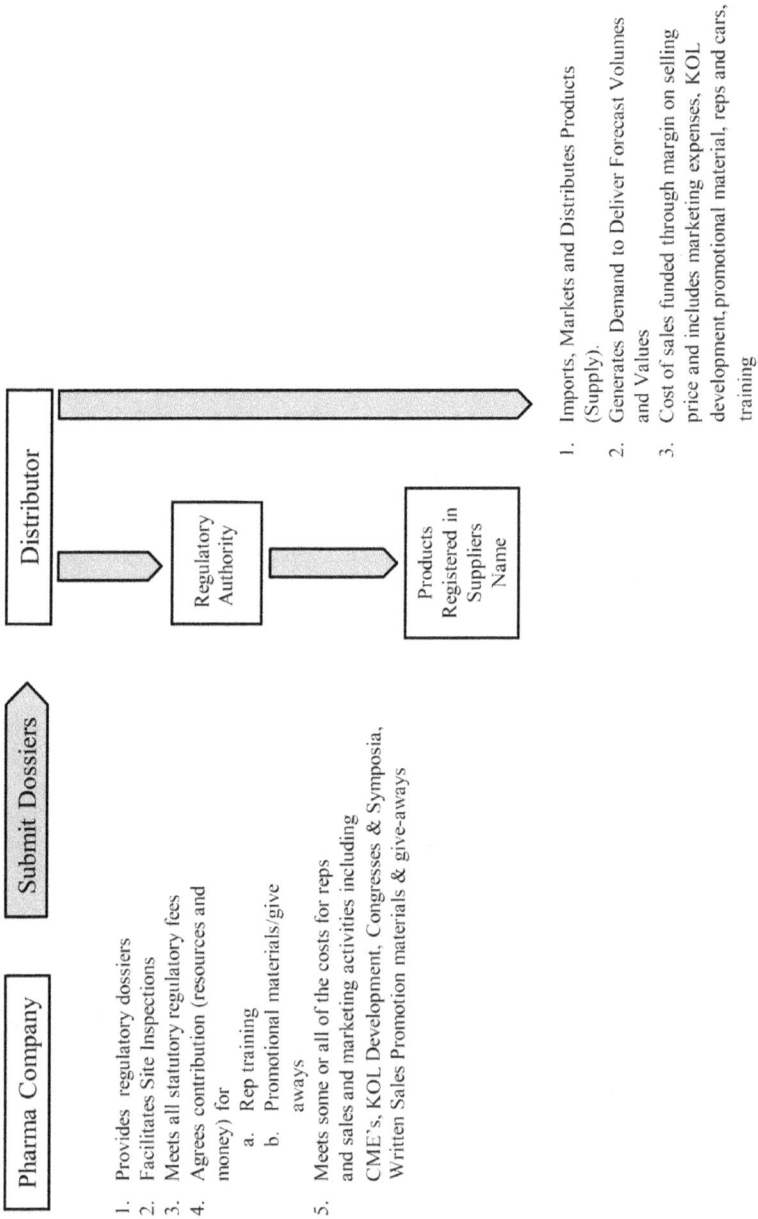

Pharma Company	Submit Dossiers	Distributor

Regulatory Authority

Products Registered in Suppliers Name

1. Provides regulatory dossiers
2. Facilitates Site Inspections
3. Meets all statutory regulatory fees
4. Agrees contribution (resources and money) for
   a. Rep training
   b. Promotional materials/give aways
5. Meets some or all of the costs for reps and sales and marketing activities including CME's, KOL Development, Congresses & Symposia, Written Sales Promotion materials & give-aways

1. Imports, Markets and Distributes Products (Supply).
2. Generates Demand to Deliver Forecast Volumes and Values
3. Cost of sales funded through margin on selling price and includes marketing expenses, KOL development, promotional material, reps and cars, training

The Pros and Cons are the same as the Hamburger Model.

There is extraordinarily little degree of control despite making some contributions to promotional costs. The distributor will only forecast small quantities as he is contractually bound to buy the agreed volumes to deliver the values set by the manufacturer. This confers no real advantages over the hamburger model for a manufacturer. There is extraordinarily little control despite contributing to some of the costs and therefore an incredibly low likelihood of achieving scaleup and critical mass.

Representative or Scientific Office Model: Basic

The basic version of the scientific or representative office model takes its name from the fact that your 'representative' (that is, your distributor) sets up a scientific office that forms the basis of starting or growing your business. The premium version of this model, if correctly set up and carefully negotiated with a distributor willing to work to this model, would be my go-to model of choice, where I wanted the greatest chance of achieving scaleup and delivering a critical mass business.

But let us first explore the basic rep office or scientific office model.

In the basic scientific office setup, the distributor manages the registrations and regulatory activities and thereafter manages all the demand activities (sales and marketing) of the products. The distributor controls both demand generation as well as supply fulfilment.

The scientific office can be a separate building leased by the distributor on behalf of the principal. Or it may be a section of his office for rent by the principal for the staff to work out of.

The costs of payroll, cars, marketing spend, and building lease are expensed and reimbursed by the principal to the distributor by monthly debit notes. Often cars are purchased outright by the distributor and amortised over a five year period to be then written off. The cars are in his name. The write-off value on disposal goes to him despite you having paid the amortised cost each month for the stipulated duration, typically over five years.

Payment for reimbursing the distributor is made from the HQ to the distributor's account in the manufacturer's reporting currency – GBP, USD, or Euro. Scandinavian manufacturers may invoice in their local currency as they are not using the Euro currency.

Alternatively, the principal may make payment to the distributor in his local currency if the bank can supply local currency (which they often will not, without high bank charges). And of course, the company is exposed to an exchange rate risk in this situation.

In the premium model, the principal negotiates the separation of the registration and regulatory activities from the importation and distribution of products (supply side). Thus, the demand creation activities (sales and marketing), and control of the sales staff are negotiated to be placed under the direct control of the manufacturer/ principal (you).

In both the basic and the premium scientific office model, the distributor appoints all the staff for the principal. The principal (you) is not legally present in the country and therefore cannot employ staff directly as employees. That is why the staff are employed under the name of the distributor and are employed under local employment law legislation.

Not all distributors will want you, the principal, to have control. Where the control is kept by the distributor (the basic model), there is little chance of achieving scaleup and critical mass.

Why is there little chance of achieving critical mass and scaleup with the basic scientific office model?

The reasons for this are many and include:

1. The distributor does not have the required level of ability in sales and marketing.

2. Distributor efforts are dispersed across a portfolio of the principal's products and usually reflect the contribution of each of those principal's portfolios contribution to his total sales income. If yours is a small value business, it will only receive a small amount of attention.
3. Distributor shares resources across different principals that are not visible to the principal. Despite paying for activities, the principal has little idea how much promotional effort is going into the brands versus the amount of promotion on the distributor's other principals' brands.
4. The distributor does not have the product knowledge or the training to develop the sales force to develop the demand to critical mass forecasted levels.
5. The distributor will not invest in the training and development of staff because these will likely be borne from his selling margin.
6. If you are starting a business or your business is small, and the distributor has a few large value principals, he will not devote time to setting up or growing your portfolio. It is not worth his time and effort to invest in growing your business. This is not a sign of a good-fit distributor aligned to your needs. You need a distributor who will devote time and effort to build your business if you are to achieve the ambitions you have promised to your senior Board.

There are many examples of a basic rep office or scientific office setup whereby the principal pays for staff costs, but there are numerous examples where the distributor has to fund the cost of staff from his sales margin. This latter practice is prevalent among generics manufacturers more often than large multinational global suppliers.

If you want to guarantee that your sales remain flat and incredibly low, tell a distributor that you will not pay for staff and that he has to pay for staff from his selling margin.

As an example, let us say his sales of your products in local currency are equivalent to $100k. After landing the goods from the airport to his warehouse, he applies a sales margin of 25% on his landed price to create a wholesale price. That margin is 25% or $25k from which he has to pay for his distribution and admin costs. Where does he have the capacity to fund a single rep on a basic salary of $20k? And with that budget, how does he finance a car for the rep and give him a marketing budget?

I reminded clients that did not want to pay staff costs but expected the distributor to fund those costs from his selling margin many times over that they had flawed ambitions that were the product of a "get rich quick" dream. Even reciting these numbers and realities, they still chose not to fund reps and issued legal agreements that stated the distributor had to meet the selling costs from his sales margin.

After a few years, such principals would let the registrations lapse and effectively close down and exit the market for their products. Then these same clients would say they could not succeed in Africa because of "greedy distributors". I found that a crazy nonsense statement.

Representative or Scientific Office Model: Premium

A scientific office model, if executed correctly in the form of the Premium Model, backed up by good analysis of the opportunity size, clarity on the segment to be competing in, getting the resource allocation correct (reps and headcount be commensurate to the size of the business) and a considered pricing model and strategy that can compete against the main competitors and focused on the right target customers, has a very high probability of scaleup and achieving critical mass. However, it needs the principal to be in control of the demand generation activities by having the skills in sales and marketing required to create demand.

Both the Premium and the Basic Models are relevant, based on opportunity size. The choice of model depends on the market, the opportunity size, and the ambitions to achieve a scalable critical mass within five years.

For example, I ran a Premium Scientific Office Model in Kenya. But in Sudan, I ran a basic Rep Office model. I had no rent to pay for the

94

distributor's office in Sudan as he managed the staff from his office. The distributor was accountable for delivering demand to forecast within agreed costs from me. He submitted the initial demand forecasts, and we negotiated the 'stretched' (higher) final value stretched by me which he always delivered. I had a better idea of the effect of the sales and marketing spend ability to create the required demand. The distributor's office was a scientific office by proxy.

A principal must be mindful of one feature in the Premium Model that is not present in the Basic model. In the Premium Model, the distributor will not be held to volume forecasts if the principal is in control of generating the demand for the products.

Think about that for a minute. He is responsible for supply fulfilment and you for demand generation.

You, as principal, oversee and control generating and creating demand to forecast. And you deliver that through the power and the control that you have over the staff and your broad cognitive bandwidth across sales and marketing before your appointment in an International Sales role. So, you cannot hold him to buy the demand forecast volumes. If the demand is not to the forecast, it is down to your failings, not those of the distributor.

You cannot have your cake and eat it. If you did not create the demand forecast to budget, it is your failing, not your distributors in this premium model.

Unfortunately, many international sales professionals fail to accept this. They try to blame the distributor for the failure when it was their failing.

On the next page, I share a schematic of the two Representative/ Scientific Office Models:

Representative or Scientific Office Model – Basic End-to-End Business Assigned to Distributor

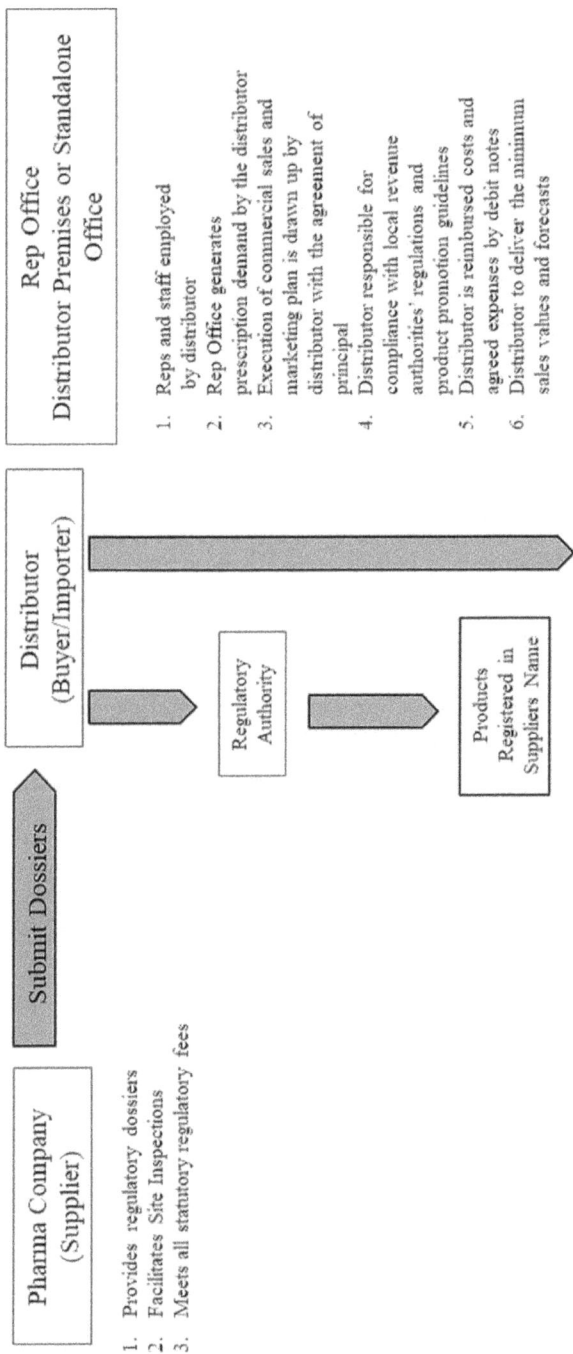

Pharma Company (Supplier)

1. Provides regulatory dossiers
2. Facilitates Site Inspections
3. Meets all statutory regulatory fees

Submit Dossiers

Distributor (Buyer/Importer)

Regulatory Authority

Products Registered in Suppliers Name

Imports. and Distributes
Products (Supply) to wholesalers. retailers. hospitals. large accounts and Government institutions.

Rep Office
Distributor Premises or Standalone Office

1. Reps and staff employed by distributor
2. Rep Office generates prescription demand by the distributor
3. Execution of commercial sales and marketing plan is drawn up by distributor with the agreement of principal
4. Distributor responsible for compliance with local revenue authorities' regulations and product promotion guidelines
5. Distributor is reimbursed costs and agreed expenses by debit notes
6. Distributor to deliver the minimum sales values and forecasts

Representative or Scientific Office Model – Premium
Supply and Demand Split Between Pharma and Distributor

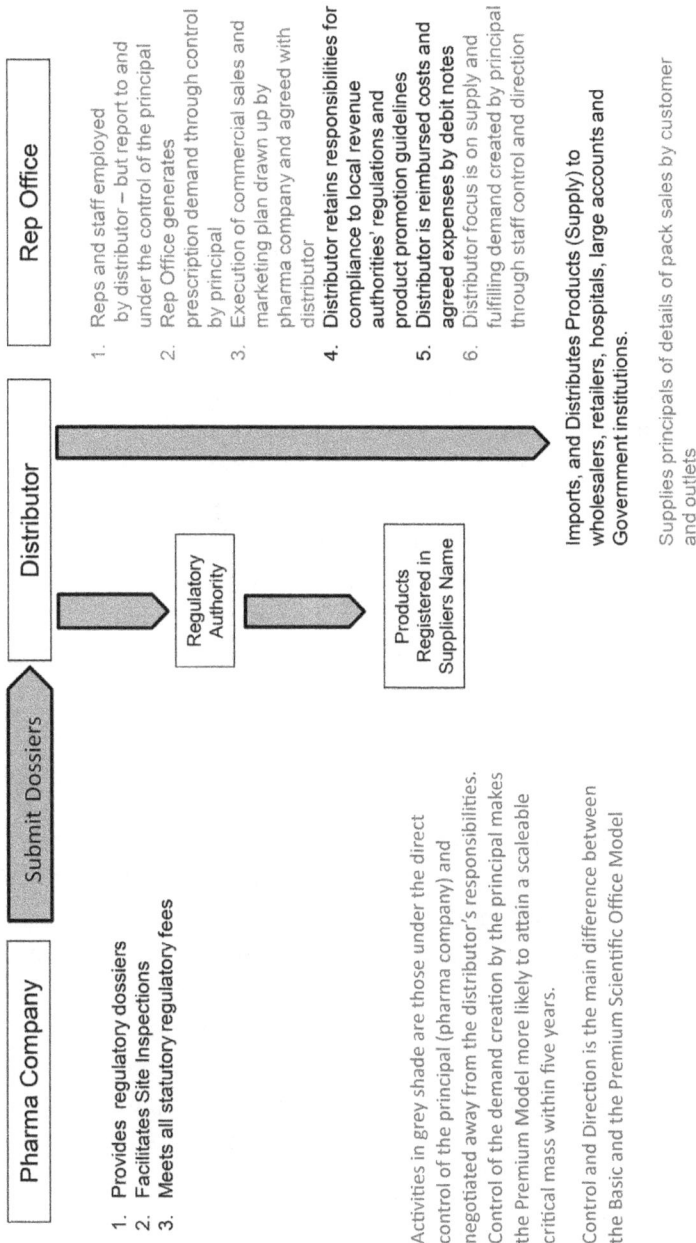

Pharma Company	Submit Dossiers	Distributor	Rep Office

Pharma Company

1. Provides regulatory dossiers
2. Facilitates Site Inspections
3. Meets all statutory regulatory fees

Regulatory Authority

Products Registered in Suppliers Name

Activities in grey shade are those under the direct control of the principal (pharma company) and negotiated away from the distributor's responsibilities. Control of the demand creation by the principal makes the Premium Model more likely to attain a scaleable critical mass within five years.

Control and Direction is the main difference between the Basic and the Premium Scientific Office Model

Rep Office

1. Reps and staff employed by distributor – but report to and under the control of the principal
2. Rep Office generates prescription demand through control by principal
3. Execution of commercial sales and marketing plan drawn up by pharma company and agreed with distributor
4. **Distributor retains responsibilities for compliance to local revenue authorities' regulations and product promotion guidelines**
5. **Distributor is reimbursed costs and agreed expenses by debit notes**
6. Distributor focus is on supply and fulfilling demand created by principal through staff control and direction

Imports, and Distributes Products (Supply) to wholesalers, retailers, hospitals, large accounts and Government institutions.

Supplies principals of details of pack sales by customer and outlets

In a Scientific Office model, the office may have a sign something like this:

"(Pharma Company) (Country name) Represented by (Name of Distributor)

This gives away that the principal (the pharma company) is not legally registered as a company in the country. There are many examples of this model – largely where the activities of supply and demand are the basic model controlled by the distributor with the principal paying some or all the costs and leaving both the supply and demand creation activities under the charge of the distributor! Smaller companies tend not to pay for staff costs – for example reps. Instead, they leave the cost of staff to be funded by the distributor's selling margin.

This situation is to be avoided. In my experience, where I did not have control over a premium scientific office model, I struggled to reach a critical mass. In both the Premium and the Basic models, you as the principal are paying the cost of operations and, in any case, if you are paying the staff costs in each model, then not taking control by splitting out demand creation to be under your direct control is crazy. You may choose not to take control of the staff if you are stretched too thin in all the other activities that go with the job.

The worst model is where you leave the reps to be funded out of the distributor's selling margin. In such a case, your distributor will price your products high and appoint very few staff. Demand generation will be non-existent leading to an incredibly low value of sales.

You can only achieve scale and critical mass by taking control and drawing on your experiences in sales, marketing, recruitment and selection, performance management, HR basics, and negotiating and spending time in the markets. Taking and having control costs money!

Put another way:

If you want to achieve a scalable critical mass within five years, you must have total control of the demand-generating activities (sales, marketing, publicity, PR, KOL development etc.) even if the staff are employed by the distributor. You must decide how many reps are in what locations through discussions with the distributor. You must be involved in the recruitment of those reps and staff because you are going to pay their costs to the distributor – salaries, on-costs, provident fund (pension fund), health insurance, cars, marketing expenses etc.

Some principals are paying for all these costs of staff but have no day-to-day involvement in the activities, nor planning and control over the sales and marketing activities in the countries. Truly bizarre.

Even more bizarre are those principals that had control, many had staff employed directly by their legal affiliate, and still failed to achieve critical mass. So, in desperation, they re-assign the staff to a distributor who has them under the distributor's payroll to take control of the staff (often reduced in numbers). This is called "handing the business back to the distributor."

But this still has costs associated with it.

The distributor is not going to take on your staff from his funds. He will want you to agree to fund those costs and simply take them off your headcount and shift them to "variable selling expenses" by sleight of hand in your financial reporting. But you still bear those costs, irrespective of how you report the costs!

This is extremely short-sighted for seniors. They reveal poor cognitive bandwidth with such an action. Imagine, if with all your expertise of your products and the expertise and support available to you within your company for sales and marketing, your company's resources that you have for providing training and development, financial accountants, and other resources, and you STILL cannot succeed!

Now ask yourself how your decision to hand the task of achieving critical mass back to a distributor that is outside of your company could be successful. They lack the expertise of your company and can never devote as much attention and focus on your business as you; so, ask yourself how a distributor can stand any chance of achieving what you yourself could not.

Many companies have implemented such bizarre practices in Africa and thrown millions of dollars of cumulative investment down the drain, only to throw more money down the drain with this bizarre move of handing the business back to the distributor!

Be clear. If you cannot achieve critical mass, then you have failed. Accept this simple message! Take solace in the fact that you are not alone. Many seniors in international business fail to deliver the results set for them by their Executive Boards, as far as I have witnessed across Africa. I reckon this is similar in other emerging markets using distributor partnership models.

The only variable is that some senior Boards are more tolerant of failure than others and some senior Boards have an abundance of indecision about taking drastic steps to solve an underperformance.

When you fail, the solution is not to hand it to a distributor to achieve what you could not achieve. That is sheer lunacy – and costly lunacy at that!

The solution (if your company has kept you on) is to close down your costs to create a cash cow model by laying off all the staff, letting the registrations lapse at renewal and retaining your distributor until renewal so that he can purchase your brands to fulfil the small demand that is there in the market that will tail off without promotional effort. Do not pay for staff costs in this situation.

Part 2: Why Do So Many Fail?

The reasons why so many fail in international sales as I have witnessed from my time in Africa (and it must be similar in other markets) are complex, with no single factor attributable to failure. Rather it is a blend of factors coming together into an amalgam that drives failure.

One factor is a lack of understanding of the markets. And that is directly proportional to time spent in the markets. The job of international sales is out there in the markets. It is not sitting at your desk in a plush office in England or Dubai or South Africa.

I spent typically 20 – 30 weeks a year collectively in my top five markets. On each visit, I would spend time with the distributor, Key Opinion Leaders, (KOLs) and maybe a competitor distributor or two. I might even meet potential recruits who expressed an interest in joining the company via enquiries received by the scientific office or through the distributor. I would arrive Sunday and work Monday through Friday evening in the market before flying home late Friday evening or Saturday morning. Being in the market for a full week at a time gave me a real feel and view of the business and the opportunities.

I would go with reps and field managers to see for myself their standards and how well they were implementing the campaigns. That enabled me to design ongoing sales training and management training programmes that I designed and delivered (I had been the UK Sales Training Manager among my many roles before international sales).

I worked for one pharmaceutical client on a project. Sales were abysmal. Seniors brought me in to assess and define a pan-African strategy. Sales were so poor that after more than 10 years under the distributor in a Hamburger Plus Model for several years followed by a more costly fully expensed Basic Scientific Office Model, they were only around $1m and they were paying for four reps and a supervisor

101

plus other costs with some cost-sharing by the distributor from his selling margin for HR and Regulatory support.

I looked at East Africa. The Head of East Africa was based in South Africa. When I interviewed this gentleman, he had upgraded from a Hamburger Plus model for several years to a basic scientific office inside the distributor premises. He had no control or awareness over the day-to-day activities of the four reps and field supervisor in Kenya. That headcount did not justify the mediocre sales performance.

I probed to find out how much time he spent in the field.

In one year, he had spent less than three full days! The prior year was similar.

That client had appointed a guy to lead East Africa based in South Africa who had left everything with the distributor despite paying all the costs for the reps and the non-existent sales and marketing of products with no idea or awareness of field activities such as how many customers are being seen, how often, and by which rep.

Sadly, for too many companies, this is the typical setup and the typical guy they employ to develop their international sales in Africa. It is highly likely to be prevalent in other geographies and markets. Seniors making such appointments should be held to account by their Executive Boards for such flawed thinking and flawed models.

I started this section by stating one critical success factor for International Sales is *"time in the market"*: *"You cannot succeed without spending time in the markets."*

If that thought is abhorrent or risks wrecking your marriage, I would urge you to think carefully before considering a move into an international sales role. The job is being out there. The job is not in an office. It is out there in the countries with customers and your staff.

I will cover this in the profile of the person most likely to succeed later in the book.

Three magic ingredients to success in International Sales begin to emerge and I will develop each of these as we progress, as well as add other factors. Right now, the three factors that emerge are:

1. **Cognitive bandwidth.** This is a product of skills and capabilities gained in a variety of roles with a consistent track record of delivery and abilities proven by results (not paper qualifications). I might describe this as a well-rounded individual capable of wearing many hats across separate and varied roles with a consistent track-record of delivery in all those roles.

   These 'distributor markets' usually cannot sustain lots of headcounts before achieving a critical mass. So, the job holder needs to be the Sales Director, Marketing Director, HR Director, General Manager, Key Accounts Director, Sales Training Manager, Commercial Negotiator and so on. He can only be in those roles if he has experienced those roles and delivered successful results consistently in every role without any gaps.

   These individuals cannot wear those hats if they have never done and delivered in those roles before being appointed in International Sales.

   International Sales nowadays require your most skilled and experienced talent. It is not a dumping ground to hide away the problem of poor performers in another part of the business. Other roles, possibly. But not international sales roles. More about this in the chapter on the profile of the person who succeeds in this role.

2. **Being in total control of activities** in the markets through well-designed best-fit commercial models negotiated with distributors. Such models should always be to your company's benefit more so than the distributor's. I have seen far too many young guys in this business who are simply incapable and incompetent and cannot negotiate. As a result, they ended up giving away far too much to the distributor without gaining something in return. That is not negotiating!

3. **Time in the market.** You cannot achieve anything unless you spend time in the markets talking to people, meeting them, understanding what drives success, and understanding the channels and players. You should also be spending time in the market to spot talent if you decide to change a key member of staff or they resign unexpectedly. It is sensible to have a pool of backup ready-now candidates per country if your GM for country X was run over by a bus. This is particularly relevant for smaller companies and family-owned and family-run businesses.

Unless you have control, your business cannot and will not scale up and achieve critical mass.

I have outlined some of the reasons why. If you do not have control, you are sinking money into a black hole without knowing where and on what the distributor is spending it. This type of setup, where you do not have control, is the reason so many principals do not achieve scaleup and deliver a critical mass. They have placed too much reliance on the distributor.

Ignore completely any distributor's claims of being able to achieve wonderful results for you. Begin with the premise that all distributors over-promise and deliver nothing. These distributors often have many principals and will spend time on their big accounts – not the tiny start-ups like you, entering a new market that requires distributors to work for a living.

You should be able to find a distributor that will collaborate with you to give you control of staff. If your first-choice guy declines to work on your model basis, keep looking until you find one who will work for your model.

The key is that they must work to your model, not the other way round.

Once you divide the activities of registration and supply from demand creation (sales & marketing and staff) you will put yourself in control of sales and marketing as well as forecasting, as in the Premium Scientific Office Model. This means you will be in full control and able to set up control measures and a dashboard of key metrics that enables you to fly the aircraft with a full array of dials and gauges to know where you are on the journey.

You will work in consultation with the distributor on forecasts and the business.

Most companies cannot achieve critical mass and scale with a basic scientific or representative model (the distributor is your representative). When I investigate why they are not achieving scale and critical mass, one feature stands out:

They have left their business in the hands of the distributor – the Basic Scientific Office Model.

As a result, they have little visibility on how the business is being run. They have also lost direct involvement in generating demand for the products. They do not spend enough time in the markets. They cannot assess the effectiveness of the promotional campaigns and the promotional mix, and they are no longer leveraging their own company's core capabilities in the sales and marketing of the company's products.

When they present to their senior Board an underperforming business woefully adrift from the budget and targets, they offer the same set of weak recycled excuses for failure. But the reality is that they do not know what they are doing. Neither does their distributor! For some lucky individuals, their Board knows little about export business and distributors and accepts the same set of recycled excuses year in/year out. Quite possibly, one can infer that the Board may not know what it is doing in this International Territory.

After presenting my findings and recommendations to a client's senior Board, I sometimes have to share with the senior sponsor of the project that they had staff who did not know what they were doing, and that they needed to address this matter urgently.

To deliver critical mass, a company needs talented folk who really understand and know what they are doing and why they are doing it. You will be surprised to hear just how many seniors are not aware they have staff running international export markets who do not know what they are doing. It is an easy deduction. If your staff are not able to deliver the numbers and budget for several years, you clearly have staff who do not know the markets, who do not know the business, and therefore do not know what they are doing!

So often, on a market visit, the distributor and the client's country head would try to dazzle me with their understanding. And so often, I had to interject and stop them and say *"I know all that! Tell me something I do not know!"* So never assume you have talented staff and partners until they prove it to you through results!

No distributor will ever know the sales and marketing of your products better than you and your company's support functions. Always remember this. Never forget it. Distributors will tell you otherwise with stories of how they can transform your brand. Until you unravel (with examples from the distributors) what his role was versus the role of the principal that owned the brands, this is largely rubbish.

No distributor will appreciate and understand the core principles of how to drive sales force excellence – the relationships around targeting, segmentation, activity levels, directed promotional expenditure, developing key opinion leaders, or designing optimum field force structure, and how to drive effective demand creation (in my case, driving branded prescriptions by name for my products). If you want to test a distributor, ask him how he implements the concept of 'diffusion of innovation' as applied to your brands and how he will identify your customers in that concept. You will receive blank stares for sure!

If you leave things in the hands of the distributor, you will not achieve scale and critical mass that is commensurate with the size of the opportunity. You will achieve sales. *But nothing commensurate with the size of the opportunity.* Do not be misled by absolute value.

$500,000 in sales in year 5 after having invested $1 million might look acceptable to you, but not to your Executive Board. They see your market share in an opportunity size of $10 million growing at 15% per annum for the past five years as "barely scratching the surface".

If you had worked for my seniors, you would be constantly reminded that only three metrics matter. In order of priority, they are:

- Market Share.
- Market Share... and...
- Market Share!

Leaving your business in the hands of the distributor acting as an incubator will be a sad result for you. You will see the year-on-year disappointment in the failure to achieve targets and budget results that I have seen over and over again with many companies. You may as well downgrade to a Hamburger model with no staff and save yourself some of the costs you were paying in the basic scientific office model.

The distributor in a basic scientific office model will explain repeatedly the reasons why your sales were not met, using one or more of the following arguments:

- Your prices are too high. You need to cut the prices at which you sell products to him. But he will not make a corresponding reduction in his selling price in the market. You reduce your margin by cutting prices as he requests. Think about it: You have already failed to meet sales, and now he wants you to fail on margin and of course your profitability target for the year.

- You need to increase the number of reps because the competitors have more reps than you. This is a red herring. You and he sat down and discussed his sales forecast, and he based it on how many reps are required and in which locations and how much share-of-voice (SOV) you need based on the competitors. In other words, to stand a chance you had to be close to matching the activity levels and the 'noise' of the competitors. Why now does he say, "You need more reps"? You must ask "What has changed"?

- In some markets, unknown to you, your reps under the distributor's control are not engaged in promotional activities on your products with customers. He will not tell you that. But I know they are being engaged as delivery boys delivering a range of his products (these may not even be your products) to customers. They are also his credit management team chasing up customers for the collection of outstanding invoices. And you have been paying for the staff to generate prescription demand whilst they remain under the control of the distributor?

This happens a lot in Nigeria. Your staff have become the distributor's delivery team that is free to the distributor because he is invoicing you their payroll and you foolishly are sending him payment for those staff costs each month on debit notes.

A clear demonstration of *"You don't know what you don't know."*

- He tells you that recruitment for vacancies was frozen by you because sales were so poor. But how do you confirm those reps existed and have now left the distributor and not been replaced because of your moratorium on filling vacancies when sales were so bad?

Leaving your business in the hands of a distributor will not enable you to achieve a critical mass commensurate with the opportunity size that drove the investment decision. I have seen examples of big Pharma using the Basic Scientific Office Model in key markets such as Ghana and Kenya that after ten years had ex-factory invoiced export sales of only $800k and $1.2million sales, respectively.

Contrast that to a similar portfolio that I set up in those same markets with a Premium Scientific Office Model that went to sales of $4m and $7m respectively in five years from such low baseline sales.

The Premium Scientific Office Model splits demand creation away from the distributor and puts it under me, the principal. I take control of the staff and all sales and marketing to create demand for the products. The distributor provides distribution and logistics and takes credit risks of payments from the customers in the country. He buys my products invoiced in USD, so I have no exchange rate risks for my reporting currency. He takes the exchange rate risks by buying USD with his Kenya Shillings.

One of my unique features as a consultant, based on my corporate life, was that I could work seamlessly across the demand-supply axis. For too long, in corporate life, I inherited a situation where the company agreements had put distributors in charge of our business.

I worked in significant commercial roles in the UK in sales, sales management, sales and leadership training, commercial development, business analysis, and major change projects on business processes but, crucially, I worked in the international Manufacturing Operations in the Global Supply Chain and Logistics business unit.

Distributors were literally *"up against it with me"* because I knew the supply side and channel management side of their business to a remarkably high standard, but I also knew the demand-creating side of their business much better than they did.

Conversations with distributors showed how poorly and how little they understood anything about sales and marketing. There were no marketing plans. No performance targets or activity reports – who was being seen by whom, and how often? What coverage were they achieving on the target customers? I asked for a list of target customers for our different therapy areas. There were not any! Then in another country, one distributor and the country manager produced a list of over 400 clinicians as target and when I asked if this was the universe or the target group, I was met with *"What's the difference?"* Two comedians who clearly had no clue!

Amazing, but true.

The Role Played by Senior Executive Board Members in Failure to Achieve a Critical Mass

To conclude this section on why so many fail, I must mention the role that senior Executive Board members play in this failure. As much as they will not want to admit it, they too are responsible and have contributed to the failure in several ways:

1. They have often allowed repeated non-delivery of the numbers by accepting inexcusable reasons for performance shortfalls for far too long. Allowing your senior leader for international sales to fail repeatedly actually makes the problem a bigger and costlier one to solve the longer you leave it.

2. When they do 'bite the bullet' and remove an under-performer, they often repeat the selection mistake when choosing the replacement. I elaborate on this in a separate chapter on how to pick winners for these types of international business models.

3. Many are remarkably impervious to offers of help by independent experts when, in reality, they desperately need it. Maybe their pride prevents them from an admission of failure that is inevitably perceived by bringing in an outside doctor. So, they tend to stick with their witchcraft traditional healer in a grass skirt to miraculously create some sort of concoction that can reverse the past failed years. But they stand to be extremely disappointed.

4. They stand to be disappointed because they fail to recognise that the new witch doctor, that they have installed is a complete bluffer. He has no clue either what he is doing. But his chants and dances around the fire dressed in a grass skirt impress those seniors and they go to bed each night with a dollar bill tucked under their pillow for good luck that the new witch doctor they installed, is going to change the results. But they are in for a disappointment. Nothing will change for the reasons below.

5. The new witch doctor is also impervious to offers of help from an independent expert. This expert knows the witch doctor does not

know what he is doing. This expert does know what he is doing and can predict the areas that need immediate attention to change the results.

The witch doctor has no clue, so she puts the issues back to her local management team in the market to address and sort out. But her trust is misplaced. Imagine asking the same set of local seniors who created the mess, and who repeatedly failed to deliver the numbers, to produce a solution that will work for the first 12 months of the new witch doctor's tenancy. Relying on those who have shown themselves to be incompetent and expecting them to define a solution that can work is sheer lunacy.

6. So, the independent expert reaches out to the senior Executive Board member at corporate HQ who confirms dissatisfaction with the results but merely redirects him to the witch doctor on the ground!

Then these very seniors at the local regional level and corporate HQ level moan with frustration that their teams repeatedly fail in the international sales delivery of numbers through distributors in Africa! And they try to blame it on their distributors and stock shortages, along with other myths and works of fiction that I can see through but those senior Executive Board members at corporate cannot.

However, they have only themselves to blame. Repeating the same incompetence, both through their own actions and through their regional local seniors, whilst expecting a different set of results is indeed lunacy!

The only solution is for a senior corporate board member to take control and bring in an outside independent expert to define the issues and propose recommendations to put the mess right. It is NOT a solution to use the helpful expert who approached you with the idea of helping you to deny his help, and instead, use the local witch doctor, who does not have the real answers and is in fact shooting in the dark.

So, the solution rests with senior corporate Board members at HQ not to put up with repeated failure as long as they do (certainly never beyond three years or three P&L cycles). And they must acknowledge and accept that repeated failure confirms their guys do not know what they are doing. They need to bring in an outside independent expert to diagnose and propose what is needed. Someone who really understands these models and has a track record of success supported by years of delivery of the numbers.

But they must choose wisely. There are many consultants out there who can sell a good story, like reading a child a book at bedtime. But in reality, they produce fancy charts and PowerPoint® slides but cannot address the issues. They will talk in terms of "the what" to consider but cannot explain "the how" to address it. They will spout textbook theories that you could read for yourself at a fraction of the consultant's cost.

In all my consulting assignments, it has been a senior corporate board member outside of Africa who has shown dissatisfaction with the present, and dissatisfaction at the abject repeated failure of his senior regional team to deliver the numbers of their guys. They no longer want to put up with the recycled excuses year in/year out and have decided to bring me in as an expert to get clear answers as to why the business is not performing. And I will answer these factors as you will read in the book.

Where I have such a senior sponsor, the engagement has been truly remarkable and fruitful. But if that senior sponsor passes me to the regional witch doctor, there is no engagement and another repeated set of failed numbers. Guaranteed.

I can only point a strong finger of blame at their senior masters – the Executive Board members – who fail to even want to act; who fail to take a grip and unravel what is really going wrong with their Business; and fail to understand why their business through distributors cannot deliver the numbers or their investment cases. And yet through this darkness, many seniors declare Africa and its undoubted opportunities were a challenge that proved elusive for them to succeed. They fail to find a flashlight or torch to illuminate their path to success. They stay and stumble in the darkness. Shooting in the dark is their norm. As a reader, if you are a senior Executive Board member, I urge you not to do this. Take decisive steps, take control, and stop listening to guys who repeatedly let you down with non-delivery.

You must be surrounded by people, and a team of senior leaders in these international markets, who know what they are doing and can demonstrate that feature through consistent results delivery of the numbers. Clearly, if they fail to deliver their numbers for two or more years, this is living proof that you do not have people who know what they are doing (leaving aside a catastrophic nuclear explosion or invasion by an aggressor or pandemic infection in your markets that closes down financial institutions and supply chains and the airports and shipping ports).

Part 3: Do You Push When You Should Pull?

In the examples I explored earlier, I mentioned that I changed the model by splitting the demand-creation activities away from the supply-side activities. This is the Premium Scientific Model. In the Basic Scientific Office Model, both the demand creation and the supply side activities are contained inside the distributor's accountabilities.

My firm view is that demand-creation is critical to attaining a critical mass. The premium scientific office has one single clear focus – demand creation (prescriptions) with high control and visibility of activities down to the level of each rep and manager whilst I was sitting in my office in the UK. I knew who was visited by an AstraZeneca rep, and what products were discussed, and I would know who was short on activity versus their activity targets and who was becoming repeatedly short on meeting activity targets. That was control! Very few have such a level of control. My office dashboard told me all that I needed so that I was in total control of what was going on and what actions needed to be taken before it was too late.

I moved the model away from the distributor's 'push' model, trying to push products into the customer channels with the company trying to 'push' products onto the distributor to continually buy more products.

Working a 'push' model is akin to putting the cart before the horse. It can never enable you to attain a critical mass. Without demand, the stock just sits there at the distributor, eroding its shelf life.

To create a 'pull' model, in my experience, distributors are not gifted with the marketing capabilities that we in this industry possess. The strongest 'pull' model is where you take control of demand creation.

I made a fundamental shift to a 'pull' model, where I created prescription demand that pulled products out of the distributor's shelves and into the hands of dispensing staff in retail pharmacies and hospital pharmacies, who were in turn putting the products into patients' hands.

There is another observation here:

In order to achieve a critical mass within five years, only the 'pull' model has the capabilities to achieve this for you. So many companies focus on the 'push' model pushing distributors to buy stock and signing up multiple distributors that each have to buy an initial three-month stockholding. This is a recipe for disaster.

Why?

The answer is simple and is another one of my oft-quoted mantras:

1. "Demand ALWAYS precedes supply."

2. "More distributors do not add more sales."

Multiple distributors (more than two) are a fallacy if they all have identical products at identical ex-factory prices. If a company has sales of $1m with one distributor, adding another distributor with the same products at the same prices adds <u>nothing</u> to the sales for the country. This is because the demand side remains the same. These two distributors share the cake. Where previously the one distributor enjoyed in-market sales from $1m import sales, they now each share it. They will then lose interest in your business; they won't want to help the other distributor have a share of the demand they have created, and your business will never achieve critical mass.

To illustrate the practical example of a basic scientific office versus the premium version, I had a control group in another market where I left the business in the hands of the distributor with a similar opportunity size within the cluster in a Hamburger Plus model/Basic Scientific Office model.

Without going into names and full values, the market I inherited at $1.6m export sales, once I took control with all staff reporting to me, with a Premium Scientific Office Model, went to $8m within five years at constant exchange rates. I had been set an aspiration target to double sales within five years ($3.2m)! I smashed that target. The other 'control' market with the basic model was inherited at $300k and in five years remained around $320k!

The Premium Model showed it was *'moving the needle'* with demand flying ahead and driving the distributor to buy more volumes of products to fulfil the in-market demand.

The other market remained flat. It never doubled sales, even seven years later at the end of my tenure.

Each market visit that I made invariably had a distributor or two asking me to appoint them with the phenomenal growth and demand I was generating from my office in England. They wanted to work on the Premium Model and learn about real demand generation.

I declined all invites to appoint additional distributors – we had trust between me and my distributor. We had agreed that I will create demand and they must hold minimum stock levels and order to the forecasts unless they could justify why demand forecasts were not going to be met.

It was hard. There was pain before there was gain – for both of us.

In the Premium Scientific Model, the distributor's focus would be solely on supply, sharing sales data and competitive intelligence on the customers buying my products – chemists, wholesalers, institutions, and hospitals. I would set the distributor's in-market sales targets by pack and by each brand to reflect the volume forecasts and budgets. The same targets were issued to the Country Manager and reps.

Note: If your import forecast is 10,000 packs of a product pack 'x' you cannot set the distributor a target of 10,000 packs of 'x'. A job holder with low cognitive bandwidth will surely fail if she does this.

Why?

Because this target does not account for the distributor holding 12 weeks of stock on the shelf at any time in a quarterly order supply model to forecast. In this case, 12 weeks of stock equates to 2500 packs to be held at all times plus goods on order.

So, the correct distributor in-market target is that sales out of the distributor to HIS customers must equal 12,500 packs in the year. If you phase that equally (not a good idea because every business has seasonality) then the in-market sales target is 12,500 divided by 12 = 1,042 packs of 'x' per month. In other words, the in-market volume target needs a 25% uplift on ex-factory import volumes if the distributor needs to hold three months of stockholding at all times in his legal agreement.

He does not open on 1st January with zero stocks. He has to open with three months of sales stock plus a quarter-one order that was forecasted and placed in September of the prior year (for delivery in early quarter-one of the following year).

Far too many job holders simply do not have a clue about the numbers needing to be delivered. This is one good example – a guy who takes the import volumes and sets a target as one-twelfth of the annual total. I would ask:

"What about the stockholding requirement in his distribution agreement? How do you reconcile those 12 weeks of stockholding into your import forecast and set an appropriate in-market sales volume target?"

All I would get would be a blank stare with a furrowed brow!

You will read later in the chapter why a job holder needs a high level of numerical as well as verbal critical reasoning skills. I have lost count of the amount of time I have had to work with a client's staff member on forecasting and budgeting and explaining the setting of the correct level of in-market sales targets. Many had no clue whatsoever.

The in-market focus should always be on volumes out from the distributor to his customers.

Setting distributor value targets is meaningless because his sales are in local currency while your sales to the distributors are in a reporting currency for your company – USD, GBP, or Euro. The impact of in-market price markups by the distributor (typically +25% on the landed cost of goods), in local currency, is meaningless.

I never set metrics for the distributor's sales other than volume sales aligned to import sales and stockholding contractual requirements. My metrics set by my seniors were solely those that made money for my company – invoiced sales out the factory gates (ex-factory sales) to the distributor in the export markets. That was what I invoiced and that was the cash I collected from the distributor.

Setting volume targets is key for a distributor business. Very few clients I worked with did this. It was blind sales management. The blind being led by the blind.

Is it any wonder why so many fail?

I took control of the staff. Where relevant, the distributor secured me a lease on premises in his name that I reimbursed monthly for rent and overheads by debit notes.

Moving the staff out of the distributor's premises gave me total control. The staff were no longer available 'on demand' by the distributor to be diverted to other tasks and activities.

I set activity targets with the Country Manager. These salesforce effectiveness metrics could form the basis of a separate book – targeting, segmentation, key measures etc.!

I set the salesforce volume targets for in-market sales out of the distributor. This became the country demand target for in-market sales. The import ex-factory target became my target delegated to Country Managers (glorified Sales Manager roles).

Reps and supervisors were measured on in-market sales.

None of my Country Managers had P&L responsibility. This was because they were employed by the distributor, and we could not share sensitive data on COGs and financial margins with any of them.

Titles are confusing. A Country Manager might present herself at the interview as a P&L holder. But I would establish instantly if that were the case by asking her for her last full set of results for % Gross Margin, and Gross Profit as a % of sales, and then ask what the target was for both metrics. None could tell me!

Therefore, my assumption is that these folk are not P&L holders until they prove otherwise. Many could not even tell me clearly their sales – some would mumble a figure. When I asked if that was ex-factory or in-market, they gave a blurred opaque reply. If it were ex-factory, I would ask if it was at Constant Exchange Rate. That floored them! They had no idea, whereas anyone who managed the P&L would know instantly. I will cover this in more detail in the section on finding good talent and how to navigate the bluffers and good storytellers that present as candidates for these roles.

Negotiate Hard

In the premium scientific office model in one market, I moved the distributor away from the straight 25% across-the-board markup he was applying to his landed cost of products he was selling. This was allowed as per his distribution agreement. I simply could not allow that for a business that had not delivered the budget for the prior three years in succession under my predecessor.

I negotiated extremely hard to get the distributor to agree to a new (lower) differential pricing model. Some companies may call this a "Tiered Pricing Model."

In that new model, I could allow him up to his previous 25% margin on old mature brands that were decreasing globally in volumes, but the new products could never survive with those sorts of markups, despite the considerable investment in market preparation and the sales and marketing mix. On new products the margin varied from +8% to +15% on his landed costs.

I negotiated the distributor to a net margin of 18% across the portfolio from this differential pricing model (tiered pricing).

119

The compelling argument why he would accept this net reduction in margin was that my five-year forecast at those prices would give him 18% of $8m ($1.44m).

This would be much better than the 25% margin he could apply across the board if we continued as-is with him running the show in the Basic Scientific Office Model.

We predicted the business in that as-is; the Basic Scientific Office Model would struggle to get above $2.5m (at best) and applying his straight 25% markup would only bring him $625k or less if he could not get it to $2.5m.

Believe me, if you have a Scientific Office or Rep/Representative Office model, you can move the needle IF you get it designed and negotiated correctly (the Premium Model). By that, I mean spending money in return for total commanding control.

The downside is that the distributor will submit import orders to your manufacturing site (and therefore your sales to the distributor) dependent on your ability to create demand for the products (the 'pull' model). You are in control of creating demand, not the distributor.

He must order to demand forecast and you must deliver that demand in the market.

If you focus on demand generation, supply always follows and budgets will be met (so long as your distributor pays you – more on that in a different section on how to choose a distributor). Importantly, a critical mass will be achieved within a five-year horizon and go on to snowball over ten years.

The "push" model, where suppliers try to push and invoice products onto distributors, is very prevalent among the mindset of international seniors because that is how they see a distributor – someone we can make sales by selling products to them and take no risks if it does not sell. The push model cannot achieve a critical mass. This is a major reason so many international scale-ups fail. As per a prior disclosed mantra:

"Demand always precedes supply."

Some companies and seniors even ask distributors in this 'push' model to take extra stocks at year-end. This is then invoiced to create artificial sales to 'pad out' and report the year-end figures. But owing to a lack of demand, these artificial or fake sales are then credited back to the distributor within three months after the year-end figures. They may also issue fresh stock free of charge to replace stock that becomes short-dated and cannot be sold.

I should add such activities with the push model can be considered summary dismissal offences on the grounds of creating false or artificial sales reporting.

If you want to succeed with a distributor model, you need to split the demand and supply.

To do this, you should go for the Premium Model where the opportunity size justifies the risks versus the returns.

Move to a 'pull' model by creating demand. Spend money on demand creation. Stop sending money to a distributor for vague and blurred 'marketing expenses' and take control.

Take control of demand – sales and marketing, targeting; segmentation; skills training; structure of field force and how many reps, how many supervisors and so on. Invest in behavioural-based skills training (not theory presented as 'Death by PowerPoint®').

Set targets for activities. Set targets for volume and value of products by pack by brand by month and cumulative.

You can only do these things by taking control of staff, ideally in an office removed from the distributor so that he is not involved in the day-to-day running and activities of the staff in your scientific office.

Technically, they are employed by the distributor. But as you are contractually reimbursing him the payroll, they report to you.

Summary of 3 Distributor Models

1. As you spend more on costs, you gain more control.

2. Control is a key determinant of success. That is, assuming you have the skills to manage, and control demand creation demonstrated by a record of accomplishment across the many roles you will be required to do in this role. You will need to wear many hats – Sales Manager, Marketing Manager, Brand/Product Manager, Commercial Excellence and Sales Force Effectiveness Manager and Sales Training Manager along with recruitment and selection experience. These are just some of the many hats you will need to wear demonstrated by the successful delivery in prior roles before being appointed to an International Sales role.

3. Taking control to create the 'pull' model gives the greatest chance of success. Take charge of marketing and promotion to create demand for your brands.

4. Leaving your business in the hands of the distributor (the 'push' model) will mean year-on-year frustrations and poor delivery of results for so many seniors. The distributors are not experts on your products, and they do not and cannot market them as effectively as you can.

5. Remember that you and your company are experts on your products and those different roles – or you should be! Otherwise, why are you in this job?

6. Each to its strengths. The distributor's focus should be on supply and logistics with support for regulatory processes and helping you set up the business for which those costs are reimbursable to the distributor by debit notes. Leaving demand generation activities to the distributor and paying him for it or, worse still, letting the distributor finance demand generation through his sales margin are both highly likely to lead to failure to attain a critical mass with disappointing results for you and your seniors.

CHAPTER 4
The Legal Affiliate Models

Part 1: The Legal Affiliate Models

In a Legal Affiliate, the company (the principal) creates a legally registered entity in the international market.

Each market has its own set of rules and procedures to be followed in setting up legally in the country. If you are considering this option, you should take professional advice from qualified professionals, including accountants, tax & treasury experts, legal, IT systems, servers and data management and backup, office and data security, facilities management (you'll be finding your premises in the market), office suppliers to kit out your offices, and health and safety officials. You will need to comply with all the country's health and safety requirements such as fire prevention facilities, fire exits, emergency escape planning in the event of fire or earthquake or disaster. This is not an exhaustive list.

There are many considerations in setting up a legal affiliate. You should satisfy yourself on all aspects of the country you intend to set up a legal entity that this is the best-fit model from the outset.

You should also conduct a risk assessment for your intended model.

The three legal affiliate models are:

1. The affiliate (you) becomes the importer, and you adopt a model as an importer with your warehousing, trucks, logistics, and delivery staff. I know of only one major pharma company in Sub-Saharan Africa that did this. It is extremely expensive, and my view is that the expense and risks do not justify whatever (minimal) advantages there may be with creating a business model where expensive resource-intensive distribution and logistics are not core to the company. I will disregard this as it will not apply

to most of the readers expanding internationally. This is a trading model in the country that has mandatory filing of financial reports and tax documents in the country, with taxes paid to the revenue authority in the country.

2. The affiliate (you) is present without your own assets for warehousing and distribution. But you are the licence holder and importer of your products. You agree and negotiate a contract with a third-party warehousing and logistics partner to land (clear goods at customs), transport, store, and distribute your products to nominee customers – typically wholesalers, major institutions, and hospitals. This third party is an "Intermediary Partner" that often falsely goes by the name of being a 'distributor' and is sometimes termed a *'pre-wholesale consignment model.'* I will cover intermediary partners and the pre-wholesale consignment model separately in its own right because several big pharmaceutical players in Sub-Saharan Africa have implemented this model without perhaps carefully considering better and more cost-effective means of supply management. There are other markets globally that use a similar model.

   If you as the importer are invoicing customers in the country that are supplied by your intermediary logistics partner, your legal affiliate may be deemed to be a trading entity subject to the same rules for financial reporting and compliance to revenue authority rules as (1) above.

   I know of one instance where a company operates this model in SSA from a Regional Hub and declares it to be non-trading. But this is high risk and could come under the scrutiny of the tax authorities in that country in SSA for failure to file proper returns and pay the tax with severe penalties and criminal charges for the Directors. When I highlighted this, the CFO in their Regional Hub believed they had a strong argument to counter any such claims. I remain sceptical. It can only be a matter of time until a revenue authority examines their trading model and opens a tax evasion enquiry that will bring that large company into the headlines.

3. You appoint a distributor to be the importer. Your affiliate has effectively become a scientific office with a high degree of control.

But as you will see, this offers little by way of advantages over a well-designed (premium) scientific office model but has the huge costs of operating as a full legal affiliate.

However, a significant advantage of this model is that clearly, your legal affiliate is not a trading entity. The distributor buys products, the title to the goods transfers to the distributor and he pays you in your reporting currency and sells the goods with a margin added to his customers in the market.

Costs for setting up warehousing and distribution, trucks, IT infrastructure, drivers, and vehicle acquisition and maintenance are all expensive for a pharmaceutical company to conduct. It is not their core business. It can be an expensive failed exercise with models 1 and 2.

Although there are three principal versions of a legal affiliate, in practice there are only two. The legal affiliate models differ only in who imports and distributes the products for the company and how it is done. Only one version of a legal affiliate model uses a distributor for importation and distribution:

The next page summarises these three legal affiliate variations.

The Differences Between Each Legal Affiliate Model

Legal Affiliate Model	Staff Employed By	Demand Creation	Importation of Products	Warehousing, Supply & Distribution in Market	Comments
Legal Affiliate 1	Affiliate	Affiliate	Affiliate	Affiliate	Huge cost & huge risks. Cost of trucks, cost of delivery operations and collecting payments from hundreds of in-market customers hugely expensive and risky.
Legal Affiliate 2	Affiliate	Affiliate	Affiliate	3rd party warehousing and distribution logistics provider (Box Shifter)	Pre-Wholesale Consignment Model. Used with a Legal Affiliate typically in South Africa for Sub Saharan Africa. Can also be found in other international markets where a legal affiliate is used.
Legal Affiliate 3	Affiliate	Affiliate	Distributor	Distributor	A model that makes a lot of sense, but rarely used when setting up a legal affiliate. Offers nothing extra to a Premium Scientific Office Model with the Principal taking control of demand creation.

Legal Affiliate Model 1 does not bear thinking about. The costs and risks are massive.

In Legal Affiliate Model 2, the legal affiliate is an importer but lacks warehousing and distribution services. It appoints an intermediary third-party transport, warehousing, distribution, and delivery provider that supplies nominated customers whom you wish to trade with in those export markets. These nominee customers can include wholesalers, hospitals, large multiple accounts, clinics, and retailers supplied on the affiliate's authority served through the third-party logistics company.

This is the model used by many large pharma companies in South Africa. It is an 'intermediary partner' model termed a "pre-wholesale consignment model".

The logistics provider and the principal deal through wholesalers. This is why I stated that South Africa is a wholesaler market. It is not a distributor market. This intermediary partner charges fees for receiving your goods and freight services, clearing goods at customs, fees for warehousing, fees for transport and distribution, fees per delivery to each customer, and fees for items of service such as invoicing and cash collection. These fees can be high. Since I last reviewed this model for a client, I estimate the sum total of these various service fees could be around 20% of invoice value by now!

If the invoice value of goods sold to a market or cluster of markets in SSA was $10 million through this model using an intermediary, a client would pay the intermediary partner $2 million (assuming their charges are at a total 20% of invoice value).

This intermediary partner fee is entirely avoidable in SSA with a different model as I will explain later in a separate section. You will wonder why anyone with any sense would use this for distributor markets. But for completeness, I need to explain it because readers will come across this model being proposed for their supply chain management.

The third-party intermediary has no market knowledge or intelligence. They are simply described as "box-shifters". The wholesalers in the country order from the box-shifter and goods move from their shelves to the wholesaler's shelves – hence the term 'box-shifter'.

They are not involved in creating demand for products. The demand-creation remains the responsibility of the affiliate.

If the legal entity in country 'x' imports products and sells them in country 'x' through its directly owned warehousing and distribution operation, it is usually considered to be a trading business that needs to pay that country's tax authorities and pay local taxes. Some argue that the intermediary model does not confer trading status on an affiliate. I am not sure. I will let readers decide after explaining how it works. At the time of writing, I am unsure if there has been a test case that challenges such an arrangement through an intermediary box-shifter as trading or non-trading.

I will cover this distribution model through an 'intermediary partner' – termed the Pre-Wholesale Consignment Model – in a separate section.

Legal Affiliate Model 3 makes a lot of sense. It formalises the Premium Scientific Office Model by creating a legal entity that can employ the staff directly rather than having them under the distributor. It retains a distributor to manage the supply and logistics. The distributor is the trader, not the legal entity. This Legal Affiliate Model 3 is rare from my experience. The key question is to consider what this model gives you, the principal, over and above a well-designed carefully negotiated Premium Scientific Office Model.

Let me explore each of the three legal affiliate models in more detail:

Affiliate Model 1: Schematic

Legal Affiliate Model 1	Staff Employed By	Demand Creation	Importation of Products	Warehousing, Supply & Distribution in Market	Comments
Legal Affiliate 1	Affiliate	Affiliate	Affiliate	Affiliate	Huge cost & huge risks. Cost of trucks, cost of delivery operations and collecting payments from hundreds of in-market customers hugely expensive and risky.

I would have to question any company that would want to set up its importation and distribution in a new country from the outset. There are many reasons:

1. It is extremely expensive. The capital outlay in buying a fleet of trucks and premises for storing and delivering products is enormous.
2. It requires warehouse inventory control systems to be set up. Expensive.
3. It requires a huge headcount of drivers, warehouse operatives, credit management, and credit control.
4. There is a huge risk of defaulting on payments from customers.
5. Involves collaborating with a huge customer base – from wholesalers, retailers, institutions, and hospitals to government authorities.
6. For any pharmaceutical company, I do not see distribution and logistics as a core business model in international expansion until a sizeable scale is reached.

I might call this a suicide model for any seniors in the pharmaceutical industry seriously considering this as a market-entry model. The costs will be horrific and never allow the attainment of a critical mass.

Some companies have gone one step further. They have moved to locally produced goods with an in-country partner to lower their cost of goods. And it may well reduce their COGs.

I have covered this in an earlier section under the go-to-market option of local manufacturing/local production. It creates enormous challenges with an in-market Boardroom structure comprising nationals and ex-pats, shareholdings, filing tax returns and financial reporting.

As if that were not enough, your affiliate is trading in local currency that may be non-convertible or it may be a blocked currency. Non-convertible currency refers to a currency that is not easily exchanged or traded on forex markets. One reason that a country may choose to make its currency into a non-convertible currency is to prevent a run on capital to offshore destinations. An example of this run on capital might be when you attempt to convert the currency to your reporting currency to repatriate it to your corporate HQ to amalgamate the cash into reporting currency for the annual statement of financial results.

A blocked currency is a currency that cannot freely be converted to other currencies on the forex markets as a result of exchange controls. Such money is mainly used for domestic transactions alone and is not freely exchanged with other currencies, often due to government restrictions at home or abroad.

Finally, some currencies have variable convertibility. There tends to be a correlation between a country's economy and the convertibility of its currency. The stronger an economy is on the global scale, the more likely its currency will be easily converted into other major currencies. Government constraints may result in a currency with low convertibility. For example, a government with low reserves of hard foreign currency may restrict currency convertibility because that government would otherwise not be in a position to intervene in the foreign exchange (forex) market to support their currency if and when necessary.

Countries with a currency that has poor convertibility are at a global trade disadvantage because transactions do not run as smoothly as those with good convertibility. For a principal affected by this, it may mean that these revenues collected in local currency may not be easily repatriable back to the corporate HQ for financial reporting statements.

An example of a non-convertible currency is the Argentinian and the Chilean Peso, as well as the Brazilian Real. Other examples outside Latin America are Ethiopian Birr, Indian Rupee, and Ugandan Shilling.

Any reader considering a legal affiliate with local manufacturing and/or invoicing customers as an affiliate and collecting cash sales from customers in local currency should take skilled legal and financial advice from their finance team, tax and treasury teams and fiscal compliance and controls teams.

Affiliate Model 2: Schematic

Legal Affiliate Model 2	Staff Employed By	Demand Creation	Importation of Products	Warehousing, Supply & Distribution in Market	Comments
Legal Affiliate 2	Affiliate	Affiliate	Affiliate	Through the Appointment of an Intermediary 3rd party warehousing and logistics provider (Box Shifter). May be presented as a "Master Distributor" or "Regional Hub Distributor".	Pre-Wholesale Consignment Model. Used with a Legal Affiliate typically in South Africa for Sub Saharan Africa. Can also be found in other international markets where a legal affiliate is used.

This affiliate model 2 makes no sense whatsoever when you look closer and consider that it is a model based on 'consignment' stockholding using an intermediary partner and does not solve the problem it is intended to solve.

The consignment model supply chain is a model whereby you as the principal, manufacture the product. But instead of selling it to a distributor who pays for it, stores it in his warehouse and distributes it to customers and carries the risks; in this bizarre consignment model, your company ships it at your cost centre's expense, to the legal affiliate in the market (typically South Africa) at either a transfer price or at an internal price based on cost-of-goods price.

This supply management in Legal Affiliate Model 2 is termed the "Pre-Wholesale Consignment Model" and involves an intermediary logistics partner.

Details of how it works are described in a following separate section.

Affiliate Model 3: Schematic

Legal Affiliate Model 3	Staff Employed By	Demand Creation	Importation of Products	Warehousing, Supply & Distribution in Market	Comments
Legal Affiliate 3	Affiliate	Affiliate	Distributor	Distributor	A model that makes a lot of sense, but rarely used when setting up a legal affiliate. Offers nothing extra to a Premium Scientific Office Model with the Principal taking control of demand creation.

Prima facie, this affiliate model 3 makes much sense. Demand creation by the affiliate is a core function of the market entry model. This gives the greatest chance of achieving scale and critical mass within five years. The importation and distribution are managed by the appointment of a good distributor in the market whose core function is importing, distributing, and supplying your products and takes responsibility for credit risks and currency volatility (the difference between his buying price from you in a major traded currency and his local currency selling price).

The distributor may be different in each of the export markets under the control of the affiliate. For example, in the case of SSA, the legal affiliate can be in South Africa and a distributor is appointed in each export market such as Kenya, Tanzania and Uganda and each distributor orders goods quarterly directly from the manufacturing site. This is the direct distribution model, not the intermediary pre-wholesale consignment model.

The distributor in each country buys products from the manufacturer's factory and imports them directly into the market (for example, Kenya). The goods <u>do not</u> go to South Africa in this example of legal affiliate model 3.

What is also attractive in this model is that the manufacturer invoices the distributor in Kenya in its reporting currency (USD, EURO, or GBP) and has zero currency exchange rate risks. The distributor takes an exchange rate risk in paying for the goods in USD. The affiliate is not a trading entity. The distributor is the trader, selling the goods he purchases from the affiliate's manufacturing sites to his customers (by proxy, they are your customers also).

Direct Shipment to Distributor Model
The Preferred Model in Most Cases

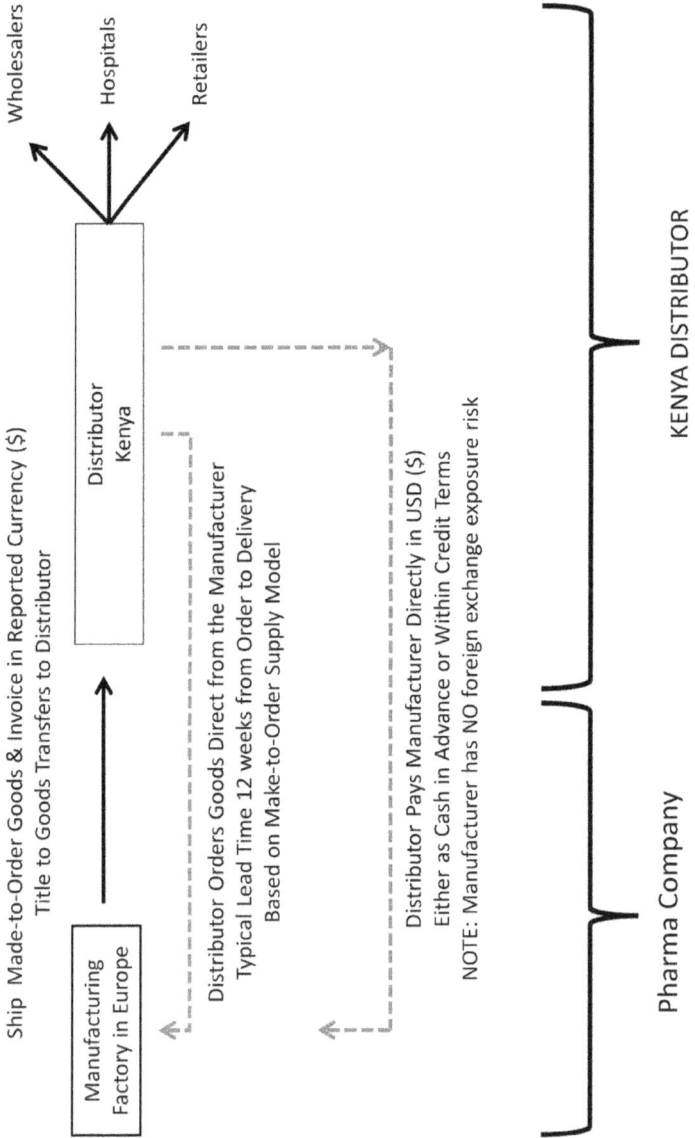

Ship Made-to-Order Goods & Invoice in Reported Currency ($)
Title to Goods Transfers to Distributor

Manufacturing Factory in Europe

Distributor Kenya

Wholesalers

Hospitals

Retailers

Distributor Orders Goods Direct from the Manufacturer
Typical Lead Time 12 weeks from Order to Delivery
Based on Make-to-Order Supply Model

Distributor Pays Manufacturer Directly in USD ($)
Either as Cash in Advance or Within Credit Terms
NOTE: Manufacturer has NO foreign exchange exposure risk

KENYA DISTRIBUTOR

Pharma Company

My observation is that, of those companies that set up a legal entity in SSA, many do not split out the separation between their office and a negotiated distribution agreement with a strong local distributor in each export market. This model has advantages:

1. There is a clear separation between demand creation and supply fulfilment.
2. It is easy to show that the affiliate is not a trading entity and not subject to that country's taxation rules or filing submissions for financial reports.

The major question with this model is:

> *"What does creating a legal entity in Kenya offer over and above a well-designed and negotiated Premium Scientific Office Model with a distributor in Kenya?"*

The costs are hugely expensive. The costs are in excess of setting up and running a Premium Scientific Office model because of the costs of setting up and maintaining the legal affiliate and the additional reporting burden to local revenue authorities. As a principal, you take on all risks in the market on the demand side and the cost of operations is high. You are exposed to litigation being legally registered in the country.

My recommendation would be that this creation of a legal entity with a distributor is a non-starter, until at least critical mass and beyond. The Premium Scientific Office Model with a distributor is to be preferred if the opportunity justifies it. It is less risky and less costly whilst giving control over the key elements of demand creation.

Very few run a legal affiliate in (for example, Kenya) with a distributor to this example. Instead, many running SSA out of South Africa run a bizarre Legal Affiliate Model 2, creating legal affiliates in SSA, and having no distributor agreements in those markets, but using a third-party intermediary logistics box-shifter headquartered in South Africa with satellite distribution depots in SSA supplying wholesalers in each of those markets.

To summarise my thoughts on this third option – the legal affiliate with a distributor that imports and distributes your products:

1. In my considerable experience and opinion, creating a legal entity in this third option gives little advantage over and above a well-designed distributor model.

2. It exposes the parent company to considerable risks and costs that are avoidable with a well-designed distributor model that will have become clear through my descriptions and explanations of the various configurations available for a 'distributor model.'

You should not rule out the Legal Affiliate option.

There are situations where it would be the preferred go-to-market model. I will share an example of where it might be appropriate and may be considered to be the go-to-market of choice.

Part 2: When Might a Legal Affiliate Be the Preferred Choice for Go-to-Market Model?

There are markets where the preferred go-to-market model from the outset is to go in as a legal affiliate. I can illustrate this with one example from my Sub-Saharan Africa experience. In all the markets of Anglophone SSA, a company must engage a distributor to file for registrations of their pharmaceutical products.

The registrations are issued in the name of the dossier holder (your company) but the regulatory activities in the market are conducted by a nominated pharmacist in the distributor's business with responsibility for interacting with the regulatory authorities in the market. Your head office regulatory staff will work with and through that nominated pharmacist in the distributor to liaise on your behalf with the market's regulatory authorities.

Any regulatory queries raised in the market are communicated to your head office regulatory team by the distributor's nominated pharmacist. Your regulatory team in turn will respond to those enquiries through the nominated pharmacist.

There is one market that is an exception and can severely affect your business ever reaching critical mass. That exception is Nigeria. There will be similar examples in other geographic territories of Latin America, Eastern Europe and SE Asia or Asia-Pacific Regions.

Nigeria is the only market in my portfolio of Anglophone SSA that uses a distributor model which is flawed from the very outset. Most principals do not realise this until they decide to appoint another distributor or change the distributor.

Remember my mantra:

"They don't know what they don't know."

"Neither did their staff on whom they relied."

In Nigeria, you believe you negotiated a good Non-Exclusive Distribution Agreement. It is your company policy to only issue Non-Exclusive Agreements. Your Agreement stipulated that the distributor shall set up a scientific office on your behalf (more of that later) where your staff (employed by the distributor) will be based. Your distributor managed all the regulatory activities through his nominated pharmacist to get your products registered whilst also interacting well with you.

Three years down the line, with poor sales and year-on-year missing budgets, and with a lot of pressure from seniors at your quarterly business reviews, you declare that you have a solution, and your seniors tell you to go out there and *"make it happen."*

That solution that you got the senior executive to agree to is that you are going to add another distributor to your Non-Exclusive Agreement, or perhaps terminate the current distributor for a 'better' one (however you define 'better').

Bang! Wait until I tell you what happens next.

Unknown to you. And unknown to your legal department. And unknown to the due diligence team that 'checked out' your distributor, you all get a shocking surprise. That surprise is that all your products are registered in the name of the distributor as the Holder of Certificates of Registration (HCR). Additionally, your distributor has registered the trademarks in his name.

Remember, regulatory authorities only issue a certificate of registration for your brand-name drugs. If your brand name is a trademark, it needs to be registered in each country. This is a separate legal process. But you did not know that, right?

Companies do not register trademarks all over the world. They register them in the major economies and markets. Your distributor in Nigeria has not cheated you. He has done nothing wrong. The ignorance is yours.

"You did not know what you did not know about Nigeria."

Let me explain how and why you have got yourself caught in a tricky situation and have probably wiped out any chance of ever recovering the business in Nigeria and quite possibly derailed your career.

The law of the land in Nigeria is that only a registered company in Nigeria can hold the licence registrations. They cannot be issued in the name of the principal (you) even by a third party acting on your behalf. An affidavit to your distributor will not enable the licences to be registered in your company name. You stipulated differently in the Agreement. You stated that the Agreement is non-exclusive, and the distributor is appointed to register the products in your name. But it is a meaningless clause in the document.

It is meaningless because the Holder of the Certificates of Registration (HCR) has to be the legally registered body in Nigeria. The regulatory authority gives a mandate to the distributor in Nigeria to produce his "Holder of Certificates of Registration" together with the Bill of Lading and other shipping documents (all in his name) at the point of import so that he can clear the goods through the customs with those documents.

Because you did not know this (a similar situation is also the case in South Africa), you did not negotiate an especially important clause in the contract. That clause is worded along the lines that:

> *"...the distributor shall on demand irrevocably and unequivocally surrender and release the product licences and all associated trademarks and copyrights to the principal or his nominee without recourse to any compensation in funds or assets for this surrender and release and shall cooperate and assist the principal in registering the product licences and trademarks and copyrights in the name of the principal or his nominee."*

I negotiated such a clause when I signed up a regulatory provider in South Africa so that, as a legal entity registered in South Africa, he could be the Holder of the Certificates of Registration (HCR) without me having to create a legal entity on behalf of my client. The client was free to choose a commercial distributor partner for the importation and distribution of his products in South Africa. The contract also stated explicitly in another clause on commercialisation that the HCR would be considered for that commercial partner in an open and transparent process with requirements and specifications fully disclosed for the selection of the commercial partner.

Back to the example with Nigeria, the registrations and licences cannot be held in the name of your scientific office that you stated to be set up by the distributor. The scientific office may exist. But it is of no value to you as it legally holds none of your intellectual property or assets.

That clause and the purpose for which it was inserted in the legal agreement are worthless. But you have a great legal team, right? Your Agreement is stated to be Non-Exclusive. But it is also not worth the paper it is written on. Because as the licence holder, your distributor has become an Exclusive importer of your products despite the legal agreement stating it is a Non-Exclusive Agreement.

Moving forward, to allow another importer to be added, or to replace him, you need his cooperation. But you had been agitated at the poor results and false promises from your Nigerian distributor. So, you started to make plans for an alternative model that could be a solution to present to your seniors. You had started to talk to possible named distributors who all promised you wonderful results if you appointed them (all humbug). You did this without talking to your current distributor because you wanted to assess the feasibility of a solution for poor sales to present to your seniors because you have a Non-Exclusive Agreement.

But unknown to you, the word has got back to your distributor that you are talking to other distributors behind his back. News travels fast among distributors! The trust between you and him has broken down. Oblivious of this, you take a trip to make the changes armed with a silver bullet in your pistol (a termination letter). But you cannot do anything as it stands.

Your distributor knows (unknown to you) that you cannot do anything unless he agrees to issue a 'letter of no objection' to a named distributor allowing the other distributor to clear the goods at customs using that 'no-objection' letter. He will not agree to issue a letter of no objection allowing another distributor. Why not? Because you are asking him to share your business (however small it is), which he set up on your behalf, with another distributor. You are asking him to share it with someone who has done nothing towards establishing or growing your business. Why would he share the business with another distributor that never did the registrations or take the risks of setting up a business for your products?

You request that he allow you to appoint another distributor by handing back the licences to your nominee (the other) distributor. Handing the licenses to your nominee distributor puts you in the same position as currently but with a different distributor. He agrees to hand the licences back to you. But you will need to set up a legal affiliate first because he can only hand the licences to a legal entity registered in Nigeria. To set up a legal affiliate comes at great cost. You will need to fund premises, carry out searches that the seller has title to the freehold and the building (which he may not have).

Your distributor will demand compensation to hand those licences back to you. He will also demand a fee to notify the Regulatory Authority that the licences are no longer in his name, and he has no liability for pharmacovigilance and safety issues or product recall. Before the licences can be handed to you, or a nominee, you will need to ensure there is a local nominated person responsible for pharmacovigilance and safety issues to interact with the regulatory authority. That means having a registered Pharmacist employed by you, on your payroll registered with the Pharmaceutical Society of Nigeria (PSN) before the licence transfer can take place.

High cognitive bandwidth was needed.

I say it repeatedly. I regularly see examples of poor cognitive bandwidth.

If you want to change distributors and/or he wants out of the contract, he will not hand the licences back to you without a substantial hefty compensation payment being demanded. These compensation sums can be in hundreds of thousands of dollars to even a few million. Your talented legal team says, *"We'll litigate"* in their ignorance of the situation that you have created.

But what you, your legal team and your company do not know, is that you will be embroiled in a bitter acrimonious court case that will last at least 10 if not 20 years, which will cost huge sums of money and without any guarantee that you will win! The courts invariably take the side of the Nigerian distributor. Corruption is rife. Endemic. Judges can be bought. Court papers can 'disappear' when you turn up to a hearing and the hearing must be postponed.

Even your solicitor in Nigeria may do a deal with the distributor behind your back to try for an early low-value settlement and receive an underhanded top-up payment from the distributor.

But let us not tarnish a country's population with the same brush. There are a few bad apples out there. Thankfully, I know the good guys who steer me away from the bad apples.

There is a quick way to enter Nigeria – it is the Scientific Office Distribution Agreement that distributors focus on, and they promise your registrations in quick time with sales projections plucked out of a telephone directory. You now know why the distributor wants this and is never fussy when you insist it must be non-exclusive.

"You did not know what you did not know."

On the other hand, there is a longer route to the market. It is a more secure way that has you in complete control of your products and assets and one in which you are entirely free to choose as many distributors as you like. That model is to create a legal entity or legal affiliate from the very outset.

But it means finding your premises and recruiting staff under your company affiliate name, as opposed to a distributor as the employer. You will have high office costs as well as high general and admin costs – you'll need staff headcount, such as a Regulatory professional initially, and then as registrations come close to being achieved, you'll need HR, Sales Manager, Marketing Manager, and reps that were provided by the distributor on a split cost-sharing basis with his other principals, but which are now 100% on your headcount. These costs will be substantial until the products are registered. That could be three years of costs with zero sales!

But at the end of the day, all the licences will be issued in the name of your company – (Company name) Pharma (Nigeria) Ltd or (Company name) Pharma (West Africa) Ltd.

You will register the trademarks in your company name. You will need a lawyer in Nigeria to conduct that activity for you. You will have a bank account in the company name in Nigeria. You will have to appoint a local Nigerian on the Board of your legal entity. You will be free to trade and agree to contracts with suppliers and vendors.

As a licence holder, you can have one or several distributors by issuing them a "Letter of No Objection" to allow them to clear the goods that arrive at customs. You will be the importer with your dedicated in-house warehousing and logistics function (even more expensive), or you may appoint a third-party logistics service provider ('box-shifter') to clear the (consignment status) goods, store them and distribute them to customers that you find through your sales and marketing efforts, or you will hire a distributor to import and sell your products. You will be in complete control, except with the supply solution if you outsource that to a third-party 'box-shifter' logistics company or appoint a distributor to import and distribute.

You will be able to have Non-Exclusive Agreements that are enforceable as Non-Exclusive. The world will be your oyster in Nigeria with that two hundred million population. But it comes at considerable risk and has the potential to become embroiled in complex tax demands by the local authorities in Nigeria. And due to factors outside your control, you may still not attain a critical mass in Nigeria. For example, you cannot influence Nigeria's fiscal policies and controls that wave in one direction and then another, or the devaluation of the currency or the raging inflation it sees regularly making it difficult for a distributor to pay you.

Furthermore, any model that involves having to build assets on the ground for local manufacturing or a partnership with a local manufacturer spells immediate danger and high risks. Think very carefully if you want to go down that route. I have seen an example where a company built a local manufacturing plant in a market claiming that COGs would be lower, and that the Government would fast-track product registrations. The first part was true. The second part was not. Registration procedures have to follow a prescribed process for every applicant.

When that local manufacturing plant was up and running, it ran at 40% of its capacity (and that's at its peak levels). Some hare-brained guy thought that they could sell those locally manufactured goods into Africa. They could not. What that guy did not know or understand is that when a product is registered, the site of manufacture and the release site are registered for the product. Changing the manufacturing and the release site is a major regulatory change process, during which time products can neither be exported from the original sites nor the new sites until the site change is affected. In other words, a period of zero sales, denying access to patients for those products. It then becomes a reputational damage issue.

That is why I state, *"You need broad cognitive bandwidth and if you don't have it, bring in someone who does."*

146

But there is a place for a Legal Affiliate from the outset through understanding market knowledge, as illustrated in this real case from Nigeria and based on my own experience.

I set up a legal affiliate in Nigeria and understand very well the risks and challenges along that journey and the multiple stakeholders that I had to deal with. I had to end a Non-Exclusive Agreement set up by my predecessor to change distributors and set up a legal affiliate. I know first-hand what is needed and how to do it. I negotiated and managed the licence hand-back to me without paying a single cent of compensation. I can tell you how to do it – but only as a fee-paying consultant!

I would steer readers to a Distribution Agreement at the outset for pharmaceuticals and other highly regulated industries. I will explain in detail why in the next section.

Creating a legal affiliate must confer a significant advantage over a carefully designed distributor model, even when a critical mass is reached. Or it should remove a restrictive impractical clause inserted out of ignorance, which is a red line for the company once discovered or known from the outset.

I reached critical mass across several markets in SSA, and seniors suggested we set up a legal affiliate. Being my senior, I did not shoot down the suggestion. Instead, I put it to them:

> *"What would a legal affiliate give us that we do not have today that has driven a stellar business performance?"*

The reply?

"Put like this, we cannot see the merit. If the licences are in our name, the trademarks are registered in our name. We have our own offices with a lease taken out on our behalf by the distributor reimbursed on debit notes, the legal entity would expose us to more risk, and we could be exposed to tax and other enquiries. Currently that exposure is with the distributor.

I would add: *"And with an affiliate, we would still need a distributor because buying trucks and drivers and warehousing and selling products to customers and collecting cash on high risk of defaulting payments has never been and will never be our core business."*

CHAPTER 5

The Pre-Wholesale Consignment Model/The Use of Intermediary Partners

Part 1: The Pre-Wholesale Consignment Model

This is a model offered by an intermediary third-party logistics company. It may mistakenly claim to be a distributor. Why mistakenly?

I defined a distributor as "someone who buys from you and pays you for the goods".

The goods and title pass to the distributor (they become his, he owns them) at a point dictated by the Inco® terms agreed. Because the goods are his, and he has paid you for them (or will do if he has credit terms) he is free to sell them to whoever he wishes in the geographical territory stated in your legal agreement. Do not lose this definition. It will come in handy to test anyone who claims to be a distributor offering to partner with you.

Be aware that not all who claim and title themselves to be distributors fulfil the definition of a distributor as I have defined it above. Instead, they carry out 'distribution'.

A distributor is a noun – a thing, a person or place. To distribute is a verb meaning it is an action or activity that involves 'to hand out'; 'to deliver'. A company that distributes may not be a distributor in the real definition as I have defined it. Some simply avoid the term 'distributor' and label themselves as "logistics specialists in supply chain management providing end-to-end distribution solutions".

Here is another example:

Some 'distributors' falsely label themselves as "Master Distributor" or "Regional Hub Distributor" claiming to offer (market themselves) as:

- *"A flexible end-to-end market access and logistics solution"* and perhaps offer themselves as

- *"Centralised logistics that simplifies trade across your markets"* and state their purpose as
- *"Building long-term partnerships that maximise opportunities for you"* and similar such wording.

Some just use the terms such as *"Your Central Distributor with Reach to Multiple Markets"* offering you a "custody of supply model" that *"enables you to fulfil demand through ensuring stock is always available via their careful management and inventory control"*.

The first test to put to anyone who calls their services as that of a distributor is to ask:

> *"Will you be buying our products to sell in these markets to our forecasted demand?"*

Followed up by:

> *"Can you tell me about the main customers and channels with whom you trade in the markets?"*

You may be in for a big surprise. After a lengthy long-winded verbose answer designed not to answer your question directly and hoping to make you forget what it was you asked, you must repeatedly bring them back on topic and ask for answers.

Then at last the nuts and bolts will emerge as:

1. We don't buy the goods.

2. We offer 'freight management' and distribution services whereby you order and import your goods from your factory, we collect the goods, clear all the formalities at the airport, transport them and store them for you in our warehouse and distribution hub.

3. We are a Master Distributor operating a Regional Hub Distributor model. The "Distributor of Distributors". One day all distributors will be this good......maybe?

4. We hold your product stock for you so that there is always a supply of product available in the market as well as our Regional Hubs for supply to your customers.

5. We supply your products to your customers on your behalf. They ring us, and if they are on your customer list that you give us, we supply them with a daily or twice daily delivery.

6. We run a full inventory control system, with state-of-the-art Enterprise Resource Planning (ERP) platform – for example SAP® or Oracle® - that you can access. This will enable you to see your stock levels at each of our depots and hubs.

Anyone who calls himself a distributor that does not buy your goods and sells them to his customers in the market is NOT a distributor. Be absolutely in no doubt. He is NOT a distributor. He is an "Intermediary" or a 'middleman' between you and YOUR customers who claims to facilitate business and trade for you and your customers.

An intermediary or middleman is a box-shifter. And an expensive intermediary at that!

EVERYTHING that he does is charged to you. He takes NO risks.

ALL the risks are on YOU. Be absolutely clear. See beyond the smoke and mirrors.

The stock is yours on consignment. You have been charged internally for it and have paid for it. You have imported the stock from your manufacturing sites. Because the goods are yours, it means that until they are sold to your customers, they remain your liability for shelf life erosion and risk becoming short-dated. If (more likely when) they become short-dated with a shelf-life that is not acceptable to your customers, the goods can no longer be sold, and they have to be destroyed to ensure they cannot re-enter circulation elsewhere.

Your workload just went up several fold – your staff need training in inventory control, stock rotation, trained in the use of various

ERP platforms, and you need a credit management team to collect payments invoiced to your customers in your market by the box-shifter.

The box-shifter can raise invoices to customers he has supplied. He can also offer to collect payments on your behalf (in local currency – more about this later). But they are all chargeable services. You have no idea how good he is at collecting cash. The goods are not his, it is not his cash that he has spent in goods.

How strong is his motivation to collect cash that he has not spent on your customers?

Those charges and costs for the services soon mount up. And it doesn't end there.

He pays on your behalf airport freight costs for clearing, collects cash from your customers in local currency (for example Shillings in Kenya). If you are dealing with the Master Hub in South Africa, he repatriates the collected payments in Shillings by converting them to South Africa Rand (ZAR). He has an exchange rate risk and incurs charges for converting the currency that he passes to you. In South Africa, you convert these receipts in ZAR to reporting currency (USD) and there is another exchange rate risk that you take on the head!

These are just the tip of the iceberg dealing with a middleman or intermediary box-shifter.

They spin a great story that many seniors are gullible to and fall for, hook, line, and sinker.

However, it must be stated that the model is appropriate in certain situations as I will go on to explain.

Sadly, I can see through all their spin story because of my time and experience in AstraZeneca's Manufacturing Operations designing and optimising supply chains and distribution models in favour of AstraZeneca's business. I know how to design and optimise supply chains and distribution logistics. The use of an Intermediary Partner, however they describe themselves, introduces (by sleight of hand and smoke and mirrors) many non-value-adding links in the chain from your manufacturing site to the end user of your products (your patients in the pharmaceutical industry). Each of these links costs you a lot of money. This has an inflationary effect on the price paid for your products by your end user and impacts on you in your selling margin (remember costs come out of margin, not sales).

Any such 'intermediary' model where that third-party does not buy the goods from you dramatically increases your costs and creates additional numerous risks in distribution and supply in the market.

These costs are ALL AVOIDABLE if you engage a 'real' distributor (the noun), not a distribution partner (the verb).

You will recall I defined a distributor as a company that buys your products from you, imports them, meets all the clearing and landing costs, transports, and stores them in his warehouse and sells them to his customers in the market with a door-to-door delivery service – all at his expense, costs, and risks. You invoice the distributor reporting currency and collect cash in reporting currency. You have no exchange rate risk. Neither do you have risks in collecting payments from customers in the market – the distributor carries those risks as well as shelf-life erosion if they do not sell.

Anyone who propositions you by offering you "an end-to-end logistics and supply management service" who does not buy products directly from your company is an 'intermediary partner' and is going to be adding a lot of costs and risks to your business.

So, ask yourself:

> *"Why do I want to take all this stock and inventory control on myself AND have to pay for the goods AND take on avoidable costs and risks that are not there in a real distributor model?"*

Be clear, are you dealing with a distributor or are you dealing with an intermediary (box-shifter)?

Let us assume that you are dealing with an intermediary box-shifter selling a *"custody of supply"* model sometimes termed a *"pre-wholesale consignment model"*.

This is a model that is used across several regions, for example, in Africa where companies hand the responsibility to South Africa to manage exports into the rest of Africa, also a similar model is used in SE Asia and smaller European markets.

Look carefully at any distributor that talks and sells you the story of *"custody of supply"* as a solution to overcome distributors running out of stocks of your products. Any such firm or body offering custody of supply solution is a box-shifter. As I declared earlier, a box-shifter takes no risks and charges you for everything.

A box-shifters customers are those nominated by you as accounts that you want to sell your products to. These are invariably 80% or more comprised of wholesalers, nominated hospitals and clinics. In that list of wholesalers will be distributors. But in this instance, they are being supplied as wholesalers. Remember, earlier I told you that all distributors are wholesalers but all wholesalers are not distributors.

The next page summarises the pre-wholesale consignment model.

The Pre-Wholesale Consignment Model (Legal Affiliate Model 2)

Typical Intermediary Pre-Wholesale Consignment Model Used in Anglophone Sub-Saharan Africa

Typical Pre-Wholesale Consignment Model Used in Anglophone Sub Saharan Africa

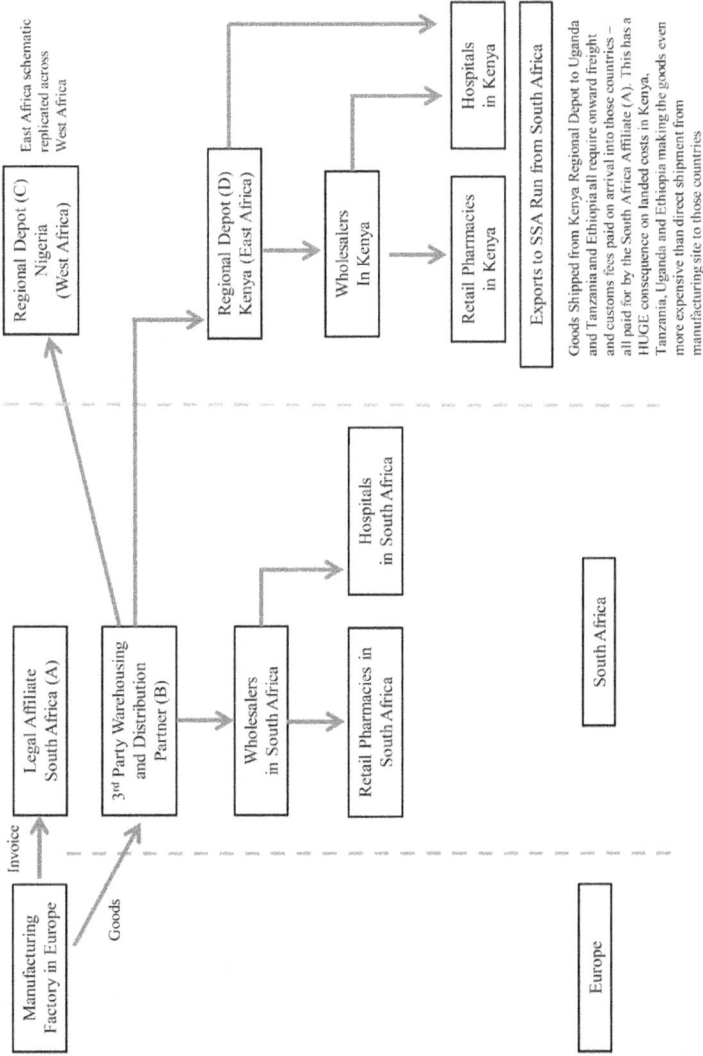

Manufacturing Factory in Europe

Invoice

Goods

Legal Affiliate South Africa (A)

3rd Party Warehousing and Distribution Partner (B)

Wholesalers in South Africa

Retail Pharmacies in South Africa

Hospitals in South Africa

Regional Depot (C) Nigeria (West Africa)

East Africa schematic replicated across West Africa

Regional Depot (D) Kenya (East Africa)

Wholesalers In Kenya

Retail Pharmacies in Kenya

Hospitals in Kenya

Exports to SSA Run from South Africa

Goods Shipped from Kenya Regional Depot to Uganda and Tanzania and Ethiopia all require onward freight and customs fees paid on arrival into those countries – all paid for by the South Africa Affiliate (A). This has a HUGE consequence on landed costs in Kenya, Tanzania, Uganda and Ethiopia making the goods even more expensive than direct shipment from manufacturing site to those countries

South Africa

Europe

In this model, the corporate office sees there is no distributor/importer. The affiliate (A) is now the importer and distributor combined. But the affiliate (A) does not have warehousing facilities, nor does it have the trucks on the ground to provide supply services to its customers. The head office of the company's legal affiliate now treats the legal affiliate internally as a trading entity. It 'sells' the goods to the legal affiliate and raises the internal sales invoice to the affiliate. This may be at the cost-of-goods price or based on an agreed transfer price.

The affiliate pays for all shipping and freight costs from the company's manufacturing release sites to the destination country (South Africa in this illustrative example) and the affiliate pays for all costs for onward re-export to the markets of Anglophone SSA as well as paying for all the clearance and customs costs at each of those destination countries. The affiliate is a stand-alone profit and loss centre.

On arrival in South Africa, the affiliate will need to clear the goods at the airport by paying all fees and duties. But you do not have your warehousing and distribution operation as would be the case in Affiliate Model 1 – for all the reasons I gave for that model.

Now, if you are that affiliate A, you are the importer of products. But you need a partner to fulfil warehousing, supply, delivery, and distribution.

So, you appoint an intermediary third-party logistics company, a box-shifter in South Africa (partner B) to land the goods at the airport on your behalf (clear customs, pay duties and fees) and store them in their warehouse. They charge you at cost plus for that service. The charge can be substantial, adding to the invoiceable cost of your products that has to be recovered through your selling price to your customers. But it is likely that, though the costs are substantial, these costs are far lower than owning your supply and distribution operation in the country.

The third-party logistics company (B) does not own the goods. They have not paid for the goods. Therefore, it is NOT a distributor in the terms of my definition. You imported and paid for the goods to your company HQ and so you are the de facto distributor in this model. What you are not doing is supplying goods to your customers with your company-owned warehousing and distribution company.

The box-shifter cleared the goods for you and held them in their warehouse at a cost to you. The total costs across the range of services provided can be up to 20% of the invoice value. The goods are still your property until they are sold to a customer – wholesalers, retailers, institutions, hospitals, and government bodies. Hence, they are on consignment (owned by you but not sold and paid for by customers as yet). As the affiliate, you issue the logistics provider a list of your customers they can supply who can order your products.

The logistics provider will agree on delivery schedules with you and a fee per delivery per customer. They can raise the invoice for you – easy for them as they have the orders. But the responsibility to collect cash and risk of default on payments is entirely yours. If you ask the logistics company to collect payments, they will charge you for it. All payments will go to the logistics company in local currency, South African Rand (ZAR) which will be advanced to you.

You will convert that local currency back to reporting currency (USD, GBP, or Euro) and you take the full exposure on the exchange rate risks in that conversion.

For cash collections in the export markets (for example Kenya) the cash collected will be in local currency (Kenya Shillings and converted to ZAR to be repatriated to you to consolidate the total ZAR trading accounts that will be finally converted to reporting currency (USD).

The box-shifter will pass on the currency conversion exchange rate risks and charges to you in South Africa.

Remember, in clearing the goods that were charged to you internally in reporting currency (USD), the box-shifter paid in ZAR and converted them to local currency based on the exchange rate at the time of clearance on importation.

By the time the goods are sold, and the cash is collected (could be months or even up to one year (if stock and inventory control by the logistics firm is poor), there may be a negative impact on the exchange rate that means a shortfall when converted back to reporting currency.

The stock on consignment is yours, it belongs to you, the affiliate. Hence the term "custody of supply model". You are the custodian of the stock that has been imported. Whilst sitting in the logistics firm's warehouse, waiting to be sold against a customer order, the shelf-life is being eroded. You are sitting on a ticking time bomb if those goods don't sell within an acceptable decay in shelf life in which case they have to be destroyed.

The model works OK in South Africa because many companies are at critical mass with several hundred million dollars in sales. South Africa is (to many) a wholesaler market, not a distributor market. The 'box-shifter' supplies wholesalers and hospitals that are much fewer in number than those dealing with retailers and high credit-risk customers. Wholesalers can order small quantities because you as the legal affiliate imported three or four months of the stock cover, in a make-to-order model, into South Africa to supply local in-market demand.

Where the Legal Affiliate Model with a box-shifter for distribution and supply breaks down is when South Africa extends this model to be the export model for (say) Kenya and East Africa by creating legal affiliates in those export markets and getting rid of the previous distributor models. Those distributors become 'wholesalers' alongside many other wholesalers in the market.

In this example of the custody of supply model, goods are re-exported back out of South Africa to a regional distribution depot in SSA – say Kenya as the commercial hub for East Africa and Nigeria or Ghana as the West Africa hub. The duplicated costs of onward transport from the South Africa hub such as freight, insurance, and carriage, as well as customs and duties to clear the goods on arrival to the regional depots, are paid by the box-shifter and charged back to you (the legal affiliate in South Africa) with foreign exchange rate risks and charges added.

These costs are duplicated and charged back to you yet again for warehousing in the regional depot in Kenya and onward shipment to Ethiopia and other East African markets outside of Kenya and similarly for onward shipment to other West African markets outside of the West Africa depot in Ghana or Nigeria.

Multiple freight and customs clearance charges are like a growing snowball of costs added to your products. Those costs have to be recovered by higher selling prices in those countries. Before you know it, your products are priced out of the market, or you sell at such grossly reduced margins that your Executive Board will question your sanity!

Be warned. Be clear. Know when you are dealing with a distributor and when you are dealing with an intermediary no matter if he calls himself a distributor or a Master Distributor or a Regional Hub Distributor. Dealing through an intermediary or middleman is going to be very expensive by incurring costs that are ENTIRELY avoidable dealing directly with a distributor that buys your products direct from the factory. These costs to be paid to an intermediary come straight off your operating margin prior to consolidation into the regional (South Africa + SSA) total.

Let us illustrate the scale of impact on your financial metrics with a box-shifter with some hypothetical figures:

Metric	Box-Shifter Intermediary 'Distributor'	Direct to Distributor in Market
Total Sales	$30 million	$30 million
Margin @ 80%	$24 million	$24 million
Less Charges	20% of invoice = $6 million	NIL
Nett Margin	$18 million	$24 million
Less Cost of Sales (25%)	$7.5 million	$7.5 million
Gross Profit	$10.5 million	$16.5 million
Profit as % of Sales	35%	55%
Additional Margin	($6 million)	$6 million
Additional Profit	($6.5 million)	$6.5 million

Say that your exports to four East African countries in a fiscal year are $30 million prior to the box-shifter charges, net of foreign exchange rate costs and charges. Say your gross margin is 80% (your COGs are 20%). Based on sales of $30 million, your margin is $24 million.

Let us say the box-shifter's total costs and charges adds up to 20% of invoice value in charges for the year. Those costs to be paid to the box-shifter are $6 million.

This $6 million comes off your margin leaving you $18 million.

Less operating and selling expenses which let's say is 25% of sales = $7.5 million.

These selling expenses come straight off your margin.
Leaving you $18m -$7.5m = $10.5 million net profit. Your profit as a % of sales is 35%.

If you had a direct supply model to a distributor in each of those East Africa markets exporting goods directly out of your factory gate to the in-country individual distributors, the numbers would be stronger by $6 million because there are no charges to be paid to the distributor for freight management, distribution or supply and no exposure to currency risks or default on payments. All those are on the distributor.

The table above shows the improvement in your numbers if you replaced or avoided the box-shifter model. This is a hypothetical example with assumptions on costs and charges. I do not have the details of the box-shifters model for pricing, handling currency exchange rate risks and precise costs for service. I have discounted the box-shifters currency exchange rate risks and charges for forex. They will affect final values (often negatively in these markets).

In addition, I have assumed that there has been no stock write-off and destruction costs due to stock becoming short dated at the box-shifter. Such costs are not incurred with a direct export to-distributor model. If the reader wants to see how stock write-off might further affect the figures with a box-shifter, we can estimate it as follows:

Invoiced value of stock written off (unable to be sold) in the year = $300,000

COGs price incurred by affiliate @20% = $60,000

Destruction cost for a third-party service and Certificate of Destruction:

Say 15% of invoice value = £300,000 x 15% = $45,000

Total cost of write off and destruction certificate = $105,000

Subtract $105,000 from the box-shifter column (Nil in the Direct-to-Distributor column) in the value of net margin and gross profit.

I have seen an example of a company that wrote off over $300,000 of stock over three years!

They did not give me the COGs, so I did not calculate the impact on their gross margin and profitability. But how can you hope to deliver your numbers and achieve a critical mass with such haemorrhages bleeding out in your business? And importantly, why did the senior corporate Executive Board allow this to happen for three years and not intervene earlier to sort out the mess?

I hope I have illustrated (albeit with hypothetical figures and estimates) the greater costs and risks in using an intermediary partner rather than a real distributor and the resultant deterioration and impact on your financial numbers.

There are assumptions on margin, COGs, estimated charges for box-shifter services and estimated costs for write off and destruction costs. The figures discount currency exchange rate risks and charges.

This example illustrates additional costs in a box-shifter model that are not there in a direct-to-distributor export model. The impact of 'custody of supply' in this intermediary pre-wholesale consignment model are considerable.

A full analysis is a feature in my client-specific projects to illustrate and identify the best-fit model for a client. The client discloses their legal agreement to me with the box-shifter as well as sharing working capital, COGs, invoiced selling prices, shelf-life stock write-off and destruction costs.

This book cannot reveal client work and analyses These examples do not represent any actual cases or any named box-shifter or distributor. Each box-shifter will have their own models negotiated individually with clients that this example cannot reproduce or validate without detailed contracts from a client.

Bonded Warehouse

Some smart guy might mention that the role of Bonded Warehouses reduces the customs and clearance costs for stock destined for exports out of South Africa using an intermediary partner in a pre-wholesale consignment model. This is a red herring. Let me explain.

A Bonded Warehouse is the term used when goods are 'cleared' without duties and taxes being paid on them and leave the airport to be placed into a sealed shipping container or warehouse termed 'bonded warehouse'. It means the goods cannot be sold in the country of storage of that bonded warehouse as they have not been cleared with the required taxes and duties or clearance charges paid. They are for re-export only, or for use in that country after duties customs and charges are paid.

However, what those clever guys overlook is that the goods for re-export out of South Africa at the 'box-shifter' (B) warehouse are mixed with goods intended for sale in South Africa and re-exported to SSA. This forces the legal affiliate to pay all duties and charges on all the goods arriving at the airport in South Africa – those for sale in South Africa as well as for re-export. It is not possible to clear just the goods for South Africa if the manufacturing site has not split out the orders by country. Such goods have different product codes, and one would need to unpack and identify by product codes those for South Africa and those for onward re-export at the airport itself – which will not be allowed. So, all the products must be cleared after paying the duties, freight and customs charges.

What the affiliate's supply chain 'expert' can see is the <u>total</u> stockholding in South Africa for both the sales to South Africa as well as export sales out of South Africa. That supply chain expert cannot see the stock for local sale (Zone II compliant) and the Zone IV stock for re-export. The third-party 'box-shifter' clears the goods and stores all of them in his warehouse. He is not going to separate local stock from re-export stock – or if he is, he is going to charge extra for that, pushing up the price of the export stock. The stock that arrived at the airport in South Africa has been cleared by the payment of all customs fees, duties, and clearance costs on the entire stock – that which is for sale in South Africa and that which is for re-export. They cannot be placed in a Bonded Warehouse now after clearing costs and duties have been paid.

The South African logistics expert in the affiliate places a top-up order with his manufacturing site in Europe for a mixed bag of stock for sale in South Africa and for re-export. Unless they are ordered by unique product code numbers bearing their Zone compliance, such ignorance is overlooked by the company's manufacturing sites – they just want to know how many products you have ordered, and they can then ship them to South Africa.

And that is where it gets complicated when we look at the regulatory potential to be out of compliance.

Part 2: An Often-Overlooked Area by Senior Executives – Shelf Life and Regulatory Compliance Considerations

In Regulatory Zones described as Tropical (Zone IV), the products must satisfy stability and bioequivalence at high temperatures and humidity. All of SSA is Zone IV. South Africa is Temperate (Zone II), as is Europe. Goods that meet Zone II are out of compliance if sold in ZONE IV. Only goods labelled as meeting Zone IV compliance can be sold in SSA.

Any company that sells Zone II products out of South Africa into SSA is in Regulatory Compliance Breach. The practice is potentially widespread because of the difficulty of identifying which packs are re-exported out of South Africa into SSA.

Some argue this is not possible because they use warehousing inventory control (Enterprise Resource Planning software such as SAP® or Oracle®). In practice, in my consulting assignments, I have not been satisfied that a legal affiliate in South Africa can categorically confirm and prove that no Zone II products were re-exported from South Africa to SSA. Corporate senior Executive Boards may be operating in complete regulatory breach of compliance in an environment where they must be able to prove they have controls and processes in place such that this cannot happen. I have yet to find a Senior Executive Board using such a model that could satisfy these requirements.

In one example, I noticed on a client assignment that there was a breach in compliance due to this disparity between Zone II and Zone IV with Zone II packs being sent to Kenya. I took up the matter with the client's regulatory senior, who informed me that "they have Kenya Pharmacy & Poisons Board authority to accept Zone II packs from South Africa, but new products registered will have to be Zone IV".

At that time, I knew the head of Pharmacy & Poisons Board in Kenya. I asked her, given some pharma companies now distribute and re-export products from South for Kenya, does the Board authorise South Africa's Zone II packs to be imported to Kenya? She confirmed *"our regulatory processes are clearly laid out. Packs must meet Zone IV requirements for stability and temperature/humidity. We do not give any company authority to waive that requirement"*.

I asked the client's regulatory senior for a copy of the letter authorising Zone II packs.

She never produced it for me. That suggests that no authorisation was given in writing and therefore the company was in breach of regulatory compliance.

Now, let us turn to an equally important area of shelf life. In Zone IV, the maximum shelf life you can be allowed will be two years if your drug meets regulatory compliance for bioequivalence and stability at high temperatures and high humidity. However, in Temperate Zone II countries the shelf life awarded can be up to four years, but typically at most three years.

Your customers (wholesalers) in the export market (say, Kenya) will be reluctant to buy your stock and accept delivery for anything with less than 18 months of shelf life – because the patients who ultimately pay for it will not accept anything with an expiry date within 12-15 months.

When the stock arrives in your country (South Africa), it probably only has 20 months shelf life from your release site due to quality controls and testing before being certified and cleared to release.

If not sold in six months, it may be difficult to sell and may not be accepted by wholesalers and other customers in your export market (Kenya). This six-month erosion is amazingly easy – time in storage in South Africa and time in storage in the Regional Depot in Kenya can easily erode the shelf life.

As a result, it may become unsaleable due to the shelf life being too short and customers will not pay for it. Such stock must be destroyed with a proof of destruction certificate to ensure that it does not re-enter circulation elsewhere or in another market through an illegal diversion.

You will have to pay another third-party company licenced to destroy your stock and issue you the certificate of destruction that must be sent back to your HQ to follow Manufacturing Operational procedures for accountability of all stocks globally sold and destroyed worldwide.

As if this was not enough. The stock initially held by a distributor as the importer is typically 12 weeks plus sales stock of 12 weeks. This is 24 weeks of stock cover based on the volume forecast for the full year.

But in this intermediary partner model, you are the importer as well as supplying stock from a third-party 'box-shifter'. Imagine the cost of stock for 24 weeks of stock cover that you will import at the opening of the business year. When that 12 weeks stock cover is sold and you are down to 12 weeks of stock cover, you re-order. The re-order is not when you have two weeks of stock cover left.

Why?

Because typically the time to make and deliver a forecasted order is 12 weeks. You need to always hold a minimum of 12 weeks of stocks on the shelf. When the new stock comes, you rotate the prior (older) stock to supply customers that order it as it has shorter shelf life than the new top-up order. But your logistics 'box-shifter' firm in the practical application has no order of control on inventory and often ships the most recently ordered stocks whilst the remaining prior older stock shelf life becomes un-saleable and must be destroyed!

Believe me, I have seen this happen. Despite claims of running warehouse management business enterprise software, these blunders can and do happen. The logistics partner ('box-shifter') has not paid for the stock. So, it has to be destroyed at your expense and considerable cost! And the 'box-shifter' will charge you to take that write-off stock for destruction to the other third party! Even more cost on you, the affiliate.

166

Can you see how bad this model is to adopt for re-exports out of South Africa by companies running their SSA business from South Africa? My take is that because South Africa is not a distributor market, these seniors in South Africa, on being given responsibility for the P&L exports to Sub-Saharan Africa, simply dismantle the inherited distributor models and extend the wholesaler model of South Africa into those export countries. Relationships with those distributors are fractured – the people so often who worked with the company to set up and helped establish the business. This leads to acrimony between the principal and those distributors who are now reduced to being wholesalers buying stock from the box-shifter.

This is nothing less than a glaring example of blind ignorance in those senior executives locally in South Africa and corporate seniors who decide to run exports to SSA out of South Africa.

When the proposal was put to me to move the SSA business to South Africa and run SSA from there, I stated it will not sell more products. South Africa is not Africa. It is a well-developed market with infrastructure and a strong Government health scheme. The only difference between South Africa and a European market is that when you look out the window from your tower block offices, you see loads of black faces whereas in Europe they are predominantly white faces! Being located in Africa does not confer any ability to do better and deliver a critical mass. I will cover location in the chapter on finding good international sales folk.

I stated to my senior Executives that all the distributor businesses I set up will be dismantled into an unworkable pre-wholesaler market model that I had seen other competitors adopt as a consequence of such a decision. South Africa is not a distributor market. It is a wholesaler market. Get that straight and get that clear! Many of these senior guys in South Africa do not understand the difference between a distributor and a wholesaler! Asking them to take on distributor markets that were delivering critical mass was asking for disaster.

But of course, no senior Board listens to the one person who really understands – the guy who turned it all around and set up winning models across SSA. So, the decision was made to run SSA out of South Africa. The rest is history, as they say.

I took an exit package and set up Samkoman Consulting Ltd because I knew there was a great deal of scope to offer my experience to help so many big pharma companies sort out the almighty mess created by the decision of corporate seniors to run SSA out of South Africa by so many (in my opinion) short-sighted multinationals.

And that is exactly what happened. Within a few months of my exit, the seniors in South Africa stopped direct exports from Europe to Kenya, Tanzania, Uganda, Ethiopia, Ghana, Nigeria and all the other markets and told the distributors that they had to buy the stock from the Regional Depots that were supplied out of South Africa and authorised other wholesalers in those distributors' countries to purchase these stocks. Previously those wholesalers were supplied by the distributors. In carrying out such a move, the seniors in South Africa effectively pulled the rug from under the feet of the distributors that had helped me to deliver a critical mass. The distributors had collaborated with me in a partnership to help create a market. They had market intelligence and provided that input to help me process the dynamics of each market. This was key to shape my success and formulate the models and strategies that could deliver critical mass. Where these distributors lacked the commercial and business planning skills that I had in abundance, we could work together collaboratively for our mutual success.

This move by seniors in South Africa completely broke the trust of SSA distributors and many lost interest in helping and supporting the company in South Africa. They stopped sharing information on the market dynamics. This information is absolutely essential if you want to know how to run the business.

Those seniors failed to realise that they needed that local knowledge and intelligence. Without it, they were lost. SSA is not South Africa and so their know-how and expertise of South Africa had little transferability to SSA. But they would find out the hard way – by failing repeatedly to deliver the numbers, where I had a clear run of seven years delivering the numbers for those markets and achieving a critical mass in the priority markets, exceeding the year-on-year growth targets set for me. It does happen that we see six dead bodies (or more) for staff running SSA in a 10-year period that could not deliver their numbers and attain a critical mass. That makes an average tenure in the role of 1.6 years! If they survive year 2, they fall at year 3 or latest early year 4. Having a clear run of 5 years results delivery is the exception.

The decision to run a wholesaler model out of South Africa was (as one distributor said to me after my exit) *"how to lose all your partners, how to demolish a successful business model and make enemies, without really trying"*!

Each market now had many wholesalers supplied from South Africa via Regional Depots in East and West Africa. The distributors no longer imported products. They became one of several wholesalers in each market and ordered small quantities that they could sell, whilst not taking any risks with stockholding. The business that we had collaboratively created and built to a critical mass was being shared among lots of wholesalers that the distributors previously supplied at a margin on their landed costs of the goods purchased.

And it gets worse, as I explain in the next section on working capital.

As I stated earlier in the book, taking a model from one market and shoehorning it into another cluster does not work. Scaleup can only be done to achieve critical mass on a country-by-country basis, never on a one-size-fits-all across clusters. This is a key lesson I want to convey.

Part 3: The Silent Potential Death Blow to a Business: Inventory and Working Capital Impacts of a Pre-Wholesale Consignment Model!

Imagine for a moment the cost of inventory or working capital on which you are sitting. The move to a Just-in-Time manufacturing model (or Make-to-Order) was to avoid all these possibilities. No company today can afford the risk of making goods and storing them in the hope that they will sell. Neither can they pick them from the shelves in the warehouse when a customer order comes in and then ship and despatch small quantities.

For this and many other reasons, the company manufacturing sites operate on a Just-in-Time or "Make-to-Order" model. In South Africa, in this example above, the local senior management runs an outdated 30-year-old model ordering goods 12 weeks in advance, importing goods, only to store them in South Africa for re-export into SSA markets until someone buys them!

Crazy but true. There are plenty of pharmaceutical companies running this model in SSA – and these companies are big, medium, and small size. No exceptions.

Look more closely at this model:

If for example, one pack of a specific product is invoiced to your affiliate by the HQ for $1 at manufactured costs (COGs) price and you have locally imported and stored, 50,000 packs, that represents 24 weeks cover (almost half the total annual volume), the stock at COGs valuation is $50,000. If the invoiceable sale price is $3, then at the lost opportunity price it is $150,000 of invoiceable stock. And if the gross margin is 80%, then it is $120,000 of margin that could be lost.

If you write off and destroy 20,000 packs, then that destruction of stock has been a cost to your local business of $20,000 at COGs valuation plus the destruction costs. Let us suppose the cost of certified destruction is set at 15% of the invoice value (not COGs).

That cost is 15% of the $60,000 invoice value = $9,000. The total cost of destruction to you of those 20,000 packs is $20,000 at COG's value + Destruction fee of $9,000 = $29,000!

This destruction cost will come straight off your operating margin!

And that is not all. The invoice cost of that product was the equivalent of $3 per pack in the local currency. At invoiced value, you just lost $60,000 in sales and $48,000 in the margin (80% gross margin on $60,000 invoice value)! And your seniors back at HQ are demanding to know why you are not delivering the numbers?

Sheer lunacy, you say?

I have reviewed this pre-wholesale consignment model for SSA for clients. My overwhelming recommendation for SSA is to end the contract and go back to a premium direct distributor model or continue with the affiliate and appoint a side-by-side distributor in the individual markets of SSA that will import and supply customers in the market.

Terminating such a contract will come at a cost to the business. This cost could be considerable.

However, in my opinion and experience, the end justifies the means to achieving a scaleable critical mass.

Consider for a moment that such termination costs are a one-off that can be accounted for in the financial reporting. Contrast this to the recurring cost on your reputation, credibility, and the cost to your career of staying with such a model that is a recipe for certain repeated failure.

Very few did reverse the model.

But as a consultant, all I can do is lead the horse to the water. The choice to drink or not to drink is up to the horse.

The model can work for legal affiliates in large established businesses with critical mass, with the importer avoiding capital costs of warehousing, delivery vehicles, and workforce through a fee structure negotiated by the affiliate and costs posted against profit in the affiliate such as in South Africa.

But remember, I told you: Sub-Saharan Africa is <u>not</u> a wholesaler market. It is a cluster of distributor markets. This is a pre-wholesale model that supplies wholesalers. The affiliate becomes the importer with this model (and takes on all the risks that the distributors took on). In SSA the distributors are the importers. Distributors carry all the risks, not the affiliate.

I hope that now, perhaps you can see why this model does not work in Sub-Saharan Africa. And compare this pre-wholesale consignment model with the distributor model and ask yourself, why would you not go for a direct distributor model?

Direct Shipment to Distributor Model
The Preferred Model in Most Cases

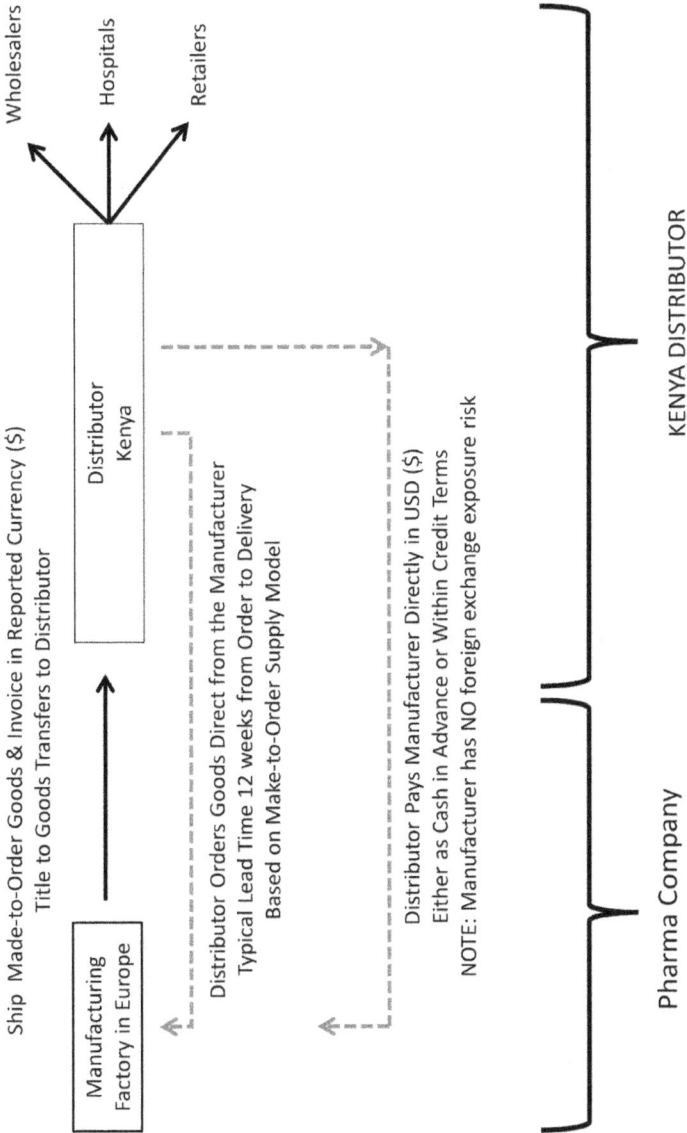

Ship Made-to-Order Goods & Invoice in Reported Currency ($)
Title to Goods Transfers to Distributor

Manufacturing Factory in Europe

Distributor Kenya

Wholesalers

Hospitals

Retailers

Distributor Orders Goods Direct from the Manufacturer
Typical Lead Time 12 weeks from Order to Delivery
Based on Make-to-Order Supply Model

Distributor Pays Manufacturer Directly in USD ($)
Either as Cash in Advance or Within Credit Terms
NOTE: Manufacturer has NO foreign exchange exposure risk

Pharma Company

KENYA DISTRIBUTOR

So why would anyone that is sitting in South Africa want to extend this wholesaler model (pre-wholesale consignment model) to their exports into Sub-Saharan Africa?

The answer is remarkably simple. For these third-party logistics providers (box-shifters) there is plenty of money to be made. They charge the affiliate between 12% and 16% (maybe even more by now when the book goes to press, say 20%) of the invoiced value of the goods for warehousing and freight management services.

Imagine if one pharma company has sales of $300 million in South Africa, the fee might be less at (say) 8% = $24,000,000.

The fee for exports totalling $30 million at (say) 20% = $6 million

Total fees paid by this ONE principal to the box-shifter = $30 million!

Of course, this is pure estimation and guesswork without seeing a legal contract between a Principal and a Box-shifter. But the sums can be considerable. The true magnitude can only be estimated with the details of the individual contract. But the use of a box-shifter intermediary partner costs the principal a lot of money!

A distributor importing your goods into the market does this for free. Then the box-shifter charges you a delivery fee to each customer based on each delivery (and some customers may ask for several deliveries a day – even more money to be made) and charge for raising invoices to the affiliates customers that they have supplied. None of these are charged to you by the distributor. If you ask the box-shifter to collect payments on your behalf (in local currency) they will charge for that service. Absolutely everything is chargeable and paid for by the affiliate. Why would anyone running a business like yours want to pay for all these costs?

Your distributor funds all these activities out of his selling margin and does not charge you for these activities. And it does not stop there. The box-shifter charges you the clearing and landing fees for clearing goods at the airport in South Africa and at each Regional Depot and arrival in each export country served by those regional depots. You, as the principal, are charged back everything. The distributor importer pays all these to arrive at his 'landed cost', from which he applies a markup to create an in-market wholesale price to his customers. He does not charge you back for these costs.

The affiliate in South Africa has hundreds of customers from whom to collect cash against the invoices raised in Kenya and the other export countries, which is all done in local currencies. These might be received in Kenya Shilling, Uganda Shilling, Ethiopian Bir and then be converted back to South African Rand (ZAR) before then converting the total exports into reporting currency (USD in this example).

Of course, the 'box-shifter' can collect the cash for you in these markets. But at an additional cost, as I stated earlier.

You will pay for absolutely everything. The 'box-shifter' pays for NOTHING. That is how they make money – charging for every item of service and distribution and warehousing fees.

Then consider that these customers in the export markets are a high credit risk. Many simply do not pay on time. Demanding to trade with cash in advance results in those customers switching your product prescriptions to a competitor that offers credit terms. You just blew away the investment of having reps creating prescription demand. Reps are expensive – but they are the most effective way to create demand.

So, that is what is in it for the 'box-shifter'. What is in it for the senior executives in the Pharma affiliate in South Africa? Now, this is where the smoke and mirrors will be revealed. Before we can answer this, we must acknowledge one reason the affiliate can miss its export budget for these countries.

That reason is stock shortages – for example, in Kenya. Your distributor does not hold enough stock. He keeps his inventory levels and working capital low. 12 weeks of stock cover plus 12 weeks on order is a lot of cash tied up in stock. He waits until the stock runs incredibly low and puts in an order at the factory. But remember, your manufacturing model is a make-to-order model with a 12-week lead time for a forecasted order. For an unforecasted order, the lead time is longer at around 16 weeks (typically).

Retailers are asking the distributor for your stock to dispense against prescriptions written for your brand that you generated through the marketing investment in staff and field force. But the stock outages in Kenya results in those patients being dispensed a competitor brand after the retail pharmacy notifies the doctor your products are not available.

You just lost a precious prescription. Demand generation with your considerable marketing spend and rep costs has failed you at the final step. This is frustrating, to be sure.

The patient has been switched to your competitor. So, both the problem and challenge in meeting sales budgets is the possibility of running out of stock at the distributor. The 'box-shifter' will then offer you a tempting solution just when you are so vulnerable to another year of failure.

He says that we can solve your problem very easily. We can hold stocks locally on your behalf and we can supply wholesalers and your other customers that you nominate from local stocks. By doing this, it will be claimed, that you will have banished all the frustrations of working with distributors who do not keep adequate stock levels.

The solution, therefore, is badged as *"custody of supply"* and it would seem to be the way to go. Take control and own the products locally and decide who should have supply from those local stocks.

Unfortunately, your senior executives in South Africa have just had the biggest wool pulled over their eyes – and all because *they do not know what they do not know,* and they *lack the cognitive bandwidth* to understand and see the stealth of the magician's hands and fingers pulling a bunny rabbit out of the hat and siphoning out funds from your bank account to the bank account of the box-shifter.

Be clear. "Custody of Supply" is smoke and mirrors. It means YOU take all the risks and pay an absolute fortune in costs and charges that are all avoidable in a distributor model. The risks that your distributor took have now been transferred to you, the legal affiliate. You have become the distributor, importing goods, and selling them to wholesalers and other customers in the market as your distributor would have done. You are about to transcend from the clear waters of non-trading to the murky waters of being classed as a trading entity. If a revenue authority can prove your model is a trading entity in its country because you are invoicing customers and collecting cash from those customers in local currency, you may fall under the taxation and fiscal controls of that country. Failure to comply with requirements of a trading entity if that is how you are deemed to be operating by that country's Revenue Authority could result in criminal charges and see the Directors face jail sentences in that country as well as repaying taxes and heavy fines.

In this 'custody of supply' model, the title to the goods remains yours until sold to a customer. Shelf life is ticking away in storage leading to expensive write-offs for the stock that becomes unsaleable due to it being short-dated or expired.

You are sitting on a huge mountain of inventory and working capital – goods with capital tied up at the 'box-shifter's' warehouses and Regional Depots. You now take on stock and inventory control for all those clusters and individual countries – a task usually beyond the capabilities of your export clerk/export executive and the P&L holder for the SSA export markets sitting in South Africa. Your distributor is good at warehousing and stock/inventory control (or should be, if you chose the right one). But not you.

I never met an export clerk sitting in South Africa that had any idea of stock levels and inventory across the markets when asked on demand. They needed days to work it out – and often the figures were flawed when adding the stock that came into the country and subtracting the stock sold!

Thankfully, all this is kept hidden from your senior Executive Board back at HQ, until I highlight this for their attention! One senior Board was amazed when I presented the stock write-off and destruction costs over a three-year period. Out of sight out of mind was definitely not a good idea for this team!

Remind yourself why your senior executives were gullible and taken in by the box-shifter's smoke and mirrors. It was put forward that the solution offered by the custody of supply model would solve the stock shortages in the markets.

And did it?

The answer, based on clients for whom I reviewed this custody of supply model (termed pre-wholesale consignment), was a resounding "ABSOLUTELY NOT!"

Beware of any partner that talks of a consignment model or a partnership where you retain 'custody of supply'.

Why did the pre-wholesale ('custody of supply') consignment model not work for those clients for whom I reviewed it?

The answer is simple.

Because the solution to stock shortages with your distributor is not to hold stocks locally!

Why is that you ask?

In the next section, I describe what the actual solution to stock shortages is. It may make surprising reading for those readers that adopted the pre-wholesale (box-shifter) consignment model with all its costs and inherent risks and failed to solve the issue it was claimed to solve.

Part 4: What is the Solution to Stock Shortages in the Markets?

Let me explain. The solution to stock shortages is NOT to hold stocks locally in Regional Depots for onward freight to markets on a consignment basis. Anybody that proposes such a solution for stock shortages simply does not know what he is talking about.

The issue begins with the new production methods at manufacturing sites operating a Just-in-Time supply model. One of the founding pillars that underpins a good Just-in-Time supply model is forward visibility of the demand for the manufacturing site that you forecast for each of your countries. Unfortunately, this is not a once-a-year event. It has to be a rolling event every month forecasting 12 months of demand on a rolling monthly basis. To create a forward view of demand you need to start with historical sales and apply an upward or downward effect based on your marketing campaigns and other factors. This demand forecast has to be in volumes sold by each pack, by size, by strength and by formulation (capsules, tablets etc).

You need to submit a <u>rolling</u> 12 months Forecast for Manufacture (FFM) that gives visibility to schedulers at your factory for production capacity and demand and balances these two important factors. These FFMs are always volume-based, never value. Manufacturing operations need to know how many of each brand (by packs, by strength, by formulation) are to be made.

The pre-wholesale consignment model makes forecasting for each of those export markets extremely challenging for the guy accountable for the P&L for those export markets. Without a view of demand in those export markets, the South Africa affiliate cannot ensure sufficient stocks are held in South Africa or the Regional Depots of the box-shifter. In client work where I have reviewed this 'box-shifter' model, the guy sitting in South Africa had no clue and forecasts were poor. This was partly a skills issue, but a larger issue was the difficulty in obtaining historical sales. Typically, the last

12 weeks of sales in <u>each market</u> are needed because the distributor is tied into four quarterly orders – approximately every 12 weeks.

This Moving Annual Total (MAT) is conducted monthly. Say, Jan 2022 – December 2022. Next month, February 2022 to January 2023 and then the following month, March 2022 to February 2023. And so on. The first 12 weeks' forecast in that MAT forecast is key because that is what the next quarterly order will be based on. Effectively, the next quarterly order is locked into the manufacturing system for production. The downstream quarterly demand forecasts can change if sales do not follow and stockholding starts to rise, so downstream orders can be adjusted. This gives the distributor leeway to change the downstream orders if demand is not met to forecast in that preceding quarter.

Distributors have no issue with this approach – the next quarterly order is locked in one quarter in advance but, if demand changes, they can revise the downstream forecast in the rolling MAT demand forecast.

This is a rolling Moving Annual Total (MAT). It is based on historical 12 weeks' sales figures projected out 12 weeks and calculated every month. Therefore, the manufacturing site has some visibility of forecasted demand (give or take 10% either way) every month. The demand is always forecasted in VOLUME, not value.

Every pack on your price list is forecasted. It is never aggregated to a total product but always stated by pack size, formulation and by strength. That is the smallest divisible unit of supply. This is sometimes termed forecasting by Stock Keeping Unit (SKU). The SKU is a unique code consisting of letters and numbers that identify characteristics about each product, such as manufacturer, brand, style, colour, and size.

In the good old days, manufacturers made goods and stored them in their warehouses and distributors ordered them as needed with minimum quantities specified in the agreement. The manufacturer picked the goods and shipped them for export.

But then, manufacturers moved to LEAN and Six Sigma processes to cut waste. One of the major changes from these initiatives was a Just-in-Time manufacturing process where goods would be made-to-order and require a lead time between order placement to order shipment. That lead time was typically 12 weeks when there was forward visibility of demand. But the lead time would be longer if that visibility were not present, and the lead time might be 16 or more weeks.

Often this rolling monthly annual forecasting by volume was not stated as a contractual obligation on a distributor when the company moved to make-to-order. Distributors got bad and lazy at doing this forward forecasting each month. The international sales executive probably did not understand this either. The result was that implementing make-to-order manufacturing was highly variable.

As stocks ran low, distributors would place an order, but the lead time meant they ran out of stocks altogether. And so, they lost you the business. If they were late at paying on credit terms, shipments were blocked until their account was cleared.

All that these senior executives in your affiliate in South Africa did, by getting rid of the distributor models and adopting the pre-wholesale consignment model out of South Africa, was to shift the burden of responsibility of forecasting demand and calculating rolling sales onto themselves instead of the distributors for each of those countries. And, in doing so, you created a third-party warehouse holding your manufactured goods in direct contravention of your make-to-order manufacturing processes! And whereas you had your own warehouses, in this situation, you paid a 'box-shifter' to warehouse your goods – usually a % of the invoice value of the goods. This could be between anywhere between 12-15% of invoice value but when other costs and charges are factored it, it could be in excess of 20% of stock invoice value!

Lining someone else's pocket other than yours is a crazy way to run a business, but it may be a necessary craze in some situations and in some markets. But not in distributor markets.

And it gets even worse when goods have to be written off due to becoming short-dated whilst in storage, or even expiring before they can be exported to SSA. These write-off costs are in addition to those storage costs!

Imagine, you have a young, inexperienced export clerk managing sales out of the 'box-shifter' in South Africa to South African customers. That is easy. There are a limited number of wholesalers and hospitals and only the stock sitting in South Africa to worry about. Even this inexperienced guy can manage the role with an abacus.

Now expand that responsibility to tracking export stocks for Sub-Saharan Africa (SSA).

He must reconcile 12 weeks of sales across all those markets every month on a rolling MAT basis – sales out of the Regional Depot in West Africa (Ghana and Nigeria individually and possibly Sierra Leone and Liberia) and 12 weeks of sales out of the East Africa Depot to Kenya, Tanzania, Uganda, Ethiopia and Rwanda and Burundi individually to each of those markets. The box-shifter's regional depots can give volumes of packs sent to each of those countries by customers – wholesalers, hospitals, and institutions.

He passes these figures to the executive responsible for the P&L in Sub-Saharan Africa who equally has no clue about demand forecasting based on these numbers. Like the box-shifter, they lack market intelligence because they got rid of their distributors.

And the export clerk in South Africa needs to do the same from the South Africa warehouse for the export markets in the Southern SSA cluster of Botswana, Namibia, Zambia, Zimbabwe, and Malawi.

Remember, all he can obtain at the absolute best is simply the number of packs supplied to each of those countries' customers – wholesalers, retail pharmacies, hospitals, institutions etc. The key ingredient he is missing is LOCAL MARKET INTELLIGENCE in each of those export markets. He asks the 'box-shifter' to forecast for each Regional Depot.

He gets a swift reply: "On your bike mate! We can give you the sales out of the depot, we have no idea of the business potential in those markets – that is your job, you should know your business better than anyone!"

The export clerk is truly caught between a rock and a hard place. He has a limited understanding of the South African market. But he need not worry unduly; he can supply those figures to a bunch of marketing and sales guys in South Africa who know the market locally and can turn them into a demand forecast for the next 12 months – on a rolling monthly basis.

But those same folk in South Africa have no clue about all those export markets, so they are not able to forecast demand on a rolling MAT every month by pack, by strength, by formulation. The guy in South Africa has no idea of the forecast of demand for those export markets.

The Regional Depots run low on consignment stock. They urgently demand stock to supply customers in Ethiopia with Zone IV export packs from the South Africa box-shifter's warehouse. Remember, packs for sale in South Africa are not compliant for export to Zone IV Ethiopia. Doing so is illegal and a serious breach of regulatory compliance.

But those stocks are short-dated or expired, or they have run out. So, the export clerk in South Africa places an urgent order at the manufacturer. But the order was UNFORECASTED, meaning that the manufacturing site had no visibility of this demand and can only supply within an unforecasted order timeline – in many cases as much as 16 weeks from receipt of the order.

By the time the goods arrive in South Africa and are then cleared and shipped to the Kenya Regional Depot, and from there exported by plane to Ethiopia, it could be (16 weeks + 2 weeks + 2 weeks) 20 weeks from running out at the Regional Depot in Kenya!

This custody of supply or pre-wholesale consignment model does not solve the stock shortage problems, which is often the key concern on which it is sold to pharma companies.

Let me be clear. The solution to supply shortage is not and never can be to hold stocks locally.

Get this firmly in your head. Do not be bamboozled by anyone that tells you 'Custody of Supply' is the solution to stock shortages. It is not. And it never will be.

The solution to stock shortages is to ensure that distributors who do have (or should have) market potential intelligence submit a rolling monthly demand forecast based on historical 12 weeks of sales by pack by strength by formulation projected forward for the next 12 weeks and beyond. And they must base their forward quarterly order on this forecasted demand 12 weeks ahead of the shipment. You must check it and sense check it by comparing the order quantities against his stock and sales report. Is it too low and risks running out of stocks? If so, you need to open a dialogue with the distributor with your proposed volumes and gain his agreement.

Note this demand forecast is only in volume, not value. And without fail, the distributor must submit every month a stock and sales report listing all the sales of every pack and the number of packs held on the shelves followed by the number of weeks of stock cover based on that historical 12 weeks of sales.

Some companies use a stock and sales report, but it is so complicated that it is paralysis by analysis! I devised a simple spreadsheet in Excel® for distributors. Some columns were hidden. For example, the value of the stock at the Cost of Good Prices, export prices and the distributor's invoice prices in local currency.

Back to the stock and sales reports, so on the first of April 2022, if the past 12 weeks' historical sales (January through to the end of March) for pack A are 30 per week, the stockholding on the shelf on the first of April is 600, then the weeks of stock cover is 20 weeks (600 divided by 30).

If in the following month, on the first of May, the past 12 weeks' sales (February through to the end of April) have moved to 50 packs a week, and stocks on the shelf are 550, in one month the stock cover has gone down from 20 weeks to only 11 weeks (50 / 550) of stock cover, which means low stocks and high risk of running out and becoming unable to fulfil prescription demand.

A forecasted order will take 12 weeks. So, he needs to place 12 weeks of stock cover based on sales of 50 packs every week = 600 packs on immediate order (50 multiplied by 12 weeks). Remember, he must have in his legal agreement a clause negotiated to state that he must hold a minimum stock cover of 12 weeks <u>excluding</u> stock on order.

The reason the pre-wholesale consignment model does not work for those clients whom I reviewed it for is that the forecasting of demand is non-existent or hopelessly inaccurate. In this pre-wholesale consignment model, the affiliate is no longer dealing with a distributor in those export markets who imports directly from your manufacturing site and pays for those goods and has title to the goods. The affiliate is the distributor!

Owing to there being many wholesalers supplied by the 'box-shifter' across every one of those export markets, neither the 'box-shifter' nor the affiliate can form a joined-up view of demand because it is the sum of all sales to every wholesaler in each country! And each country will have many wholesalers dispersed nationally plus some direct delivery customers, such as clinics and hospitals!

Had you adopted a direct-to-distributor model, your distributor could tell you instantly his sales to all his customers by pack by strength by formulation and those sales form a picture of the demand. If the distributor adds his market knowledge and intelligence, he can uplift or downgrade that demand forecast because he can see the trend in prior 12-week sales blocks of rising or falling demand.

The 'box-shifter' has no market intelligence. The box-shifter's job is only to move goods from his shelves onto the shelves of customers that you nominate for them to supply when an order comes in and then the box-shifter will charge you a fee for doing this. Such services are not charged to you by a distributor. I know of an instance where a multinational moved from a direct-to-distributor model to a pre-wholesale consignment model using a 'box-shifter' and did not realise that multiple deliveries to a customer on the same day were each charged as unique deliveries rather than a single fee for unlimited deliveries that day to the same customer!

The distributor was in a far better position to forecast demand because he was importing directly and selling in the market to wholesalers, retailers, hospitals, and institutions. He is running a business with his own money or loans secured against his assets. The box-shifter is running a business with your funds. That is a huge difference in these two models between a distributor model and using a box-shifter third-party in a pre-consignment wholesale model.

The distributor likely had five or six large accounts that purchased the imported goods he bought from your manufacturing sites, which may account for a high proportion of in-market demand sales giving more accuracy than the scattered add-up of sales to wholesalers in the pre-wholesale consignment model.

So, the distributor is in a much better place to shape and form a view of demand more accurately than the export clerk sitting in South Africa seeing sales to so many wholesaler customers but not knowing any of them personally enough to consult them for a picture of demand.

However, your senior executives in charge of SSA, and based in South Africa, got rid of the direct shipment distributor model set up by a predecessor that understood and knew how these 'distributor markets' work. They dismantled it all and moved to this complex, costly, risk-laden wholesaler model that still did not address the primary reason for its implementation – to solve the stock shortages that can happen in the export countries.

Stocks and demand became blurred beyond any recognition. These senior executives became blind and deaf pilots trying to fly an aeroplane without the senses that are vital to navigate and fly the plane.

Again, narrow cognitive bandwidth is very evident along with *"they don't know what they don't know."*

Part 5: My Preference & Guidance for a Go-to-Market Model

Imagine for an instant reflecting on the simplicity of the direct shipment to a country's distributor and the immensely complex, risk-laden, costly, smoke-and-mirrors evident with the custody of supply or pre-wholesale consignment model. Then consider your senior executives who dismantled a direct distributor model and replaced it with this custody of supply model and ask yourself:

"Do I have the calibre of senior executives running SSA and exports that I require?"

The evidence in my experience is no, you do not, and this is based on my experience consulting with many big pharma companies. The answer is a plain and simple no.

Anyone who dismantles a direct-to-distributor model or sets up a model other than a direct-to-distributor export model has questionable credibility with me. Such persons are (bizarrely) dismantling a direct-to-distributor model or creating a new market entry model that trade in local currency with all its inherent foreign exchange rate risks as well as numerous other risks that are entirely avoidable in a direct-to-distributor export model.

So many companies do not have the calibre of seniors required to run exports into complex markets such as SSA and emerging markets in general, often described as distributor markets or partnership markets. The export sales know-how of business models has been lost and there is a skills shortage of folk who understand these models intimately. When laid out as simply as I have done, why would anyone replace a direct distribution model with a pre-wholesale consignment model that is founded on 'custody of supply' with all its inherent risks?

My preferences and guidance are very clear and based on over twenty years in international export sales and scaleup development:

1. The direct-to-market distributor model is the preferred model up to attaining critical mass and very possibly beyond. There is no trigger that attaining critical mass means creating a legal affiliate. I attained critical mass across major markets, but I did not create legal affiliates when critical mass was achieved. I was unconvinced it would give me anything more than the model I had in place that delivered critical mass without exposing me to higher costs and great many additional risks that would be incurred with the legal affiliate.

2. A legal affiliate, if it is to be the go-to-market model, in my view must satisfy the following. Either it must:

   a. Remove a significant obstacle present with a distributor model. However, if you choose a legal affiliate for this reason, it should still use a distributor to import and sell products to your customers in the market, as depicted by legal affiliate model 3 in my previous chapter, where the distributor is the importer and manages supply and logistics.

   AND/OR

   b. It must present a clear-cut advantage over and above a Premium Scientific Office (Distributor) Model that justifies the additional costs and risks of being present with a legal affiliate in the country and clearly shows the capability to achieve a critical mass quicker or higher than a distributor model.

3. Anyone who states a legal affiliate model can *"move the needle"* has little understanding of how to move the needle and even less understanding of what does and does not move the needle. In my experience, such humans belong to a Darwinian species still in existence and in abundance today – The Ignorant Buffoon (Homo ignoramus)! A legal affiliate does not move the needle! In fact, it may be a severe obstacle to attaining a critical mass never being realised. I know of one prospect that created a legal affiliate in a market. After 10 years, ex-factory (FCA) sales remained at a mere €2m-€3m after the failed launch of new brands and considerable investment. That company handed the business to a box-shifter to take on the staff and manage the business. It was literally drowned in costs that were never justified through low value of sales.

4. To attain a critical mass in the defined period set by corporate seniors, of the various distributor models, the Premium Scientific Office Model offers the optimum fit between costs, risks, and likelihood to deliver the required results. In the Premium model, you take control of the staff and manage the demand activities. You will be (or should be) better at doing that than a distributor.

5. If you elect to choose a Basic Scientific Office model, you need the proposed distributor to convince you that he has the skills and capabilities in marketing to create demand for your products, train the reps and manage them against the background of all his other principals. Many of his other principals most likely have a more highly valued business than yours as you start on the journey with him. So, why would he make the effort on your tiny business?

6. There is only ONE critical success factor that can achieve critical mass – DEMAND CREATION.

7. But there is one critical destructive factor that will prevent you from achieving a critical mass. That destructive factor is your choice of distributor, and if he lacks liquidity. If he cannot afford to pay you, then you will never succeed. So, you need to choose wisely and carefully. I will explore this in detail in the chapter that covers how to choose and find a good distributor – this is another area where many people have got it so drastically wrong. Ignore distributor liquidity at your peril.

8. To succeed in international sales and scaleup development, demand ALWAYS precedes supply. Too many companies fail to acknowledge this reality and mistakenly focus on the distributor. They begin with supply. This is akin to putting the cart before the horse.

9. Get the demand creation correct and export sales will follow. Appointing a distributor (supply side capabilities) does not deliver a critical mass. That is why so many companies end up with a sprinkling of export markets with small value businesses that are nothing spectacular versus the size of the opportunity.

And their results are hopelessly short of the financial projections they put forward for the investment in the first place. You need to persuade seniors that you have control over how you will take market share from competitors or create a new market – in other words, how you will create demand and create the market for your products.

A recent development with the pre-wholesale consignment model is where a company has failed miserably with its scientific office setup, employing their own staff with their legal affiliate turning to these box-shifter pre-wholesale outfits.

They hand the business to the box-shifter who takes on the costs and payroll and invoices the principal each month for those costs. They assign a staff member in charge of the principal's sales force to manage them (an additional cost to the principal) and they will agree on the marketing and sales budgets that the principal will reimburse. There may be a reduction in staff numbers and expenses under the box-shifter so the principal may see a reduced cost exposure of running an ailing, miserably small value (failed) business after many years of frustrated investment. The box-shifter may present a basic scientific office setup with or without a consignment stock model.

You may recall earlier what I said about handing the business back to a distributor. It is an opportune reminder with more emphasis this time:

> *"Even more bizarre are those principals that had control, failed to achieve critical mass, and then re-assigned the staff to a distributor to take control of the staff (often reduced in numbers). This is called 'handing the business back to the distributor'."*
>
> *This is extremely short-sighted of seniors, and they reveal poor cognitive bandwidth with such an action. Imagine, if you, with all your expertise of your products and the collective expertise within your support staff in sales and marketing; with the resources that you have for providing training and*

staff development and with all such resources being leveraged, you STILL cannot succeed. Then answer the question of how, by handing the task of achieving critical mass back to a distributor that is outside of your company and knows even less about your products and marketing than you do, can that outside party possibly stand any chance of achieving what you could not achieve?

When you fail, the solution is not to hand it to a distributor to achieve what you could not achieve. That is sheer lunacy – and costly lunacy at that!

The solution (if your company has still kept you on) is to close down the business, cut your losses by laying off all the staff, let the registrations lapse at renewal and retain your distributor until such time as renewal so that he can purchase your brands to fulfil the small demand that is there in the market that will tail off without promotional effort. Do not pay for staff costs in this situation."

Box-shifters are not distributors unless they purchase goods directly from your factory and take risks of stock expiry and exchange rate risks to pay you in your reporting currency. Having a background of supplying wholesalers on behalf of legal affiliates that import goods on consignment, it is highly likely that they do not have the intelligence on demand opportunity and forecasting. So, they may only purchase small quantities to reduce their risks.

The biggest blunders are failing to achieve a critical mass and being unable to identify the problems or develop workable solutions. This is then compounded by giving up and handing it to a distributor or a 'box-shifter' expecting better results whilst paying them for staff costs. Or if you negotiate no costs, you gain nothing – the 'box-shifter' does nothing to drive demand and just services the current low levels of demand that will deteriorate over time. And the box-shifter will charge you for such services!

It is impossible to see any box-shifter or distributor take on your staff and run the business for you free of charge. Life simply does not work like that. Any staff member who puts forward this proposal to their Executive Boards should be considered the one exception to the old 'don't shoot the messenger' adage. He or she has revealed he has no clue about running your international business with such a proposition and deserves to be shot!

Some simple lessons that I hope you, the reader, have digested fully. They are especially important IF you want to succeed and deliver a critical mass within the defined expectations set by your corporate senior executives and stand out from the herd in my mantra:

> *"The plains of Sub-Saharan Africa are littered with the corpses of corporate heroes who bravely went in declaring them to be lands of opportunity. They were excited to meet the challenges set by them, only to find that they needed to beat a hasty retreat within two years, admitting defeat with a career that was quickly derailing and leading towards an enforced exit from the company."*

Where Sub-Saharan Africa is concerned, there are plenty of these above folk. It is highly likely a similar situation exists in other geographies also.

The message for senior corporate executives is that you must demand proof of the concepts in these last nine summary points from whomever you trust to deliver results for you in exports and emerging markets. The section on how to pick winners will be a real help to such seniors because, so often, the real failure is seniors appointing the wrong person into these roles.

Square pegs do not fit into round holes, despite many seniors trying to do this very task and wondering why the results are sub-optimal.

The next page has a full-page summary of all these options for quick reference.

The Seven Go-to-Market Models Summary

At a Glance Parameters by Model	Distributor Option 1	Distributor Option 2	Distributor Option 3	Distributor Option 4	Option 5	Option 6	Option 7
	Hamburger Model	Hamburger Plus Model	Scientific or Rep Office (Basic)	Scientific Office (Premium)	Legal Affiliate Imports and Distributes with Own Logistics (Legal #1)	Legal Entity Imports & Distributes via 3rd Party[1] (Legal #2)	Legal Entity with Separate Distributor as Importer/ Supply[1] (Legal #3)
Degree of Control	None	Very Low	Low	Very High	Total (But at Huge Operating Costs)	Very High	Very High
Costs to the Principal	Very Low	Low	High	High	Extremely High	Very High	Very High
Likelihood of Achieving Scale & Critical Mass	Zero	Very Low	Very Low	Very High	Low[2]	Low[2]	High[2]
How Commonly Adopted	Very Common	Very Common	Very Common	Not Very Often	Very Rare	Quite Common[3]	Rare

1 Principal acts as importer and distributes via 3rd party logistics partner
2 High operational and running costs impact on ability to achieve scale and critical mass
3 Many medium to large pharmaceutical companies have setup legal affiliates and adopted this pre-wholesale distribution model. Very few have a Distribution Agreement in parallel with a distributor importing goods.

194

CHAPTER 6

Finding, Choosing and Selecting Distributors

Part 1: How Not to Find a Distributor

I often get asked, "How did you go about finding distributors?"

The answer invariably began with the mistakes I see so many seniors had made, and I would describe how not to go about it. So, I am going to share some eye-opening facts on how NOT to find a distributor.

1. Do not look for a distributor by attending trade fairs and exhibitions.
2. Do not look for a distributor through Government initiatives in your country that subsidise overseas trips and introduce you to several distributors in the market you want to enter.
3. Do not be tempted to discuss distributorship with an inbound enquiry from a distributor.
4. Never start a discussion with a box-shifter. They do not have the local intelligence and forecasting ability of the business potential for your products.

Why do I say these methods should be avoided?

The message is simple. Finding a distributor is a long-term venture. A little bit like finding a marriage partner – but with some differences.

You expect your distributor to know the market, to have contacts and connections and be prepared to roll up their sleeves to collaborate with you to set up and prove that your business can attain a critical mass in a target of five years from obtaining your registrations.

You expect that your partner is not on any "unwanted" lists of frauds or debts or being litigated or has been litigated for non-payment; has the liquidity to pay you; is prepared to share risks with you; and above all, you need a partner that you can trust from the very outset.

You cannot confirm any of these things in the above four "do not" scenarios.

I know incredibly good distributors across West, East, and Southern Sub-Saharan Africa.

None of them attends trade fairs and exhibitions looking for new principals.

None of them is on any Government trade export lists for their countries.

These Government export bodies just use a yellow pages telephone directory approach, and it is highly likely they will not personally know the distributors they are introducing to you.

That personal connection is key as you will learn in this chapter.

None of the good distributors I know sends prospective emails to pharma companies to want to represent them and be their distributors. Equally, none of them reply to mail enquiries from principals asking them to be distributors for them.

The reason is that cold enquiries from principals usually turn out to be timewasters who want market knowledge free of charge. Such enquiries have a strong chance of cutting out the distributor after the first few 'exploratory' talks by a principal. These are termed 'unqualified' leads and such leads are usually timewasters.

Many emerging markets have independent experts that are rich with personal networks and contacts and connections. These personal networks can offer qualified leads.

ENORMOUS difference.

The guys who approach you are 'unqualified' and are in it for themselves – not for your interests. Remember what I said earlier in the book?

Ask *"What's in it for him to be approaching me"* and then ask yourself *"What's in it for me?"*

Some distributors want as many companies as possible to sign them up, on the back of huge promises and a façade of presenting knowledge and understanding of the market. You do not know how well they understand the market. Why?

Because *"You don't know what you don't know."*

The reason these distributors want as many companies as possible under their umbrella is that they would rather have your products under their model where they can control your rate of penetration into the market. They do not want you to pick a smart, shrewd distributor who will put a lot of effort into creating a market for you that could be a threat to their current business with their current clients. Very few principals understand this when I make this point.

You need high cognitive bandwidth to see this as a possibility.

This is a seduction that many principals fall prey to. They are impressed that someone is interested in their products and keen to stand for them – but without taking a measure of how good a fit there is between the parties.

In my consulting life, one feature of clients who could not succeed and achieve critical mass was a severe mismatch between the distributor capabilities they needed and the poor choice they made in the current distributor.

Why do such mistakes happen? And why so often?

The reason is that nine out of ten of these principals never started at the very beginning by answering the one simple question that I always asked and based my choice against:

"What does an ideal distributor for my products look like?"

If you omit to address this very first basic question, it means that you pick any distributor.

A bit like Alice in Wonderland® in the book by Lewis Carroll, when Alice asks the Cheshire Cat:

Alice: *"Would you tell me, please, which way I ought to go from here?"*

The Cheshire Cat: *"That depends a good deal on where you want to get to"*

Alice: *"I don't much care where"*

The Cheshire Cat: *"Then it doesn't much matter which way you go, any road will take you there."*

It sounds surprising to so many, but believe me, so many principals have made poor choices of partners because they never took that first step to define what an ideal partner looks like and thus did not define which way to go. So, like Alice, they ended up with any distributor, be they a good fit or otherwise.

And getting that initial choice wrong and then trying to correct it comes at a huge cost, risk and your reputation will very likely be damaged in the market. Severing a bad-choice distributor is rarely a clean-cut surgical incision. There is a bloody nose for both of you and blood on the carpet – shed mainly by you, the principal, I hasten to add. The severance compensation and demands just go one way – upwards. You will go back to your Executive Board and Finance Director with a rising tide of costs to sever the relationship. They may keep you on until you complete the dirty work. After that, your career may be derailed, or they will give you some role in the broom cupboard under the stairs as training manager or "Africa Policy Advisor."

So, in the next part, I will examine how to optimise your search and find a good distributor partner.

Part 2: How to Find and Choose the Ideal Distributor

In the most direct basic way, the ideal distributor can pay you, has liquidity, has good reach into the channels and segments for your business, and is well connected with regulatory authorities to ensure few delays in regulatory approvals. Ideally, he should have no competing or conflicting products versus your portfolio. This last point is not a red line for me. I would simply choose an alternative distributor for the products that had competing interests in my #1 preferred distributor with a commitment to review the two of them within x years to consolidate to the strongest player. One would lose my portfolio and the other would win the whole portfolio.

In the market, the distributor must take credit risks, otherwise, he will not supply your products to his customers if they are overdue on their payments to him. This results in a lost opportunity for your precious prescriptions that you invested costs in sales and marketing to generate.

After taking credit risks, he must still be able to pay you and place orders to the demand forecasts.

He must hold the minimum stock levels and have finance in place to make four quarterly orders over 12 months (maximum of six orders every two months) to ensure efficient production and sale of your products from the manufacturing site (made to order) to the destination.

Anybody that wants to order trickling small quantities every month or every few weeks was a no-go. The admin costs and freight costs are too much and charged back to my P&L account.

Besides, we ceased making goods and holding them in a warehouse until an order arrived back in the 1990's. Therefore, it was not possible for distributors to order stock on demand when they ran low. We operated a made-to-order model in manufacturing that required rolling 12 monthly forecasts of demand and orders needed to be placed 12 weeks before delivery. This ruled out tiny peddlers and hawkers and market-stall traders, and wholesalers. But I did not rule out smaller distributors if they could meet my criteria. If they were committed to sharing risks with four quarterly orders, and they met a lot of other criteria, these players were often preferable to large distributors who would not be able to create a demand-driven business from ground-floor up.

You may notice that some large distributors are lazy. They have liquidity. They can do four quarterly orders per year. BUT they are not good at creating demand. Their business model wants to rely on you doing all the work to generate demand and they delight at creaming off that demand with a nice 25% (or higher) margin supplying orders to the demand that you created.

They want an easy time and not have to work for their margin. They do not want to share new product launch costs with you or help recruit staff by agreeing to pay them the first three months trial period out of their costs without being reimbursed or being able to charge it back to you.

Very few principals demonstrate they consider all of these aspects in choosing a distributor.

I replicated the process with clients that I used for testing my distributors for best-fit.

Again, I used a spreadsheet to define the criteria and together with the principal we agreed for each criterion, a weighting so that the sum of the criteria came to 100%. We would hold talks with prospective shortlisted distributors exploring each of the criteria and score them out of ten on each criterion. We multiply score x weight and add these up and it gives a total score for the distributor.

Unfortunately, I do not want to share with you my comprehensive spreadsheet that I used to score and evaluate distributors because I only use it with fee-paying clients.

I then compared the total scores and narrowed my focus to the three or more distributors that best fit the client's ideal distributor profile so I could complete further assessment. Often, a smaller distributor scored more heavily than a large volume distributor when using an objective evaluation and approach.

Before you can define your ideal distributor criteria, you need to understand the basic tasks and functions a distributor conducts and then define what you want to look for in his capabilities under all these tasks and activities for engagement. Further on, I share a diagram of a distributor's main activities. Your portfolio will demand attention on some activities and channels more than others.

If you want the Premium Scientific Model where you control demand through the sales and marketing of products and you want complete control over staff with your dedicated premises, then not all distributors will be able to partake in this model. It needs a distributor that has the liquidity to commit to spending for you until being reimbursed.

The distributor may insist that you issue him a float of his likely monthly expenses incurred on your behalf that he will need to reconcile monthly. This could be many thousand dollars in value. He would be reasonable in asking for this cash float to manage expenses on your behalf.

I had one distributor to whom I issued a cash float of $250,000 to avoid him sending me bank charges on loans incurred in running my business and the delay in being reimbursed from his submitting me debit notes of expenses. You need to think carefully about such a float. Anytime when you give out cash, it needs to be signed off by your compliance team and the finance director. You must amend the distribution agreement to mention the float and it must be reconciled each month with six monthly or (at the least) annual statements of confirmation that he holds your float, its value and confirms that it is to be returned on demand by you or your nominee.

Where I ran a premium scientific office model, the Country Manager would send me each quarter an itemised budget required for the following quarter. I would scrutinise all costs proposed, and we would agree the next quarter's costs budget to be advanced. Once advanced, the Country Manager would reconcile each month how those funds had been spent and the balance remaining. We had already agreed the annual budget, but I had to ensure those funds would not be exceeded.

You will be surprised to hear that there are folk out there who exceed their cost budgets (lack of adequate controls) and fail to deliver sales and profit targets. They are more common than you can imagine.

Distributor Activities and Levels of Engagement

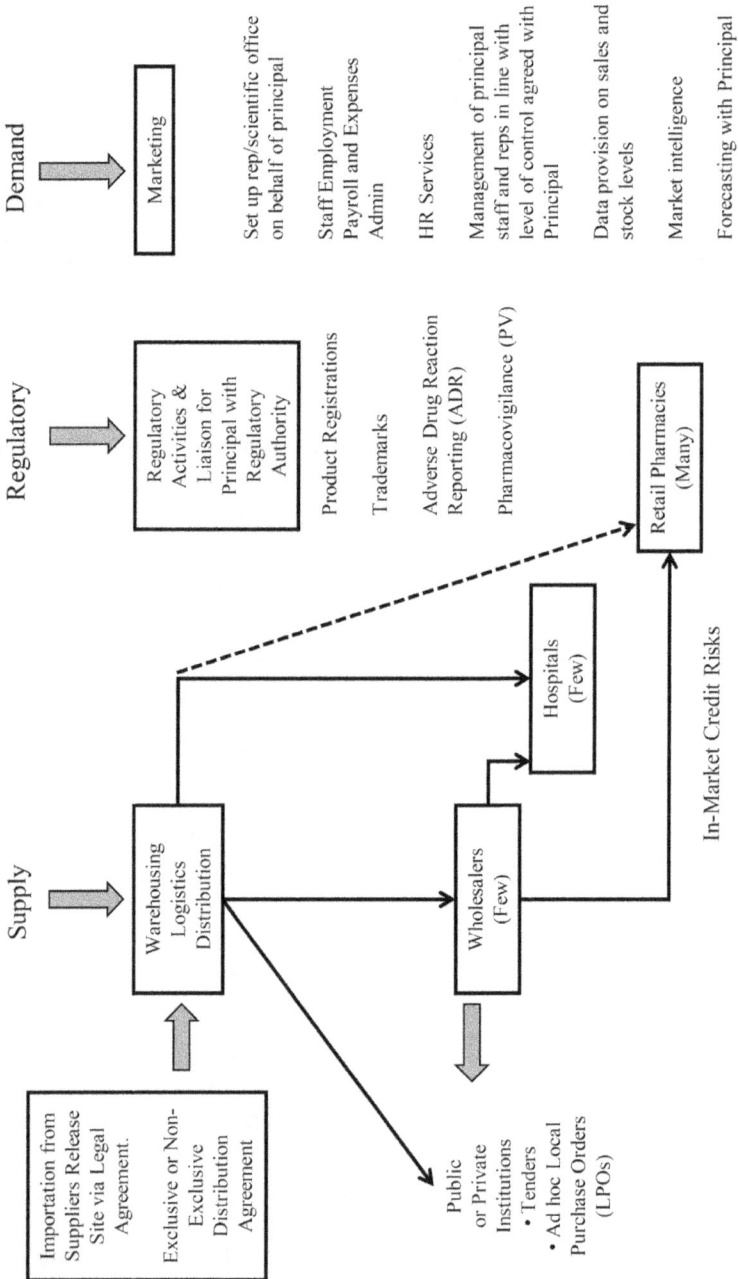

Supply

Warehousing
Logistics
Distribution

Importation from
Suppliers Release
Site via Legal
Agreement.

Exclusive or Non-
Exclusive
Distribution
Agreement

Public
or Private
Institutions
• Tenders
• Ad hoc Local
Purchase Orders
(LPOs)

Wholesalers
(Few)

Hospitals
(Few)

Retail Pharmacies
(Many)

In-Market Credit Risks

Regulatory

Regulatory
Activities &
Liaison for
Principal with
Regulatory
Authority

Product Registrations

Trademarks

Adverse Drug Reaction
Reporting (ADR)

Pharmacovigilance (PV)

Demand

Marketing

Set up rep/scientific office
on behalf of principal

Staff Employment
Payroll and Expenses
Admin

HR Services

Management of principal
staff and reps in line with
level of control agreed with
Principal

Data provision on sales and
stock levels

Market intelligence

Forecasting with Principal

The distributor needs to have a payroll admin function and an HR function for recruiting and dismissing staff to comply with local laws and submit tax details to the local revenue authority.

He must own a wholesaler licence with relevant and up-to-date certification for warehousing facilities and cold-chain facilities (if needed) issued by the Government Regulatory Authority.

In addition to such certification, he must be able to produce a recent quality inspection report and certificate or licence to operate as well as being able to produce a registration certificate for his Superintendent Pharmacist registered with the regulatory authority who will carry out the regulatory work for your product dossiers.

He needs a registered Superintendent Pharmacist to be the liaison with the regulatory authorities. He may ask you to share these costs or insist that you appoint (via the distributor) your own dedicated HR person and Superintendent Pharmacist solely active on your company matters and not shared with other principals.

If he suggests sharing resources, he may ask for a cost towards the payroll admin and HR and Pharmacist Regulatory function expressed as a % of the salaries and on-costs of those staff based on how much of their time they spend on your company matters per month. The difficulty is in knowing if those staff – to whom you are contributing – spend the declared time on your portfolio or if you are cross-subsiding them with time towards other principals' portfolios, who are also contributing to those staff costs.

I had distributors try this out on me wanting me to contribute a % of the HR and Regulatory (Superintendent Pharmacist) headcount. I refused and never agreed to this. Others have done. My refusal was based on the fact that I have no way of assessing what % of time these headcount are spending on my company activities versus the other companies and principal at the distributor. I'd firmly and politely point out that those are costs that go with running his importation and distribution business. Then I'd turn the table on him and ask:

"How would you feel about contributing to the staff costs in our export team that plan, prepare and ship your orders that are costs I am bearing at corporate?"

The distributor would back down and agree, that this is a necessary cost of doing business for him and not one to be shared with a principal. They try it on all the time! I was sympathetic to genuine partnership cost sharing, but not this cloudy murky sort of cost-saving.

Always remember, whenever you concede to meet a cost or expense, it comes straight off your margin, not your sales. You need to preserve your margin to meet your essential costs because once those are taken out, what you are left with is Gross Profit before central costs and overheads.

Anything that you agree or rule out as inadmissible will need to be captured in writing in the legal agreement. This may include such things as if you concede to issue him a float to help with the expenses of running your business and how it is to be reconciled each month and returned in the case of a termination of the agreement.

Once you define what an ideal distributor looks like for you, you can compare each against that template and score them on those criteria. This gives objectivity and consistency. Without this framework, your choice may turn out to be gut feel or who seemingly impressed you the most with his bullsh1t!

I have a very comprehensive template already populated with criteria that I use to facilitate this discussion with clients on fee-paying projects. Clients put a weighting as a % on how important each criterion is and then score the distributor out of ten against these criteria with my help and guidance.

We multiply the score by the weight; total it up and compare the two or three distributors with the highest scores to create a shortlist of four or five distributors.

The basic criteria for the initial choice of four or five are those that will:

1. Work inside the model the client wants to adopt for the market – hamburger, hamburger plus, basic scientific office or premium scientific office. We arrive at that choice through a facilitated discussion between me and the client.

2. Align with my or the client's demand for a Non-Exclusive Agreement or a workaround that I used to use that effectively made a Non-Exclusive Agreement an Exclusive Agreement.

3. Have the liquidity and cash flow to be able to place annual volumes in four quarterly orders with rolling monthly annual volume forecasts. Some cannot do this – they do not have the cash or the appetite for risk to buy four large orders. This can be established easily at the outset. Some distributors pose as distributors but are wholesalers and cannot work to four large quarterly orders. You will never achieve a critical mass with such distributors. They lack liquidity and will not take risks in offering credit terms to their customers in the market. You can never attain critical mass with a market stall trader or street hawker or wholesaler. Although they are plentiful.

4. Have no competing interests and, if they do compete, make sure they are prepared for you not to offer competing products but agreeable to you to offer such products to a non-competing or competitor distributor. In other words, the distributor is prepared to accept split product lists.

5. Be strong in the primary channels for the clients' products. Every portfolio has channels that drive volume sales. Your distributor must be strong in the channels you operate in. A good example is a client that failed to attain critical mass having a distributor heavily active with 75% of sales through the Public (Government) market. The client's portfolio was 100% in the Private (self-funded, out-of-pocket) market! Is it any wonder the client's sales were so abysmally poor? The distributor was not strong in the private sector and the client had no business in the Government market due to the pricing of the client's products. This just shows the poor decision-making process of clients in selecting distributors – or suggests even the absence of a process.

These five basic considerations define the distributors to be approached and eliminated if necessary. There are others that I used that I cannot go into within the scope of this book as they are in my client consulting toolkit.

This sounds logical and rational. But my experience from client projects is that very few prospects and clients select a distributor with such a structured approach. If they did, there would not be the significant mismatch that I see between the client's ambitions and the choice of an unsuitable partner and inappropriate go-to-market model through whom those ambitions can never be realised.

If you take the time to choose the best-fit model with the best-fit partner, you have optimised your chances of achieving success and delivering a critical mass within the five years agreed with your senior executive board.

How do you find distributors, you ask?

I use word of mouth through my networks and connections that propose good candidates versus the client portfolio on the project on which I am working.

But if you do not have a network?

In that case, I recommend a scouting visit to the country for a few days. Talk to the Regulatory Departments for suggestions on whom to contact using your pre-determined list of the Ideal Distributor Criteria. Asking for an introduction is always preferable. Leverage the personal connection and network for the introduction.

Talk to hospital pharmacists and retail pharmacists in the country. You need to make reconnaissance visits. The job is out there! It is not sitting in your office.

Some names of proposed distributors will come up more often than others.

You now have a starting point. Reach out to them. State that you got their name from a market visit and that you would like to arrange an initial Zoom call to explore if there is mutual interest and fit between the two of you. From that, you may then decide to meet in person with a market visit to see their setup. You must inspect his premises to satisfy yourself that the premises exist and that the 'warehouse' is not a garden shed or his conservatory at home piled high with boxes of stock.

You can also talk to other seasoned International Sales folk for suggestions and introductions.

Note the absence of searching via trade fairs and exhibitions or low-cost Government International Trade Department advice and their offer of subsidised low-cost market trips.

It takes time and money to get to a shortlist of candidate distributors in a country. Do not rush into it. If you do, you are highly likely going into an area 'where Angel's fear to tread'.

Part 3: Big Distributors versus Smaller Distributors

I am sometimes asked my view of whether it is better to go for a big distributor or a smaller more agile distributor. This is also tied to the enquiry about appointing a regional distributor present in several markets or choosing on a market-by-market basis.

Let me start with the second half of the question:

Regionally Present Distributors

My views on distributors that are present regionally are simple and clear.

Rule #1 <u>No</u> distributor is strong in a pan-African or pan-Regional context across all his markets. Check for other geographic areas outside of Africa.

I have seen some clients seduced by the offer of a distributor that is present across several markets. For example: "Tom Jones Distributors, Kenya/Tanzania/Uganda." This is an East Africa Regional presence.

If Tom Jones Distributors is also in Ghana and Nigeria and in Sierra Leone and Gambia, then this becomes a pan-African distributorship. That is, it extends beyond one region. In this case both East Africa and West Africa.

But the reality is that such an appointment is a lazy man's way of international expansion. In my experience, this is very often sub-optimal and cannot achieve a critical mass for you, very often in any of his countries where he is present.

Every one of these regional or pan-Africa distributors started in one country – their home territory. In that territory, they <u>may</u> be a strong player versus other competing distributors in the territory.

But in many cases, their expansion to other markets is driven by a strong desire to grow their business beyond their home turf. Sadly, their business development ambitions are rarely matched by their understanding and connections with channels and key players in those other markets.

My experience is that there is usually a stronger player in those other markets – that you would have identified if you had taken the time to adopt my process to find suitable partners and ignore the rhetoric claims of *"we can take your business into several markets through us as a single point of contact"*.

This is an example of a Regional or pan-African model within a cluster of countries that share a common language and colonial ties – in this example, Anglophone SSA.

But in the past two decades, we see Francophone distributors expanding into Anglophone SSA.

This is an example of a Regional or pan-African model that extends beyond language and colonial ties.

You may recall that the Anglophone SSA opportunity is much bigger than the Francophone SSA opportunity.

Not surprisingly, these French distributors want to claim a stake in that larger opportunity.

But just as I mentioned that the South African market is a wholesaler market, not a distributor market, the Francophone SSA market is closer to a wholesaler model than it is to a distributor model.

The Francophone model relies on a monopoly supply model, which means that export sales must go through a France-based exporter.

Whilst South Africa operates a pre-wholesale consignment model, and the French model does have such a model too, more often seen is a pre-wholesale model without the consignment element.

In other words, the French exporter based in France buys the goods from the manufacturer.

In this way, he is a distributor sitting in France. He has regional and country offices across Francophone SSA where he exports the goods he has bought and creates sales demand on behalf of the pharma company by conducting the recruitment, management of staff and sales and marketing. The fees and expenses are agreed upon with the pharma company – often whilst sitting in France. The pharma company principal sells products to the exporter in France and is paid in France in Euro or his reporting currency.

The model is typically the Hamburger Plus or the Basic Scientific Office Model where the principal has little control over the sales and marketing activities.

The visibility of the principal's stockholding across SSA is variable.

The exporter is estimating collective volumes across the markets, but the stock could be sent to those markets that have more demand than predicted and others that have less demand than predicted.

The difference is that in this model, the exporter in France is carrying the risks for the stock – shelf-life erosion, working capital and inventory and the potential cost of destruction. The exporter receives sales and marketing support from the client's international sales executive (often sitting in France), but the payment has been made when they purchased the goods in France.

The rest is then catch-up to try and sell it.

These exporters have little commercial intelligence as they are categorised as 'box-shifters' buying what they think they can sell and keeping low inventory levels.

They will be cautious with what they order from their pharma client because this is not a consignment model. Title transfers to the exporter because he has paid for the goods and the goods become his.

The model has limited prospects of ever achieving critical mass. Firstly, because of the smaller opportunity size and secondly the major flaw in the model through the monopoly supply of exports through France and thirdly, the lack of direct control of the staff.

These exporters know less about your products than you, and yet they are controlling the staff, and they are doing the sales and marketing. Not many pharma companies operating out of France exporting to Francophone SSA operate a Premium Scientific Office Model.

The model of practical implementation as I stated earlier is the hamburger plus model or the basic scientific office model. Some also operate the hamburger model – only interested in selling the exporter what he forecasts as an annual volume and committing to it and paying for it upfront.

These Francophone exporters have ventured into Anglophone SSA.

For a client to choose one of these partners in Anglophone is a blind-leading-the-blind model.

In that, neither the client who is new and does not understand Anglophone SSA and the indigenous distributors, nor does the distributor know well because he is new to Anglophone SSA. These distributors do not understand Anglophone SSA as well as they understand Francophone. If they did, they would be able to demonstrate that with stronger sales in Anglophone SSA markets.

The regulatory processes are different between these two former colonies of France and England, as is the language.

The distribution and supply models are different.

The French model is more like a pre-wholesale model, but the Anglophone markets are distributor markets.

Rule #2 I never recommend any executive wanting to venture into Anglophone SSA to use a Francophone SSA distributor/exporter. In a similar vein, I never recommend an Anglophone SSA distributor for Francophone markets.

The reason is simple.

Look at any Francophone SSA distributor/exporter website and look at his global sales by region.

You will notice first that a huge % of his sales are in French-speaking Africa and Overseas French Territories. This is not surprising given his core business is in French-speaking markets and running them out of France is the model.

But then look at what % of his sales are in non-French speaking markets, such as Anglophone SSA or Lusophone SSA. It is usually a low figure. Typically, around 10% to 15% of his sales are in combined Anglophone and Lusophone SSA. Making his French territory sales 85% to 90%!

Then look at that % over successive years in his Annual Reports. You will notice it stays at around that 10% to 15% for markets outside French-speaking territories, meaning he is not penetrating those non-French-speaking territories, even though they are the bigger opportunities. That is because there are better stronger alternative partners in Anglophone SSA.

You would be a fool to go to Anglophone SSA with a French company that is regionally present in Anglophone SSA. Remember, you need a distributor who understands the markets.

The above performance figures for total sales breakdown by region do not suggest such a Francophone distributor understands those markets in Anglophone SSA better than other distributors in Anglophone SSA.

By the same token, if you want to expand into French West and Central Africa, it would be ludicrous to appoint a distributor from an Anglophone West Africa market such as Ghana or Nigeria.

The monopoly supply model means that exports must go through France. So, the best-fit choice would be a Francophone distributor who will receive goods from France directly from his HQ into the

French-speaking market to sell to wholesalers, hospitals, and pharmacies.

The difference with the South African model is that in the Francophone model, the distributor in France has local in-market intelligence supplied via his offices in the French-speaking markets of West and Central Africa because the markets have scientific offices and can form a picture of the demand and business opportunities. There is no third-party logistics box-shifter. It is the distributor in France running scientific offices and distributing out of regional depots to each of the markets.

Big Versus Small Distributors

Turning now to the first part – whether it is better to go for a big distributor or a smaller agile distributor. The answer is not clear.

Why?

Because it depends on what you want the ideal distributor to look like for you and your products.

If you are a new entrant, you are highly likely to put a heavy emphasis on the following criteria:

1. Not being a box-shifter but confirm he is a real distributor. Your initial go-to-market model should not begin with a box-shifter. Start with a distributor.

2. Having a strong knowledge of customers and channels and reach for your products.

3. Having a proven track record and history of establishing and growing a new business from start-up to scaleup with financial numbers to support it.

4. Being hungry for new principals and being prepared to roll up their sleeves and be immersed in establishing your business. Their business is approximately evenly spread between the current principals and no one principal stands out as a high % of their total sales.

5. Having a level of liquidity that would allow them to be able to pay you. More on this in Part 5.

6. Demonstrating the ability to hold the level of stock cover you require and work to four deliveries a year.

7. Being prepared to share risks with you, share launch costs for new products or pay initially three months' salaries for new reps as a probationary period under his costs before you start to pay for them thereafter.

8. Having in-licenced brands that they are focused on growing whilst the margin from other principals subsidises the growth of his brands? This is a disadvantage to you.

The big distributors that you talk to will highly likely struggle to meet #2, #3 and #7.

There are some big distributors I know who can tick #2 and #7. But the reality is that, in a big distributor, so often a small handful of principals makes up more than 80% of his sales. This makes meeting #4 challenging. These 'large accounts' as principals are where his focus will be. He simply cannot risk letting those accounts down – holding stocks, taking credit risks in supplying their products to customers and, therefore, growing your business will be an extremely low priority.

Some big distributors have in-licenced their products as own-label branded generics from other pharma companies and their focus is on being able to grow their portfolio, not that of the client principals. They use your funding and sales income to invest in the development of their own in-house brands. If he has in-licenced brands, that will be a strong business development focus for him.

Some distributors can see that their reliance on growing through principals is limited as more principals move to take control of the operations and change the choice of partners. When principals moved from a single distributor model in a country to multiple distributors, the distributors realised that such principals look after only their own business.

So, these distributors shift their focus to rely less on their principals' products and instead take charge of their destiny by buying product licences to market their own-label brands that often compete alongside the principals to fulfil the demand already present in the market and substitute it with their own-branded generics.

I had a big pan-African project for a client. I went with the client's senior executive to Nigeria, and he proudly introduced me to his new distributor (whom I knew very well from my corporate life).

That evening, over dinner he asked me the $64 question: *"What did I think of them securing one of the biggest distributors in Nigeria after an acrimonious termination with a smaller partner?"*

My response floored him!

I told him it was the worst choice he could have made, and I went on to explain why.

The reason is that three to four accounts of large global multinationals accounted for almost 90% of that distributor's sales in the country, amounting to over $15m. If the margin was 33%, that distributor earned just under $5m from those sales in the margin, less their operating costs.

The client's business was minuscule at a few hundred thousand dollars versus the millions of dollars from his top four principals. In contrast, they stood to earn around $100k in the margin on this client's portfolio sales of around $300k.

Why would they work their socks off to grow this client's business and earn a tiny margin like that?

The client did not identify what their ideal distributor looked like. The client needed somebody to roll their sleeves up, recruit and manage a sales team to establish a new business after an acrimonious termination with a prior smaller distributor that decimated his business within an 18-month termination of the agreement when there were no stocks in the market for the client's products.

The current choice would never do that. It is too much like hard work for a business worth a few hundred thousand dollars. This distributor was large and mostly a box-shifter.

The four large accounts ran a Premium Scientific Model in control of sales and marketing to create demand – the 'pull' model. The distributor fulfilled that demand by supplying products against prescriptions and made an easy margin with little to no effort.

The only risk they had was credit risk that they managed tightly, meaning that some orders remained unfulfilled due to overdue invoices. This indicated that the principal's investment in sales and marketing to generate prescriptions was wasted.

I explained so often, that "biggest is not the best" in international sales and distributors.

What that client needed was a smaller lean outfit that was aggressive to manage reps, generating demand and taking some risks with credit with their customers to fulfil prescriptions. They would do this because they did not have a large multinational principal in their portfolio and were motivated to do a good job. To a smaller player, a $100k margin was not to be turned away.

You can now see why starting with that Ideal Distributor Criteria profile would have led them to a different choice of distributor.

But repeatedly, my experience is that clients have no structured process or approach to defining, finding, and selecting a distributor. So often, my early findings with failed businesses are that the client has not got a good partner and, additionally, the wrong model with the partner. And to compound these issues, they had the wrong guy running the business!

They had literally "shot themselves in the foot" as a large global multinational with tiny sales in that big market believing that a big distributor could achieve critical mass for them. That idea was entirely wrong, as that individual discovered in a few years when the results had not been delivered to their senior executive team's expectations.

Whenever 'big distributors' make claims with their scale and size and boast about their reach across several markets, consider asking them basic questions such as:

- Who are your other principals – and what % of sales come from your top five accounts?
- Do they operate a wholesaler model where they buy stock from you?
- Ask for major competitors with the distributor that would be a red line for your portfolio under that distributor.
- Do they have in-licensed brands that they bought from pharma to market for themselves under their name?
- What is their reach into the channels and players for your portfolio?
- What is their credit policy for in-market customers? How good is their credit control?
- Do they have the liquidity to pay for four quarterly orders per year, based on sales projections of x million dollars? I would illustrate it with a specimen figure, assuming our prices are acceptable for the market. I might say, "We see $3m in year 1 rising to $5m by year 3 and $7m by year 5." Each year will require four orders for those values. I would go on to explain: "We do not supply small quantities on demand or in monthly orders. We want a distributor that can place quarterly orders to demand forecasts and can pay a quarter of those annual forecasted values in a lump sum payment. We may consider credit options after two cash-in-advance orders." Many simply backed out with unease – they did not have the liquidity or the appetite for risks. They wanted me to

take all the risks. I did not want a one-sided relationship where I would take all the risks and he would take the cream with a nice handsome margin at my efforts.

These give you some good ideas if it is even worth exploring further.

Remember: We can see some reasons emerging why clients fail to achieve critical mass:

1. **Wrong model** – for instance Hamburger or Basic Scientific Office or, worse still, legal affiliate with a 'box-shifter' pre-wholesale consignment model for supply, warehousing, logistics and distribution. And in a hamburger or Basic Scientific Office model expecting the distributor to fund the marketing promotional costs and staff costs from his sales margin. This is a recipe for disaster.

2. **Wrong Partner** (Distributor) on several possibilities: Too small and lacks liquidity. Poor reach to your customer segment (it might be strong in Government tenders, but your business is in the Private out-of-pocket market). Too big to even care about your portfolio and is well looked after by other large principals – some of whom may be your competitors.

3. **Wrong Person** was appointed as the Internal Business Development and Partnerships Manager. Mis-fits are common. I have seen numerous cases as a consultant to large global multinational Pharma companies. There are more misfits than good fits!

4. **Flawed Pricing Model.** I will not cover pricing strategies in the scope of this book. But I can assure you that, so few companies have any real idea on pricing, too often allowing themselves to be led by a central HQ policy that is aligned to reimburse top six global markets, with the result that their pricing model in distributor markets quickly becomes expensive beyond comprehension. I could author a book on pricing and market access. It is not possible to cover such an important topic such as this within the scope of this book but it is worthy of consideration for a publication in the future.

Part 4: Multiple Distributors in a Market or a Single Distributor?

I worked with some clients that had multiple distributors or were considering adopting multiple distributors alongside their current distributors in a market. This would often be a dinner table conversation with a senior executive curious to know my thoughts on this matter.

Before I answer this with my actual opinions, let us just remind ourselves of the context behind appointing multiple distributors for the identical product range, as opposed to split distributors each with different products in the market.

The reason that clients so often want to have multiple distributors reveals their remarkable ignorance of distributor models and emerging market scaleups. That ignorance is seated in the myth that having multiple distributors increases sales.

Let me dispel that immediately. Adding to the supply side does not increase sales. It just means that the sales currently enjoyed by one distributor are simply shared among all the others. I explained this earlier in the book. The cake does not grow bigger. The same small cake that seniors are unhappy about is simply shared among all these multiple distributors. Each one receives a smaller portion of the cake or pie.

They simply push initial stocks onto each distributor (typically 12 – 24 weeks) and invoice it, thus creating artificial or false sales for their corporate Board at Head Office. This pushing of stocks onto distributors is a "push" model that does not work. These additional distributors may take initial invoiceable stockholding. But they will not order top-up stocks unless there is demand from their customers.

So, what senior Boards must be on the lookout for, and the Financial Controller in particular, is a large spike in sales initially but a

AMIT VAIDYA

forecast or latest view for the year-end turnout that remains below or at budget – not above budget. Careful checks must be kept on issuing credit notes.

Those initial stocks, if not sold because of a lack of demand, will require credit notes (returning the cash those distributors used to purchase the initial stockholding). Alternatively, fresh free-of-charge replacement stocks may be shipped. Keep an eye on free-of-charge stocks being shipped out of the factory gate. I think issuing credit notes and free of charge stocks needs to be validated and endorsed by two seniors above the guy requesting it. This is because the business is giving away cash. So higher levels must be made aware when this is being done.

Under financial reporting, creating artificial sales and reversing those sales like this, by signing up distributors that must take initial stockholding of between 12–24 weeks of the annual demand forecast, is falsifying sales under fiscal compliance and reporting rules. In my corporate life, this was a summary dismissal offence. There is a clear warning for Corporate Senior Executive Boards and the Finance function.

Adding more distributors and then wondering why sales still fail to reach a critical mass is puzzling for seniors. That is because they do not understand what it takes to achieve a critical mass.

There is only one way to attain a critical mass. It is to create demand, as I've stated earlier in the chapter on distributors. In pharmaceuticals, this means creating prescriptions for your products. Create demand and you create a strong "pull" force that draws on stock from your manufacturing site to the distributor in the country to supply his customers.

To create maximum pull, use the distributor model of Premium Scientific Office, where the distributor manages supply and regulatory and pharmacovigilance and you have the staff reporting to you and you manage the demand creation through sales and marketing strategies and implementation with relevant support on training and development for skills. This model should be supported with forecasts that demonstrate a critical mass opportunity.

There may be merit in having split distributors with different products, as I had in Sudan. One was supplied ex-Sweden and the other was supplied ex-UK. Sudan did not allow two or more distributors with the same product range and prices.

Splitting products across more than two distributors presents complexities for stock controls and stock and sales reports. Forecasting becomes difficult but still very much doable. But it may be useful to avoid a range of products at Distributor A that has competing products, so you sign up Distributor B with those competing products to avoid a conflict of interest with Distributor A.

I know of instances where some companies appointed more than five distributors, each with the same product lists and prices. Such companies struggled and ultimately consolidated down to one or two. When I see such blunders, I see a company headed up by a person who has no clue what he or she is doing.

Please do not do this. You will not succeed. You will change the model very quickly and lose credibility with your Executive Board. You may end up with litigation from those you are terminating, and they may, and many do, write to the CEO and Chief Legal Counsel making allegations that draw attention to you that will prompt an HR investigation if you are not careful. Your reputation and credibility among seniors can be so easily lost.

Part 5: Why Does Liquidity Matter in the Choice of a Distributor?

I stated the one critical success factor that delivers critical mass is demand creation. That is, the ability to find new customers for your products and sell more products to existing customers. Demand creation is the foundation of a 'pull' model. In contrast, 'push' models cannot deliver critical mass. This is because push models are supply-focused, not demand-focused.

However, there is one critical destructive factor that can override the success factor of demand creation. That destructive factor is liquidity. Allow me to elaborate and explain:

Business liquidity is the ability in your distributor partner to cover any liabilities, such as loans, staff wages, running costs and expenses, and taxes. Strong liquidity means there is enough cash to pay off any debts that may arise and fund your activities whilst waiting for reimbursement from you the principal. In addition, liquidity involves the trade-off between the price at which an asset can be bought and how quickly it can be sold, and how quickly the cash is collected too.

Now overlay a factor that none of us have control over. That factor is the foreign exchange rate. Your distributor buys goods from you. You invoice him in your reporting currency (USD, GBP, Euro as examples). He needs to buy currency locally to pay your invoice.

Let us look at a practical example with Nigeria and let us assume that access to foreign currency is not an issue (it is but let us disregard that for this illustration).

You invoice the Nigerian distributor $1. In January 2003, he needed to buy USD at the rate of $1 = 125 Naira. By January 2023, to buy $1 he needed to buy USD at the rate of $1 = 490 Naira. And by August 2023, the inflation was so rampant in Nigeria, that to buy $1 he had to pay 790 Naira!

If he had struggled to buy $1 in 2003, by 2023 he simply cannot buy your products due to the local devaluation of the currency. In addition, his operating costs have soared due to raging inflation at 27% as at November 2023. No matter how much demand that you create, your distributor simply cannot fulfil demand with products that he cannot afford to buy from you! Your in-market prices will be inflated due to this currency devaluation and raging inflation as he is forced to pass on inflated operating costs to his customers. Patients may decline to buy your products owing to their elevated costs and prioritising spend on food, fuel, and energy. Your business will fail, and you will be exposed to reputational damage from patients who started on treatments that they no longer have access to or can no longer afford - all because your distributor cannot afford to buy them from your factory.

If he can buy your products, their price in local currency will shoot up, making them too expensive for patients – again killing your business. If he has a USD account outside of Nigeria, he can purchase goods from you from those funds, providing there is compliance in the documentation listing a consignee in Nigeria but with the payment coming from funds outside of the consignee (this is called a triangular payment). You need to take skilled financial and compliance advice to judge whether this can be done or made possible without breaking any financial reporting rules. Your Trade Finance person or Finance Director are best placed to advise you.

To overcome such challenges of liquidity, a Nigerian distributor may make a side arrangement with an EU or UK based intermediary that you send the goods to, and the distributor draws supplies from that intermediary. The intermediary is different to the prior term we used for an intermediary in that he buys the goods from you. The intermediary is the consignee (to whom your goods are shipped) not the Nigerian distributor. The invoice is always made out to the name of the consignee.

You can see the complexities emerging already, can't you?

- The distributor in Nigeria has a view of the demand and the size of the opportunity. The forecasting of demand is carried out in Nigeria by the distributor jointly agreed with the principal (you). The intermediary is not party to the agreement of the demand budget.

- The consignee in England has no view on the demand or the size of the opportunity in Nigeria. He has a relationship with the distributor to order the demand forecast quantities that the Nigerian distributor will pay him to cover the invoices from you (the principal) to the consignee. He may also have a side arrangement with the distributor to be paid for providing this facility, because otherwise, there is nothing in it for him in the UK to take on the debt and rely on the Nigerian distributor to pay him to cover his invoices to pay you (the principal).

A dangerous game is about to unfold.

So long as the Nigerian distributor is creating the demand in Nigeria and collecting the cash from his customers, he can purchase the invoice currency and repatriate that currency to pay the intermediary in the UK. But what if the Nigerian distributor took his eyes off your ball and started a new venture, or he simply lost focus on creating demand for your products, or both? To compound matters, he became slack at collecting his overdue payments from his customers. Distributors struggling to collect cash from customers they supplied is quite common in partnership markets. And what if the Government imposes tight fiscal controls severely restricting the availability of foreign currency such as the GBP or USD or Euro? The distributor struggles to pay for the goods.

Now the stock at the intermediary is sitting in the UK not being drawn to fill demand in Nigeria. But the consignee has a deadline approaching to pay you.

Nigeria is not the UK or the EU. Fiscal policies and fiscal controls change with alarming regularity to the point that the Nigerian distributor cannot purchase forex to pay the intermediary and he has pages and pages of creditors that he supplied that have not paid him at 60 days and 120 days outstanding due to currency issues, soaring inflation and tight fiscal controls imposed by the Government.

The consignee says he cannot pay you because Nigeria has not paid him. But that is not your problem. That is his problem with Nigeria. He is your debtor, and he must pay. Fortunately, as the intermediary is in the UK or the EU you can close his business, forcing him into bankruptcy by calling in the debt. You have no jurisdiction over the Nigerian distributor; he is not your direct debtor.

However, in doing so, you destroy your business in Nigeria because you chose a distributor that did not have the liquidity to withstand the economic volatility in his country.

The message, therefore, is that no matter how smartly these arrangements appear to solve liquidity issues, you must be incredibly careful. Such arrangements may just turn out to be too good to be true. As in this illustrative example where the UK intermediary does not solve the issue of defaulting on debt. Unknowingly, you can set foot on an Improvised Explosive Device and have your legs blown off because as the Head of the Region, it is your responsibility to collect the cash.

Debts may be wiped out. But understand how that wipe out happens. The company takes that debt off your revenue line. If the debt is $1m, and your revenue total is $5m, you now have revenue of $4m after the debt is extinguished in the reporting format.

Then there is the issue of the budget to be delivered. This is going to hurt. You may have £1m in debts to be collected from the intermediary against a budget of £4m. You are £3m down and need to find that £3m from additional sales across your other markets. To do that, you need to find more customers from your other markets.

Finding customers is the difficult bit. It is the bit that so few know or understand how to do. There are an awful lot of textbook marketers and academic MBAs out there. But very few of them can show their abilities through their results to find new customers for their products and sell more products to current customers. If you cannot make up that £3m shortfall, you are still held to deliver the profit line by taking out costs – laying off people, not spending on marketing expenses and anywhere where you can slash costs.

In another version of this, a principal struggled in West Africa's Ghana with its distributor. But Ghana's currency (the Cedi) has been devaluing with soaring inflation. Imagine, back in 2003, there were around 3 Cedis to 1$. Today, it is close to 12 cedis to $1. However, a distributor's liquid assets struggle to keep pace with inflation. This means in real terms they erode in value. Legitimately, the distributor switches to buying small quantities that he can sell and collects cash quickly to pay the principal.

The principal decides to appoint multiple distributors so there are a total of three distributors in Ghana. But of course, this will not help to deliver the budgets. Why? Because:

1. This is supply focused. To deliver the budgets, it needs demand creation. None of their distributors can address the demand side of the equation. Two out of the three are 'box-shifters'.

2. Nobody will take risks with such volatility of currency, especially not a 'box-shifter'. And if they adopt a pre-wholesale consignment model, they may face heavy destruction and write off costs if the stock does not sell due to being too expensive in the market through that massive exchange rate of 12 cedis to $1.

As an example, let us say the landed cost is $1. That would be 3 cedis he paid a long time back. If he applied a 25% mark-up as his wholesaler price it would be selling for 3.75 cedis. If today he bought that pack for $1, and that was the landed cost, it is equal to 12 cedis. His wholesaler price to sell to his customers with 25% margin would now be 15.00 cedis. Now if that pack had a trade price of 33% markup it would be 19.95 cedis and the trade to retail price (to the patient) would be a 33% markup = 26.53 cedis.

The price to the patient has gone up four-fold (6.6 versus 26.53)!

Way back at 3 cedis to $1, the wholesale price was 3.75 cedis. The trade price would have been 5 cedis and the retail price would have been 6.6 cedis. The first thing is that patients cannot afford it at 26.53 cedis. The distributor's stock accumulates, and sales drop off because he stops ordering products or severely reduces the size of his orders. The distributor does not order in line with forecasts due to the drop in demand. Patients and customers will go without your products as they prioritise limited cash on essential household items. The principal will not meet his sales budget.

This example illustrates why demand is so important. But demand on its own is not enough. You need liquidity in a distributor so they will be able to ride out currency volatility and still be able to pay you. There will come a point with rampant inflation and tightening of fiscal rules and controls when the distributor will demand a price adjustment from you, the principal. I faced this a few times. It is not easy to produce a scheme to adjust the prices through rebates outside a band of volatility in the currency. It is too complex to be covered in this book. And if I told you how I came up with a solution, I'd have to shoot you! This solution is developed with fee-paying clients because it requires a high degree of customisation and is dependent on a number of key factors specific to each client's approach to these risks.

You need to be careful when negotiating any deal around currency volatility and devaluation because this is outside the control of both you and your distributor. You have no control over fiscal policies or fiscal controls in a different country.

You can probably gather that running an international sales business is complex and requires constant vigilance and renegotiation as well as an appreciation of what drives the business and what hinders the business from delivering a critical mass.

CHAPTER 7

The Need for Continuous Review: What Was Best Fit Then; May Not Be Best-Fit Now

"Never Take Your Eye Off Opponent: Even When You Bow"

This was a line from the 1973 Bruce Lee martial arts film "Enter the Dragon".

Whilst I am not drawing an adversarial or combative analogy between a principal and a distributor or partner in the market, it does sum up the need to be vigilant and buffered from any surprises in your international business. Let me explain.

One feature that was remarkable among clients I worked with was the level of dissatisfaction with their business performance through their distributor. But what was equally remarkable was the number of clients that had done NOTHING about it and had stayed with the same underperforming model and distributor for many years. The analogy was they were trapped in an impossible marriage where the spark in their relationship had evaporated, and both suffered from loss of libido.

One of the features of distributor models I impress on my clients is that the young bride you married then may not still be attractive today after several years of relationship. There is no fun to be trapped in a lifeless marriage where you, your distributor, or both of you feel trapped, unable to break away and start a new relationship.

I always kept all my distributors under constant review by making notes on their performance, how they were to work with, their payment history, their cooperation factor to drive business and their willingness to share risks with me on such things as contributing to new product launch costs.

Remember, I spent a long time in my major markets each year. Each of my visits was for one full week, arriving Sunday morning and flying back late Friday night or on a Saturday morning flight. At each visit, I made it a point to meet the distributors in the office as well as socially with an evening meal, when we would talk off-the-record about what was happening with other principals and staff movement, who left for what reasons etc.

During my consulting projects, it became evident that clients did not spend enough time in their markets or with their distributors. They missed a very good opportunity to gauge their distributor's interest in their products and unearth if the distributor was losing focus and perhaps going into new or different ventures that would take his eyes off the ball (and therefore losing focus on driving my sales) or worse still, underhandedly about to sign a competitor against my major brands with an attempt to disguise it.

I would find this out because I also met those who were not my distributors but were interested in becoming a distributor; for these people this local intelligence about my distributor was unbelievably valuable to share with me. In this way, I identified potential distributors that may be of interest to me if I was thinking of making changes. I would often ask them about new or different opportunities for our business that my current distributor was not leveraging.

When it was appropriate, we would sit down and appraise the relationship between me and my distributor. I was brutally honest in my feedback, and I demanded the same from them. In reality, they had not grown up in a culture of feedback as I had, so this was uncomfortable for many of them.

I would support and illustrate my feedback with examples of behaviours and the impact that those behaviours had on me. Significantly, I would state explicitly what I would like to see moving forward in terms of what they should do, how I wanted to feel and what I wanted to see more of in our relationship. I documented these discussions – something that few folks actually do, instead relying on word-of-mouth discussions.

I recall on several occasions' distributors telling me that the budgets will not be met. I would state explicitly that they would need to come up with proposals of how they intend to correct the situation because they submitted the forecasts, and they know their market. I cannot go to my boss and declare "I am not going to make budget". He will tell me exactly the same thing – go away and tell me how you will correct it across your markets if you have to. Feedback was important for me to give distributors as it was for them to give me feedback.

This exercise is such a valid relationship builder and an opportunity to state if the marriage was hitting the rocks. They always sat up and listened. In one instance, I stated that I was done chasing payments. In another instance, I stated that I was done with his late placement of orders causing shipping delays from the factory owing to the make-to-order model, meaning that we were coming (avoidably) too close to missing budgets. In another instance, unpalatable as it was, I moved the distributor to Confirmed Irrevocable Letters of Credit at Sight – this had a huge financial impact on the distributor, but he accepted the need for us to do this.

I am trying to share with you, the reader, that if you are not having such formal reviews with your distributor but are putting up with sub-standard performance and accepting weak excuses or late payments or missing budget numbers, then you are missing an opportunity to come to mutually agreed solutions.

Some distributors had mentioned to me that their principal just came on a visit with a bunch of heavies from the legal department and the HR department and issued a notice of termination where there was no prior sharing of dissatisfaction. It came as a surprise to the distributor. Refrain from giving surprises. They are not helpful.

It happens. Many companies' international sales folk are reluctant to open up and hold uncomfortable discussions. But my distributors always knew that nothing ever came as a surprise hearing it from me. I was straight-talking and told everything as it was.

The decision to terminate and change the model in one country came about because we were not realising anywhere near the size of the business commensurate with the opportunity. The distributor had been appointed by predecessors but the climate in the company was hugely different to those times. The frank exchange between us was to state the model had to be changed (citing clear reasons why it could no longer continue as it was) and how it would work. The new model would mean the current distributor had a role in the new setup but on a completely different set of legal terms and conditions and would involve a new model with several players with split products between different distributors.

My message to readers is simple but clear. Never ever be afraid to change the model or the partner or both if the results are not being delivered and where you can clearly identify the poor results are due to the model or the partner or both and not your inability to create demand. Your apathy to confront the situation head-on may just be the force that derails your career. And if you are uncertain how to approach this confrontation, then engage an independent expert to advise and guide you. Much depends on 'how' you approach the discussion rather than on 'what' you say.

My senior Executive Board was intolerant of performance when the numbers were not delivered. They wanted strong leaders that could grasp the nettle, set high ambitions and deliver them. They wanted strong leaders that could make uncomfortable decisions along that journey of ambition and demand the best from everyone they interacted with and never afraid to take the path of greatest resistance if that path was the right path to delivering the ambitions. Apathy and a willingness to accept and tolerate a sub-standard performance by you reflected in your poor business results are strong factors in derailing careers.

I wish that more senior Executive Boards were as demanding and as intolerant of failure as mine, and as able to make decisions that such sub-standard performance cannot be tolerated. This would then trigger a time to bring in someone who could help them when their regional seniors have failed them repeatedly and consistently.

Far too many seniors put up with sub-standard export performance and fail to take control of their dissatisfaction with the present. The easy (lunacy) route is to hand the issues back to the same management team that repeatedly failed to deliver.

By far the most challenging route is to take control of those underperforming local seniors and bring in an independent expert to diagnose the issues who will also recommend what needs to be done to make the business sustainably better.

If you are a senior Executive Board member reading this book, perhaps this last paragraph resonates with you. Were you too tolerant of failure and substandard performance from your local senior management teams? If you had been as demanding on results as mine were, and as intolerant of failure, maybe you might have enjoyed a different set of results because your dissatisfaction with the present and past disappointing performance drove you down a different path. You would not have accepted repeated failure but instead taken control over those local senior teams and brought in an outside expert to really tell you, as a sponsor for the project, why the business is not performing.

I leave you the reader to ponder that point for a moment.

Now, when I see a client with sub-standard performance, it would be unusual if changing the partner or the model or both did not require attention. Many simply fumble and stumble on in the darkness recreating the catalogue of failures of the past. With such a high body count in international sales, a new incumbent does something that is beyond belief to me:

1. Makes promises to his Board without changing the model or the partner or worse, without changing the people that created the failure.

2. Relies on the very team that created the mess over successive years to be able to identify what went wrong and how to put it right despite years of having tried first this, then that with no success. Such a team has shown repeatedly and consistently that it does not

know what it is doing. So why does the new senior with his head on the block look to that team to produce answers and solutions?

This is incredibly naive and bizarre. In Einstein's analogy, it is doing more of the same and expecting a different set of results, demonstrating the first sign of lunacy!

So often, what is required is a completely new fresh appraisal to identify the causes of the poor performance and the failure to deliver the numbers.

The lucky few who admit that neither they nor their staff know what they are doing, will bring me in and breathe a sigh of relief as we identify the causes and how to put things right through my independence and experience. It is like a doctor diagnosing what is causing their pain and how to treat it. They feel the comfort of *"a safe pair of hands"*.

To be clear, no distributor was a bad choice – at one time!

Whichever of your predecessors chose the model and the partner did nothing wrong.

You were not around at that time. You must assume that the choices were the right ones AT THAT TIME, for reasons that were probably well-known (or not).

But at that time, the business was more forgiving of mediocre results and the inability to deliver the numbers. Now the business has set ambitions at a higher level and requires those ambitions to be met with greater operational velocity. And the attitude and mindset of the Board has become less forgiving if those standards and results are not met – quicker and higher is now in vogue. There are still Executive Boards tolerant of and forgiving of failure, but they are slowly becoming intolerant and less forgiving. They bite the bullet and bring in a new guy.

As the new guy, selected by your Executive Board, it is down to you to sort the mess out. And to sort the mess out, the first thing you need to do is to look carefully at the legal contracts and see where they need to be renegotiated.

You need to examine the choice of partner carefully and continuously and be aware of changes in the partner's business, such that a new decision may be required after an exploratory discussion.

You need to go back to basics – the model, the partner – and diagnose the causes of the repeated failures of either you or your predecessors.

And above all, if in doubt about anything, bring in an outside independent expert to help you.

In the final section of this chapter, I will cover danger signals in your distributor that warrant an immediate review of your relationship.

Ten Situations That Warrant an Immediate Trigger to Review Your Relationship

I recommend every company operating in these partnership or distributor markets be cognizant of situations that should trigger a review of either your go-to-market model or your choice of partner or both. They should also be trigger points for seniors at one level above the accountable person you have running this business and should also raise the question: *"Do we have the right person in the role?"* I recommend that at an annual business review during the planning of the following five years forecasts and business plans, the senior executive one level above the accountable person should present these checklist areas and invite the accountable person to comment and answer questions as a standard part of the business presentation.

In my view, the following 10 signals are immediate grounds for opening up an uncomfortable discussion with your distributor or partner or your person accountable for the P&L:

1. Any change in the senior Executive Board composition in the distributor.
2. Any change in shareholding between the directors at the distributor.
3. Any change in the composition of his portfolio of companies.
4. Any diversification of a distributor's business into new areas that involve financing loans and a high degree of gearing.
5. A diverging venture from importing finished goods to local manufacturing of assets.
6. A proposed acquisition or merger of your distributor by/with another company.
7. High staff turnover where the staff are employed on your behalf by the distributor.
8. Repeated history of late payments by your distributor.
9. Repeated failure to deliver the numbers.
10. External factors that drive hostilities against your success.

Let me explain each in greater detail:

1. **Any change in the senior Executive Board composition in the distributor.**
   This may herald Boardroom disruption that is never good for a business because it can lead to in-fighting, divergent activities, and a lack of focus on your business. The last thing you need is a distributor not focused on growing your business. A change in composition of the Board can happen by the CEO or one of the partners stepping down to retire. Or maybe a partner has decided to leave and has sold his shareholding and may or may not be replaced. There may be a loss of intellectual capital of the business, its customers, and creditors. Your legal counsel will probably insert a clause for this possibility, and it shall (unreservedly) result in a review that can lead to termination or renegotiation of the legal agreement.

2. **Any change in shareholding between the directors at the distributor.**
   An example might be a potential friendly new partner or investor. If that partner has a majority share, alarm bells should ring because the business may change direction and models. You should be prepared for changes that may not be beneficial to your business.

3. **Any change in the composition of his portfolio of companies.**
   Distributors branch out into generics and own-brand generics. This may be due to feelings of insecurity that you will change distributors or bring other distributors to share the business with the current distributor. With generics, he can reach a wider market at the base of the pyramid and with his own brand generics he can reach your wealthy minority with a substitution claim that his is as good as yours but a saving in price. Another change might be that he becomes a distributor for your competitor products. He can share with that competitor who are the customers for your competing brand, and they direct their sales efforts on those users of your products. He can substitute your branded demand with

his generics or a competitor's product off the back of your marketing investments. This is most undesirable. Believe me it happens, and it has caught out some principals.

4. **Any diversification of a distributor's business into new areas that involve financing loans and a high degree of gearing.**
   This puts you at risk of delayed payments and loss of focus in your business. This happened to me with a distributor who decided to set up his own confectionery manufacturing plant – of which he knew nothing. It did not go well. Within 12 months he must have defaulted on loan payments because the bank took control of the business to collect payments to start to call the debt in. This strangled my business because the bank had a first charge on clearing his debts. Everyone else had to wait. He owed me a fortune (that I got back eventually after visits and putting pressure on him to make payments). Really bad news. I had to get rid of the distributor and change the model. I terminated the agreement and set up a different go-to-market model with a different partner where he was also listed. But he fell away due to lack of liquidity as the other partner became stronger. Watch out for this one. He kept this hidden from me and I learnt from the experience, never to repeat the mistake ever again. Ask directly, keep asking and repeating the questions in different ways until you get consistency of answers. Until you get consistency and congruence of replies, the distributor is lying until proven otherwise.

5. **A diverging venture from importing finished goods to local manufacturing of assets.**
   This can be related to (4) above. This heralds a change in business direction for your partner.

   He will likely have steep learning curve ahead of him, probably heavily geared and financed through loans from a bank. The bank will have a charge over the business. This comes at the expense of potential loss of interest and loss of focus on your business. This partner is destined for termination. You cannot expect to deliver critical numbers and critical mass with a guy whose interests wonder elsewhere. Find another good distributor.

6. **A proposed acquisition or merger of your distributor by/with another company.**

   This can so often be the kiss of death for your business. The acquiring partner and the current distributor make promises that they intend to carry on the business as it was. This is absolute and utter rubbish. This simply is never the case. Why acquire a business to keep it the same? A decision to acquire is made on the basis that the acquiring company believes it can run it better than the current owners. This involves a change in the way the current model works.

   The variable is when they will make the changes. They may choose to keep things as currently for a year or two, but then make big changes aligned to their ideas for the business that rarely align with your requirements. They are acting in THEIR interests in making changes. NEVER in your interest. Never underestimate the impact of an acquisition of your distributor by a third party. The distributor is likely to risk losing his major customers (that were buying your products from him).

   Across Africa there have been some acquisitions. A client was considering a good distributor in East Africa that I knew well. When the client asked me what I thought of that distributor, I remarked *"he WAS very good"*. The client asked; *"Was?"*

   I then went on and explained:

   > *"You do know he has sold out to X from Y country? So, if you choose this distributor the only guarantee I can make is that the business will be different after the takeover acquisition. His very good rating went out of the window as soon as he sold out. That business was one man – him! Lose him and you lose the rating. The rating now is unknown with change on the agenda and risks with little clarity on how it will operate going forward. You simply do not know what will happen now after having sold the business to a third party".*

   I explained: *"You would need to start afresh with your distributor selection criteria exercise with the newly acquired partner and see how they score. They may not score as high as previously with many responses to your criteria not answered or answered with opaqueness".*

If you have been considering reviewing your business partner but never got around to raising this matter, an acquisition gives you the simplest of reasons to review and perhaps terminate your partnership because he is no longer the best fit against your criteria. The partnership is going to go through change. Some pain and turmoil will be there as well as staff changes. This situation gives you the easiest reason to terminate and appoint a better-fit partner. For me, this is an automatic action to terminate. It is sometimes a refreshing change. If you were good in the role, there will be a line of people wanting to be your distributor. Never fear. The next guy could be better than the current one. Or worse. Choose carefully with an objective selection process against your Ideal Distributor Criteria.

7. **High staff turnover where the staff are employed on your behalf by the distributor.**
   If you were operating a scientific office model and you experienced a high turnover of staff, this needs to be explored to establish the reasons why. You do have a clause in your legal agreement that any vacancies must be authorised by you before recruitment can proceed? Sounds obvious, but not all principals know the staff employed on their behalf or are involved with their recruitment. They leave it to the distributor after confirming how many reps and managers he will pay for. Are those staff actually employed on your business or shared with other principals that have opted not to fund reps but told the distributor to fund reps from his margin? It is tempting for the distributor not to lose his margin but use your reps. They realise they are working too hard and leave. If you invested in staff training and development, staff turnover wastes your investment, and another company benefits from the investment that you made. Investigate staff vacancies. Try to arrange staff that leave to meet you when next in the country to understand why they left and get feedback on the distributor as an employer.

8. **Repeated history of late payments by your distributor.**
   This is simply intolerable. I offered credit terms. And still some distributors tried it on with late payments citing that they were owed money in the market from <u>their</u> customers!

My reply? *"Why is this my problem?"* They had no answer.

If he could not guarantee clearing his overdue payment inside 2 to 4 weeks with a goodwill payment immediately, I would consider putting them on a payment plan with a legally drafted letter spelling out in no uncertain terms that this will not be tolerated, and the offer of a payment is exceptional for this one instance on the terms outlined herein:

a) The maximum fraction of payments stated in writing to be no more than 3, within 3 months to clear the overdue payment.

b) Payments to be phased as follows: First payment 50% of overdue payment as cleared funds by specified date; Second payment 30% and Final payment of the balance of 20% all received as cleared funds by specified dates. Do not divide it into three equal payments.

c) A future default on payment by due dates may result in other measures taken to secure payment through either Irrevocable Letter of Credit at Sight or a demand for a cash deposit as insurance on future default covering a value equal to one quarter of the annual budget value or a combination of the two.

The key is that default on payments should be like a burn – intense, sharp, pain and give a jolt or a shock to let the distributor know that (i) we take stern actions if they cannot keep to their side of the bargain when we give them generous credit terms and (ii) let them know that moving to Letters of Credit or a Cash Deposit or a combination of these will be very painful to his cash flow.

If you do not want to issue a payment plan, state this possibility, and confirm it in a letter.

The options available to you then might be moving straight to abolishing credit until further notice and put them on cash in advance or move to a Confirmed Irrevocable Letter of Credit at Sight for payment terms and consider a cash deposit to be made by the distributor held in an escrow account in case of future default. Capture everything in writing and if there are legal implications have your legal counsel construct the letter and you issue it (not the legal guys).

As a senior executive accountable for the P&L, you have to get used to having these forthright demanding discussions and negotiations. If the thought of opening this sort of discussion and holding these demanding negotiation makes you break out in a sweat, think carefully if this is really a job for you.

Distributors try it on at every step and every way they can in a manner that benefits them but disadvantages you. You have to be vigilant and confront them. Otherwise, you are not going to deliver that P&L with missed payments and potentially having to write off that debt. YOU pay the price for overdue payment and debts. The risk is very high if they do not pay you and their debt has to be written off against your sales.

An interesting example arose with a distributor that I was trading on 90 days credit terms.

This is an example of how distributors 'try it on'. During a market visit, the distributor, and his finance manager at the end of the day after a long series of meetings asked if they could have a discount if they settled their invoice before the 90 day term. The basis of this was down to when they had a favourable exchange rate in local currency against the invoice currency of GBP. Of course, I dismissed their request immediately. Why and how?

First the why. When the invoice is raised at 90 days, that is the amount to be collected. If I agreed (say) 10% discount, I would have a shortfall versus the invoice showing as a debt on the ledger. We would have to 'reverse' the prior invoice with a credit note, then raise a new invoice for the new value of 90% of the original invoice but it would still have the original 90 days credit terms unless I changed the credit terms to 'at sight'. I would have given him a 10% discount for nothing that I would have to make up because the budget figures do not change.

How did I dismiss his request? I told him that we are not in a position to start changing the price lists with discounts;

but if he wants to pay early, I would be pleased to change his terms to 30 or 60 days. Not surprisingly he was not keen for me to do that.

On the topic of foreign exchange rates, I reminded his finance manager that as an international business you can hedge the risks with foreign currency, and I suggested maybe they should consider hedging as an option and then they can pay us early on the full invoice value.

Don't fall for it. The topic was raised at the end of a long day of discussions reviewing the business performance. The hope was that I would be tired and concede. Far from it. Never let your guard down. Or as Bruce Lee tells his martial art student in the film Enter the Dragon:

> *"Never take your eye off opponent:*
> *Even when you bow".*

9. **Repeated failure to deliver the numbers.**
   More often than not, repeated failure should start with exploring the person that you have in the role. Anyone can be forgiven for getting it wrong in one year. But repeating it the following year suggests that failure is starting to become a habit. The maximum to be tolerated should be no more than three consecutive years of failure. Anybody who fails to deliver the numbers for three consecutive years should prompt you to ask whether you have the right internal person running your business. This may reveal that you may not have the right go-to-market model, and the right choice of distributor partner. My experience suggests that it is two of these if not all three, rarely a single factor of the three. Why do I say this? On what basis?

   I have seen examples where companies have replaced their internal guy, but the failure is repeated, many times over with each change of internal guy. The one thing that each new incumbent does not do in the role is he does not do anything really different from his predecessor. And so, he disappoints seniors. When I am engaged to help such a company after a series of dead bodies have accumulated, I invariably find a poor go-to-market model and/or a poor choice of partner for that company's portfolio and channels of operation. The business models do not match! Hence, I state that repeated failure is down to two if not all three of these factors – wrong person in the role; wrong go-to-market model and wrong choice of partner.

10. **External factors that drive hostilities against your success.**
    Often these external factors cannot be addressed by you and in many cases by the distributor also. But they can have a severe impact on you delivering your numbers. Examples could be:

    a) A country's fiscal policies unable to manage inflation impacting on the cost of operations for your distributor. Food, fuel, and energy prices rise steeply with rampant inflation. He has to pass on his increased overheads on the prices of your products. In a price sensitive market, this may make them unaffordable to that small segment of the population that are now squeezed to buy at these prices.

    b) Foreign exchange controls and currency devaluation are potential death blow for your business and your distributor. Devaluation of currency makes it more expensive for your distributor to buy foreign exchange to pay you in your invoiced reporting currency. While foreign exchange controls could make it difficult for him to pay you because the banks limit the release of foreign currencies such as the USD, GBP, or the Euro. The situation is especially acute where the country has a non-convertible currency, such as Nigeria (the Naira). Negotiating with a distributor in Nigeria, you may need to explore what reserves he holds of forex to pay you if the fiscal controls are applied limiting release of forex to pay you. Large distributors may have a HQ outside of Africa from where they can make payments against your invoice (the triangulated payment where the goods go to the consignee in Africa, but the invoice is paid by another part of his company in an 'inter-company netting' model).

    You will need to seek the advice of your finance director and the compliance team if this triangulated payment can be achieved in a compliant manner.

Whilst you are not able to address these external factors, you should compile a risk register highlighting and identifying risks, their probability of occurring in the budget period of three or five years and their impacts on your business. For each risk, you should list actions that you would take to manage or mitigate the risk. I call it "If this; then that" in other words if this happens, this is what we will do.

In order to be aware of all these situations, it requires you to be in the market. If you are sitting blue-sky gazing out the window from your office in a tower block in Istanbul or Dubai or Johannesburg, you will not be aware of what is happening on the ground to unearth these situations.

As I stated, the job is out there, in the market meeting customers, Government agencies, distributors, your office and your field staff. You need to keep a close ear to the ground to know what is happening around you in your markets. If you don't, you might just get caught out and find yourself stepping on an Improvised Explosive Device having blown your legs off.

Be warned! If time in the market is not possible, think carefully if you want to do this job and have a fighting chance of delivering the numbers.

CHAPTER 8

How Do You Find Good International Business Managers?

Part 1: Setting the Challenge in Context

It may come as no surprise that finding good candidates for International Sales Development is not easy, judging by so many job holders on social media staying in the role for short tenures and moving to new companies every 18-24 months. Some are even shorter. The fact that some are resigning with no job to move across to is certainly suspicious and points to questions in regard to abilities and performance shortfall possibilities.

Before I continue, I should declare to the reader that what I am about to write in this section on finding and retaining good international sales professionals are my own views, based on my real-life experience. This book is about my experience. Other views strongly contesting my views and experience will exist, so I make no apology for this. Not surprisingly, there may be a vehement challenge to this chapter from HR and Talent Partners that readers should be prepared for. Such folk will attempt to dismiss my content. But I am only reciting my personal experience that have formed my opinions on HR and Talent Partners. There may be an exceptional HR or Talent Partner who is quite talented and different from those I have worked with and experienced.

What is it that drives a high failure rate in finding good high-calibre candidates?

The answer is amazingly simple. Poor recruitment practice and relying too much on traditional 'interviewing' conducted by HR and Talent Partners. Going by the high failure rates in recruitment by HR and Talent Partners that I worked with, as well as clients that engaged me, they understand little or nothing about how to pick winners for these roles. I kept HR at arm's length on my market recruitment. It was easy. The staff are employed for me by the distributor and therefore do not comprise headcount FTEs (Full-Time Equivalents) on the payroll. That changed later when the requirement was to submit all staff engaged exclusively in AZ business through distributors had to be disclosed as FTEs. But even with that change, I kept them away from being involved in my recruitment across my markets.

There are many flawed assumptions in recruiting for these roles. And we all know what happens when you assume, don't we?

For those who did not understand what happens, you make an ASS out of U and ME when you ASSUME.

Allow me to list some of these flawed assumptions:

1. **A rising star in a big affiliate model makes a great candidate.**
   Wrong. A rising star in a big market is unlikely to succeed in these smaller international markets for many reasons. The principal reason is that he has had a lot of headcounts doing things for him and these roles require a person with firsthand experience and capabilities.

   In this environment, he will not have the luxury of having a huge headcount or any direct-reporting headcount until the business reaches a critical mass. It is unlikely such a candidate has the firsthand coalface experience that is needed to succeed. You need a guy who has metaphorically gone down the coalpit and worked at the underground coalface in the dark dusty environment. Drilling for coal, pickaxe in hand striking the coalface, shovelling the coal onto the trucks, wiping the sweat off his brow in the heat and the dust and spending prolonged periods in darkness where he cannot just rely on sight but must rely on his other senses. He needs to have developed stamina for long shifts in dark dusty coalface conditions.

2. **We have a star performer in marketing or sales management who we need to prepare for a senior role in a big market.**
   Wrong. This candidate most certainly will not do well and will be sent to these markets like a lamb to slaughter. This is the young

246

late thirties or early forty's pelvic thruster who has impressed local seniors with his collection of 12-to-18-month stints in several successive roles in the company, locally and possibly abroad. But such seniors are short-sighted. Any fool can look impressive over a 12-to-18-month period. I have seen it numerous times in a corporate career where a rising star appears to have been spectacular in the role, who is then moved up to a bigger role and again appears impressive for 18 months. But this can so often be an illusion. I have seen the person who followed that 'star performer' in the new vacancy, and that follower unearthed serious business issues that his predecessor created but managed to keep hidden from seniors in his desire to maintain the illusion that he was a star performer. Some have been serious compliance issues covered over and not addressed. Instead, they are dressed and presented well to seniors who were short-sighted enough not to look any deeper.

3. **An approach along the lines that "vital skills can be learned."**
   A good example of this is a sales manager or a marketing/brand manager in a legal affiliate that has "commercial experience" but no demonstrable experience or track record of negotiations and no experience in turning those negotiations and discussions into legal contracts, nor understanding or managing large value negotiations and lacking an understanding of impacts of discounting and delivering margins and profit. Such a candidate is a lamb being sent to slaughter in these roles. He simply cannot survive against the strong tactics used by distributors and supply chain partners in these markets. He cannot learn negotiation skills 'on the job' and will be a huge liability. Neither can he learn the financial skills and understanding 'on the job'. The Legal Counsel's job is to turn the negotiations into a legal contract. It is not the Legal Counsel's job to design the commercial go-to-market models and to negotiate these deals. This job holder needs to be able to design and negotiate with distributors and partners and at the same time challenge his Legal Counsel and ensure the right legal contract is in place for success. Legal Counsel is risk averse. The job holder needs to be able to understand and explain those risks and how they will be managed and mitigated for inclusion in the contract.

4. **Employing a candidate from other emerging market territories, for example, SE Asia (such as Cambodia, Laos, Vietnam, and Myanmar), and parachuting him into Anglophone Sub-Saharan Africa's top markets of Ghana, Nigeria, Kenya, Tanzania, Uganda, and Ethiopia to work miracles.**

These two territories are chalk and cheese. What works in one territory does not necessarily work within, let alone translate into, a viable commercial model in another. What is key is not his success in those other geographies, but rather to share his understanding of the success factors and destructive factors in this book and how he managed them. The candidate may have been a star in SE Asia. But in Sub-Saharan Africa, he is a fish out of water and an absolute disaster! The latter is one of the most complex and demanding territories in which to succeed over a sustained period. That last bit of qualification is key – <u>sustained period</u>.

Any fool in Africa can show results for 12-18 months. What is important is that the candidate has the cognitive bandwidth to assess and devise market models and strategies based on a deep market understanding assimilated in a short period of time.

Any fool can look good in distributor markets over a 12-18-month period.

How? You ask.

Simple. Just load the distributors with stock. This raises a sales invoice, and, in turn, he makes a promise to the distributors to give credit or fresh stock if it expires, which it will.

This makes accepting this (indecent) proposal a zero risk to the distributor. But only if the job holder is authorised and empowered to make such promises. Invariably he is not.

All the legal contracts I negotiated had a clause that the supplier (you, as the manufacturer or principal) would not be responsible for credit for expired goods or goods that become short-dated whilst in the distributor's possession. Offering such a favourable zero-risk promise to raise an invoice to create a 'sale' and then reverse it again with a credit note is a serious breach. Under Sarbanes-Oxley rules, it is false reporting of sales.

But how would an HR and Talent Partner know how to find out whether the candidate in front of them, with an impressive two-year history, overloaded distributors, and breached compliance by manipulating ('fiddling') with his sales figures?

They cannot. But I can! And I will explain:

Shelf life is often only two years for these smaller markets due to temperature and humidity exposure. Distributors can be overloaded with invoiced stock in year 1 and up to late year 2. Year 1 looks impressive. Year 2 struggles but the half-year review showed signs of not meeting the budget. The candidate in front of you has left his company with a reasonable set of year 1 and half of year 2 results based on false sales reporting. But by the end of year 2, the business is well off track. Distributors will not 'buy' more stock. Instead, the company will start to give credit for expired or short-dated goods. The company fails to meet the budget AND gives cash back to the distributors! And that might be the guy sitting in front of you. He has no job. He 'resigned' claiming difficulties with his boss and that he was set unreasonable unachievable sales targets. This is usually nonsense.

Assume it is nonsense and allow the candidate to prove you wrong. He probably got caught out because any decent company with good financial controls has systems in place to alert seniors across finance and other functions when free goods are being issued or when credit is being given to customers (wrong flow of cash). Often such proposed transactions require second or third-level senior authorisation. The guy in front of you thought he was clever. He was not.

Do you honestly want such a guy working for you to scale up and expand internationally? Why are you wasting your time even bringing him in for an interview?

5. **The final flaw I will mention in my limited space and time is appointing candidates who do not have a demonstrably sound understanding of the financial side of running a business. Instead, you assume that they will pick it up on the job and you mutter to yourself *"in any case, the finance guys do all this stuff anyway."***

Earlier on, I set out that the challenge is not in establishing an international business. The challenge is how to deliver a scalable critical mass within five or ten years. So, if you are appointing a P&L role, it is so easy to appoint a sales manager or marketer who was good in that prior role of managing sales within costs. But remember, they will have little or no clue about managing the P&L because so many of them have little understanding of the broader financial side of running a business that a P&L requires if he is to succeed. These sales managers or marketers so often cannot explain such things as "gross margin", "gross profit" or "cost-of goods (COGs)" or the inter-relationship in the golden triangle of Price, Volume and Margin.

They do not understand the impact of price discounting through offering bonus goods versus a straight price discount. Allow me to illustrate this example that is based on real experience:

For example, if I offer 50% in bonus goods, this is not a 50% cash discount. It is equivalent to a 33.33% cash discount! I know of people who made this mistake, and they were managing a P&L! The impact on the margin is the same whether you discount as 50% in bonus goods or as a 33.33% price discount. I used to ask candidates to evaluate their understanding of this point. None could explain why the impact on the margin is the same by offering 50% in bonus goods or a straight 33.33% price discount. They failed miserably.

The advantage of offering a discount through free bonus goods is that the recipient values them at their invoice price but, in actual fact, you are giving them away at your COGs price (what it costs you to make them).

Hopefully, with these five examples of flawed assumptions, I have illustrated why such mistakes happen. So, I will now look at what you need to establish if you want to pick a winner and I will explain some of the techniques I used. These flawed assumptions should already set your cognition wheels in motion and alert you to understand the skills that you need that are missing or not demonstrable. In some cases, they may be present in the candidate, but the recruiter had no idea how to find if they were present in the candidate.

Part 2: How to Identify Good Candidates

For this, we are going to do some stargazing. By now, I can see your furrowed brows as you squint and ask what has stargazing got to do with picking winners. Is there 'a mystic Gypsy' to consult or a crystal ball gazer to pick winners?

Imagine this analogy:

A wise senior in corporate will explain stargazing. He will begin by stating one of the key traits that you need in a winner for these international sales development and P&L roles.

And to illustrate it, he would do this:

He would begin by getting some aspiring candidates together and point to a member of the group and ask:

"What can you see above you in the night sky?" the colleague would reply:

"I see stars."

He would ask what he notices about those stars.

That colleague would say "Some are bigger than others."

AND? He would ask.

"Some are bright, and some are not-so-bright," replies the young aspiring candidate.

Anything else?

The reply would come: "No, nothing else as I can see in the night sky."

That senior would then remind the group that these observations were good and probably what you all would have replied. Yes? They would nod. Apart from one member.

That member is a star performer in the role of International Sales Director and is not an aspiring candidate. He was planted in the group and would be asked to come forward and gaze at the night sky. He would be asked the same questions, and this 'candidate' would repeat the same answers as the other member.

He would be asked again, "What else do you see in the night sky?"

He would look again and after a brief pause, would reply: "I can see how those stars are arranged into constellations. I see The Great Bear, The Plough, I see Orion and those three stars are his belt."

Over there in the distance, there is a star with a different glow – orange in complexion – that is a planet. It is Jupiter. It is not a star."

That senior would tell the group, "That is why he is doing the job that he does (very well, I might add), the job that you aspire to but have not realised in your career as yet."

He would explain further: "He sees patterns between disparate objects that you fail to see. He can see connections in complex problems and the implications of actions not just immediately, but on other parameters. For example, in these P&L roles, he understands that a price discount creates a fall in the margin that MUST be compensated by volume increase. He agrees to a price discount from his markets but in turn, he understands the impact on his margin to be delivered and therefore commits the distributor to increased volumes to offset the margin and profit loss.

AND he commits the distributor to those volume increases no matter how uncomfortable that discussion will be. He negotiates hard."

He tells the young group of aspiring international sales directors to-be: "Every distributor will ask you to lower prices. But very few will want to hear this person's reply: *'We can look at that, but in turn, it will mean you will have to buy greater volumes to offset margin erosion from the lower prices. Are you prepared to do that? If not, we do not need to discuss lowering prices again.'*

"Fools offer discounts without negotiating and without demanding more and cannot hold uncomfortable discussions.

"This International Sales Director is at ease holding those uncomfortable discussions. You, my colleagues, are not ready for that just yet."

With that last sentence, he would walk away and leave the others in awe.

In many companies, the HR or Talent Partner would have a high chance of selecting one of those remaining members for the role with disastrous consequences. Is it any wonder then that, in the territory I worked, my mantra resonates so painfully for so many fallen horses and corpses:

> *"The plains of Sub-Saharan Africa are littered with the corpses of corporate heroes who bravely went in declaring them to be lands of opportunity. They were excited to meet the challenges set by them, only to find that they needed to beat a hasty retreat within two years, admitting defeat with a career that was quickly derailing and leading towards an enforced exit from the company."*

I hope that you can now see how certain characteristics are coming into sharp focus of what it takes to succeed. In my personal experience, the following are particularly important factors:

- **Coalface experience** – having done things attributable to one's efforts and results. Not the results of those under you. Do you pick people with coalface experience or those whose success was attributable to the efforts of others? Do you even ask to dig deep and find out what this candidate did himself or if it was done by others?

- **Problem-solving and Critical-Thinking Skills** – identifying the real problem and not going by how the problem appears. Getting to the root factors behind the problem. This is addressing the cause, not the symptoms and being able to identify those root factors that often are disparate and unrelated – the stargazing ability I mentioned. Strong questioning skills to define and confirm the problem. My boss used to say to me, "In four questions, you should be able to define the problem with confidence."

The challenge was constructing the right four questions and the speed and agility of processing the replies!

- **Analytical thinking** – the ability to identify the data, draw accurate conclusions and rule out assumptions based on that data. The ability to challenge numbers through numerical dexterity and data.

- **Negotiation skills and experience at the coalface** – not that which was done by others in the team or the department. As an example, the candidate MUST have demonstrable examples of having negotiated high-value contracts or setting up a brand-new business from scratch. I bet no HR or Talent Partner person ever asked for such examples from candidates at an interview! And if they did, I bet they could not validate the candidate's responses with appropriate interjections and clarifying questions.

- **Concern with impact** – being able to couch your words and decisions in language, choice of words, style, tone, and voice that demonstrates concern for the effect of those messages on the listeners. This is about HOW you communicate over WHAT you communicate. This is essential when dealing with others internally in your company but especially important when dealing and interacting with distributors.

- **Strong, clear critical reasoning skills** – the ability to be able to understand written and spoken text for what it says and very importantly, to discern what it does not say. Candidates who can apply this skilfully can make valid assumptions, they can rule out invalid assumptions and deduce accurate conclusions from the replies. The language will usually be English, but it could be another language, such as French, Spanish, or Portuguese or a local language in another country. A large part of the job is communication – written, spoken and oral. The candidate must score highly on critical reasoning skills to be able to author accurate reports, assimilate emails and legal documents quickly, and accurately respond with precision through a careful choice of words that must be watertight if legally challenged by a distributor, a government authority, or a customer, or a member of staff.

- **Financial skills and numeracy.** Employing a candidate into a P&L role without sound financial understanding is a sure-fire recipe for failure. Managing a P&L is extremely demanding. Understand that from the outset.
Managing sales within costs (a sales manager or a marketing manager) is amazingly easy in comparison. I know this because I have done both jobs – Sales Management as well as P&L holder (third-line management level). A P&L holder has additional metrics that can mean delivering sales within costs may still result in missed profit and margin targets.

  To understand finance, a candidate needs a high degree of numeracy or "numerical critical reasoning skills", where the candidate can deduce and make conclusions and decisions based on the data presented. Basic financial skills are key, and you must take steps to ascertain that these are present in a candidate. I cover this in the section describing in detail my recruitment process.

  It is a sad fact that numerical critical reasoning skills have been seriously lacking since my education at a Grammar School in England where children were segregated at age 11 into those that went to Grammar School (more intensive education for the smaller percentage of academically brighter children) and those that did not go to Grammar School but were very good in other areas, such as arts and crafts. Many of these latter children went on to trade skills, such as carpentry, welding, plumbing, electrician and so on. They were particularly good with their hands.

- **Vocational skills in the context of your industry** – sales management, brand management, marketing, sales and management training, business analysis, designing commercial models at distinct stages of a product's life cycle from launch through to maturity and decline, launching new products and market preparation. Everything should be supported by results versus targets. More on this later.

- **Stage in the candidate's career.** More in a separate section on this.

One feature that stands out to me in companies recruiting a role to expand internationally, or to review and restructure a business that is not delivering the numbers, is the remarkable number of companies that recruit a local in the market for these challenges. You know, the roles such as Country Manager or Regional Manager East Africa. There is nothing wrong with appointing locals. However, you can guess there is a big BUT coming up:

There is nothing wrong with appointing locals **BUT** they need to have demonstrable coalface experience of having done what you want them to do in that role.

So, if you are looking for someone to set up a new business, then make sure you interview and recruit candidates who have demonstrable coalface experience of having done this expansion into new markets. Ask them how they went about it, how they found a partner, how they decided which partner and how they negotiated the deals. If you look deep enough (and if you are good at questioning and looking at the body language of the candidate as the answers are given), you may discover that actually all the candidate did was to be the mule or the donkey for a much more senior manager sitting in a regional office or carry her handbag for her in discussions with potential distributors.

Appointing such a mule or handbag carrier and expecting a spectacular set of results is not going to happen! So be careful. None of my staff in the markets had authority to select, negotiate, hire, or fire distributors. Neither did they have any authority on setting prices or devising market access strategies, devising bonus schemes, or setting salaries and bonus cash payments. Input, yes. Authority to do any of these activities, no. They were tasked with the day-to-day running and managing of staff and the business and managing the distributor's customers for our products. Very much a tactical focus implementing strategies and models created by me sitting outside of any of the markets.

Do not allow the bluffer sitting in front of you to pull the wool over your eyes. Many locals in export markets lack this coalface experience. The serious setting up, reviewing and restructuring is often carried out by someone outside of the markets in his corporate office or regional hub as I have just illustrated. But they are not going to tell you that. Instead, they will tell you they have lots of experience in this. You will find out they do not know how to do this when it is too late – after offering them the job!

In a similar vein, the acts of reviewing and restructuring are often not carried out by a local manager. It is done either one or two levels above her in the food chain by someone sitting in a regional office or multiregional hub in Dubai or Turkey or Singapore or Vietnam.

Just make sure that the candidate that you are interviewing has actual experience of what you want them to do and explore deeply and broadly until you are satisfied.

In my experience, you will find many are not qualified for the roles that you are seeking. Very few will have negotiated a termination of a distributor or negotiated a new distributor. Owing to the high risks of reputational damage and litigation, the person who has done this is NOT the guy sitting in front of you, no matter how convincing he sounds!

On the other hand, he could be. So, satisfy yourself that you have a guy who has done what you want to be done in the export market.

Part 3: Are You "Good with Things" or Are You "Good with People?"

In my more than forty years in the pharmaceutical industry, I made some observations and generalisations that have proven to be remarkably accurate in my experience.

I noticed that, of all the people I worked with as well as those I managed, they were either good with 'things' or they were good with people. And there was no shortage of people in either camp.

Let me explain. Some people were good with concepts and abstract ideas. These were often suited to marketing roles devising brand campaigns, ads, media, and journal publication plans. But notice one thing? They did not deliver those plans through people. That task fell on the other group to implement and deliver – those that were good with people.

These 'good with people' folk knew how to interact with their staff to coax and persuade them to implement and deliver centrally-constructed plans into locally deliverable results – market share and revenue within cost budgets. They could see the human side of interactions and how to bring out the best in people.

Often, results were disappointing. This was probably due to the fact that they were likely to have been those that were 'good with things' charged with delivery of results where what was needed was someone who was 'good with people'. As a result, some were disastrous in the role because they failed to see the human side of interactions and the psychology of persuasion and motivation, and they were managed out or were moved into a role that better used their attraction and appeal with 'things' rather than people.

But there is a third and exceedingly rare category of persons – those who are good at both managing people and managing things. On a scale of scarcity, they are not as scarce as hen's teeth or 'Wooden Rocking Horse Poo' but are certainly scarce compared to the other two categories.

To be strong at P&L delivery, a candidate needs BOTH traits – to be good with 'things' and to be good with people. A bias towards one or the other leads to distinct but different performance issues. All P&L candidates will have some sense of bias toward one or the other. The interviewer must explore where that bias is and how strong it is in either direction.

Bias to Being Good with Things

If this is a strong bias, these tend to be backroom General Managers akin to photography enthusiasts developing photos in the dark room. Their staff rarely have an opportunity to meet or interact with them. They do not even know all their staff by first name terms. It is not important to them. Creating empathy is challenging work for them. Out of sight out of mind describes them well. "Give me the new brand plans to review and comment" is their preference any day. They prefer that (and that too by email) over having to talk to the team about the business. They believe talking and communicating with the staff is the job of their other members of the team or the distributor. But tasks that attract conceptual ability and conceptual thinking attract them like a magnet. They tend to be introverted thinkers who like to study data and make decisions based on data and logic. They are 'here and now' and 'today' people. They are often described as 'sensing' because they use their senses to make decisions. They are realists and often avoid taking decisions for fear they could be wrong. They struggle to make decisions without every tiny fact and data and evidence. In these international scale-up opportunities, the data simply may not exist, or it may be unreliable at best compared to data in developed markets. Under pressure, they become more sensing and even more introverted. They literally 'freeze' with fear over the risk of making poor decisions. They cannot rely on gut feel and intuition and that is an area of development for them.

The people's side tends not to be their comfort zone. So, results-delivery struggles. Staff turnover and staff morale may be an issue as a sign that you have a misfit in the role unable to meet the minimum of people skills required.

Bias to Being Good with People

These love to be among people to get their kick and energy. In contrast, these may be described as 'Extroverted Feelers' with strong intuition and the ability to use 'gut feel' in their decisions. When asked why and how they made that decision? They reply, "It felt right, my gut feeling said it was the right way to go." But this can also be a severe weakness – and may go against what the data and evidence point to. They may come across as 'flying by the seat of their pants'.

Unlike introverted thinkers, these "extroverted feelers" may veer towards being starters but not finishers. They start many things but lack the concentration and focus needed to see them through to completion. Their attention span wanes very easily – in stark contrast to the former category who are well focused on completing tasks.

The good ones are remarkably good at motivating and managing their staff but often struggle to hold uncomfortable discussions around poor results and lack of performance. When asked by a staff member "How am I doing?" they gloss over the answer and assure that staff member that he/she is doing good. That is until I objectively review that staff member's performance and hold the manager to task for why they have not addressed that member's performance, which is not to the declared standard. These people love to be liked.

With the right blend of abilities that define the good ones, they are a real asset. Many of them fall short and are in the 'like to be liked' category. They are poisonous and toxic and can kill any chance of delivering results. They will avoid aligning themselves to the business strategy with phrases to their staff such as "I do not agree either, but it is what 'management' wants" and in doing so can create incitement and mutiny by the staff to the business strategy. This is the last thing a senior P&L holder needs, a staff member who blames management for his shortcomings and lack of results delivery. A P&L holder needs staff aligned on the strategy and goals and to support the same. There is a risk that some in this group show support for your strategy on their faces, but their behaviours with their staff and teams do not. This can be devastating in terms of executing strategy through their people.

I realised that I had first-line district managers such as these that were submitting ludicrous salary recommendations for people who did not deliver budgets. I knew that I had a bunch of misfits who like to be liked. I designed and delivered a training programme on their role – holding uncomfortable performance discussions, reviewing performance objectively against pre-set criteria and standards that I introduced and, above-all, accountability through tight performance management. The benefit of having been a sales training and management development manager in a prior life meant I did this myself without paying for outside resources. Most staff managed the painful transition. Others did not. Of that group, I moved one or two into separate roles that were better suited to them.

What Does a P&L Holder Need to Be?

A P&L holder ideally needs to be skilled at BOTH being good with things and being good with people. Very few are. It is a rare ability. I earned a name as being demanding but with supporting, coaching, mentoring behaviours; investing in training, and demanding the extremely ambitious set of results that I agreed with my seniors. If you can show compassion with a fist of steel, it can stand you well. I called this the iron fist in a velvet glove approach.

I had developed the ability to hold uncomfortable discussions very easily. Because I had learnt to be truthful with people and couch it in an encouraging way. I never said they were doing good when in fact I needed to say, "Your performance is that of a lesser experienced person and I would like to see it set to a higher standard reflecting the greater experience that you have. This is how your performance should look..." Then I would illustrate it with examples of results and behaviours. If they can change their behaviours, they can change their results.

The ability to change behaviours is a key requirement in a P&L holder. Closely followed by 'how' they do that and the ability to 'take the people' with them. And I include third-party business partners such as distributors in that ability to 'take the people with you'.

Distributors always knew that I was straight-talking and able to hold 'uncomfortable discussions' on performance or pricing or legal changes to the terms of the legal agreement as easily as I could shower praise and encourage them to higher levels of performance. They knew I could be having dinner in the evening but the next morning we could equally be holding an uncomfortable discussion around their performance or the terms of our legal agreement that they will want to contest and challenge.

Finding people who are good with both 'things' and good with 'people' should be the aim of any recruitment in these roles. My experience suggests this does not happen enough and probably hampered by the relative scarcity of such folk.

I blame this squarely on the recruiting senior managers and the flawed guidance they receive from HR and Talent Partners. Too often HR and Talent Partners are listening to the absolute rubbish spewed by recruitment consultants whose only interest is getting their fee or commission for the placement of a candidate. Or the rubbish is spewed directly out of the mouths of HR and Talent Partners.

My numerical and negotiation skills were remarkably high. But I could also combine them effectively with managing both people and managing things. These are aspects of the role that can be learnt. I developed them through several roles and, of course, the mistakes that I made along the journey.

Some skills and experience and competencies simply must be present, and you would be ill-considered to approach such capabilities on the basis that the candidate "will learn and acquire them on the job." Learning on the job can be a serious distraction to the company – the job holder may learn but still fail to deliver the results agreed upon and expected.

I made my fair share of mistakes, but one thing stood out for me: I never repeated the mistakes. That is evidence of continuing professional development.

The job as P&L holder for me in my corporate life was numbers focused with metrics for everything! I regularly held open sessions with staff where they could ask any question they wanted about the business without any pre-submitted questions. It gained me credibility. My staff stated I had an ease of approach and relaxed style that allowed me to comfortably take questions 'blind' from the floor. If I could not answer a question, I would say so and why. Either I did not have an answer, or I had an answer, but I would tell them I could not divulge that information at this time.

A person who is good at both managing things and managing people has the best chance of delivering the array of metrics your senior team demands of you.

But you need to construct a reliable process in your recruitment that allows you to assess for these and other capabilities. Judging by the high failure rates in recruitment and selection where HR and Talent Partners participate in the meddling, I guess that their process (if they have one beyond a one-hour first and a one-hour second interview) is fatally flawed. No wonder so many fail!

I will describe the process I used for reader consideration. It is not rocket science, but it does require common sense. But if there is one thing I have observed, it is how remarkably uncommon, common sense really is.

Again, the section titled "How Do You Pick Winners?" is based on my own personal experience and there may be other readers or your colleagues who may hold quite different views. I make no apologies if this is the case.

I do not talk as an expert on this aspect, but I simply share my experience of what I did and how well it worked for me.

Part 4: At What Stage in a Candidate's Career Are These Roles Best Suited?

In my personal view, this is an important consideration. It might come under fierce criticism from HR and Talent Partners, but I will explain why this is an overlooked feature that is often responsible for the deaths of many souls selected for these key international scale-ups and business development roles.

I do not subscribe to the view that a person can spend two years in small emerging markets and then be appointed as a General Manager in a larger value legal affiliate in Europe or the US or Japan or, indeed, in large emerging markets such as Brazil, India, China, and Mexico. For too many, this is a chasm to be traversed and many fail to make it to success on the other side of 'The Valley of Death' – often having fallen quite quickly in the emerging markets 'development opportunity' role that was intended to develop or prepare them for bigger things.

A candidate needs to spend, as a minimum, five continuous years in the markets under their control to demonstrate sustained results. Any fool can show results for two or three years (though many do not even manage that!). I started off by saying the challenge is about achieving and delivering critical mass in five years or ten years. But a ten-year window needs to have a milestone at five years divided into each of one year time frames that must be delivered each year if a candidate is to demonstrate potential for a new larger role in a larger value business elsewhere for the company.

That five-year milestone requires delivery of results for five consecutive years if it is to be delivered. A feat that eludes so many candidates appointed into these roles.

So, the first point is that a job holder needs to be in the role for at least five years. A young pelvic thruster is unlikely to want to stay in the role for that period. Such candidates expect to stay in the role for 18-24 months and then move on to a different, bigger role. There is a major mismatch of expectations between such a candidate and what the company expects before progression into another role can be considered.

Appointing such a candidate, the company loses out on two counts:

1. A candidate that takes few or no risks and just keeps the status quo with a focus on keeping his nose clean, not raising his head above the parapet, and adopting a low profile. The business stagnates or declines because these roles in these markets involve setting and delivering ambitious targets, taking calculated risks and strong thinking skills to keep the company ahead of the competition through intelligent strategic thinking and execution for deliverables. Creating and managing change is a constant in the quest to attain a critical mass. This ability to create and manage change (constantly) goes together with the role. Two years is simply too little to measure such a candidate.

2. The bigger loss, though, is the lack of results through a candidate that has not developed all the skills and competencies I proposed earlier. A feature of these markets is there is no luxury of headcount – marketing manager, brand manager, sales manager, HR Manager, Finance Manager, Logistics and Forecasting Manager. Until the business can achieve a critical mass, costs are tightly controlled using the distributor staff. In the case of the Premium Scientific Office, the candidate will have control of staff employed by the distributor, but with low-value sales to begin with, there is no budget for all these roles. Even if there were, it would be highly likely that it would prove difficult to find good candidates in that country for those roles and functions. But there is a necessity for those functions.

So, there is a necessity for such roles but neither the budget and usually neither the ready-now skills and experience to recruit in that country. That necessity MUST be fulfilled by the candidate wearing all those different hats. If you pick a guy in the early to mid-career stage on his ascendency, there is a risk that the candidate has not spent enough time in all these roles to prepare them for such a demanding P&L role AND to wear all those different hats that are required of him.

And this explains a huge reason for the failure of recruitment for international expansion and scaleup. That failure is recruiting people without the time-in-roles and the track record; people who are unable to demonstrate and produce evidence of their ability through results. At interview, they need to prove their aptitude in their different roles, evidencing that they are able to wear all those hats and switch between them as and when needed.

I already stated earlier that there were several flawed assumptions. This example illustrates the flawed assumption of recruiting candidates without coalface experience and demonstrable vocational experience in the context of the job – such as sales management, marketing, and financial understanding. This leads to a deficit in skills and competencies and the result is a poisoned chalice containing a lethal cocktail that kills the candidate's career and kills the company's investment in a suicide pact between the company and the candidate created by the recruiter. Only a small dose of the narcotic, alfentanil, is more toxic than this recruitment mistake.

So, as contentious as it might sound, I say that, for me, there is a persuasive case for considering candidates at the tail-end of a career after they have spent time in all these roles and demonstrated their ability through sustained results.

In my case, I spent time in the UK and internationally in Sales, Key Account Management, Sales Management, Sales Training, Management Development, Business Analysis, Commercial Development, Programme Management, Facilitation and Change Management, and Supply Chain and Logistics before progressing to P&L holder for Africa based in the UK.

This was an ideal 'coalface experience' with a documented history of results delivery across all the roles I had held. It was the ideal blend of skills. I could wear many hats and did not need lots of headcounts to do those roles.

I was in my late forties and that is how long it takes to get the required experience to hold down such challenging roles. Due to an

Asian heritage (sadly, yes, it does matter) and despite having grown up in England from the age of six, my belief is that I made it to senior grade P&L holder around eight years later than my white cohort peers through inherent discriminatory actions. By that cohort's own admissions, they always felt that I had been somehow held back in my career and that I should have been propelled into these roles before they were. C'est la vie!

Notwithstanding this, based on abilities and results delivered, I would have been appointed in early 40's if HR had enforced a meritocracy environment devoid of considering where someone was born. Such discriminatory practices are subtle and difficult to prove. But I always can sense it.

A candidate below the age of forty is unlikely to have the experience and maturity to hold down these roles. If they joined at age twenty-five as a sales rep, they would have needed fifteen years of experience across these sorts of roles with top-tier or upper-quartile demonstrable results delivery supported on paper on company-headed letters and internally documented assessments of performance. That might be typically three years in each role of sales management, sales training, brand marketing, business development, commercial negotiations, and key account management skills.

My career move after seven years in the P&L role across Africa (18 markets) would have been to be GM of a larger value legal affiliate – in the Asia-Pacific region, such as Thailand or Vietnam or cluster GM for Vietnam, Laos, and Cambodia or perhaps GM Philippines or GM Indonesia and Malaysia. Closer to Europe, there are the smaller affiliate markets in Central and Eastern Europe that could have been open to me. The Baltics (Latvia, Estonia, and Lithuania) and Balkans (Croatia, Romania, Bulgaria, Slovakia, Slovenia, Serbia, and Bosnia), for example, all conduct business in English. Latin America GM roles could be in Central America, such as the Costa Rica cluster or Peru, Argentina, Bolivia but not Brazil. These Latin American markets all (ideally) require Spanish as a business language, so would not have been open to me.

The commonality across all these markets is that they are distributor-based partnership markets with some having a legal affiliate and head office in the country and they are not based out of the UK. Some may even have a similar value of some distributor-only markets, so the gap in business size is not overwhelming for the candidate in the succession to these areas.

In terms of the candidate life cycle, a stint at these (next stage) markets for a candidate in their mid-to-late forties might be a five- or ten-year terminal stint before retirement.

Mature markets for succession planning for these candidates might be Australia and New Zealand. They offer large geographies but tiny populations and small healthcare sales business that is nowhere comparable to a smaller EU market. Both these examples are 'mature' markets and ambitions for performance reflect that stage in their life cycle for innovator R&D products.

But located at the other end of the world, it can be useful to post someone there to be out of mind and out of sight until they retire! I always used to remark in senior surroundings that if I had a problem senior, we should look to posting them out of sight in a metaphorically speaking role as GM of Ascension Islands or GM Falkland Islands!

Outside of the Big Markets of the USA, Japan, and the Top 5 EU, there are plenty of smaller markets that a job holder succession pathway might lead. The common feature is they all need maturity and a blend of skills and experience. The Big Markets tend to attract talent from a different pool of candidates and succession pathways.

The feeder to GM France, or Germany – two powerhouse economies of the EU – is a different succession pathway and talent pool. I personally do not think candidates in that talent pool are strong candidates for these international scaleup emerging markets on the basis that they spend two years there as 'development opportunities' to prepare them for these bigger markets. In two years, they will be dead bodies!

In Pharmaceuticals, one can predict rising stars destined for the main board. They have exposure to big markets. The market may have sales of $1 billion and costs of $400 million. These markets represent a high percentage of the global total. Examples are the USA (up to 55% of the global total revenue), Japan (maybe around 10% of global revenue), Top 5 Major EU markets (makeup about 15% of global revenue).

Managing such large numbers requires a distinct set of skills. The impact of poor decisions can be huge. They need to be careful to ensure good risk identification and risk management.

The skills they require are not coalface. They need to deliver results through managing a high headcount of diverse roles all picked as top-tier talent to support the GM of these large value markets. "The buck stops with them" no matter what.

They have a Finance Director, HR Director, Marketing Director, and a Medical Director to support the GM – all of whom came up through the ranks and identified as top-tier talent. It is unlikely that an HR Director in Nigeria or Marketing Director or Finance Director in Kenya will be on a pathway to these large value markets.

The job of the GM in these big markets is people management and total focus on numbers achieved through others. The ones who are good survive typically four or five years before being moved into less stressful roles. Or they may progress to becoming Senior or Region Vice President of a Major Region, such as Europe, Asia Pacific, or Latin America, with several GMs and Cluster GMs reporting to them or perhaps an Area Vice President China and Area Vice President SE Asia reporting to them. From there it could be an Executive Boardroom appointment by their late 40s or mid-50s.

Others simply failed to cut it once appointed. The only real test of a candidate's fitness for the role is after they are appointed. It is not during the recruitment process. The recruitment process simply identifies those that have a good chance of success – but not a guarantee. Some candidates interview very well but are disastrous once in the role. I have seen it many times.

As an example, I have seen repeatedly these candidates appointed to Africa become dead bodies within 18-24 months. They really struggle to understand how this business and the different models come together to deliver results year-on-year, let alone deliver them for five successive years. They lack the blend of different skills and experience and many lack the coalface experience, having relied on delegating to staff under them in their career to do the actual work. They do not know where and how to begin working at the coalface!

You can gather I am more supportive of longer service, more mature candidates who can demonstrate coalface experience across many roles supported by evidence of results in international scaleup success to deliver a critical mass.

I think young pelvic thrusters may be an exceptional choice, but you have more likelihood of finding a candidate that can be a success from the mature older pool of candidates. For them a succession plan could involve a larger value affiliate business in different geography and infrastructure of head office with supporting staff roles.

These mature candidates are more realistic in terms of succession ambitions and do not need close first-hand supervision from a senior versus a small value of the business on a risky trajectory to deliver critical mass in five years. With the right blend of skills and experience, married to the maturity of years, these candidates can deliver critical mass with the right models, the right partners, and the right people. Their experience gives them the ability to find all those 'right' elements that are the foundations for successfully delivering critical mass. They do not need their hand holding in complex high-value negotiations and their experience means that they do not shy away from taking the path of greatest resistance in meeting a challenge. Their domestic situation is usually such that extensive travel poses no problems. A young pelvic thruster risks wrecking his marriage if he is to spend the required amount of time in the markets required for the role.

Any senior leader wants staff with those qualities and capabilities that a mature candidate is very likely to bring. If you want to set an ambition to deliver a critical mass defined from the outset, how do you do it with a candidate that lacks the skills and experience and was probably appointed without producing a shred of documented evidence of past performance? Believe me, it happens!

Do not believe HR if they say that you cannot ask for that evidence. You can ask! You can ask every candidate for evidence of capability and results delivered in prior roles in prior companies. If you did not, then you probably appointed a complete bluffer and buffoon in the role and there is every possibility that he may leave of his own volition, or he is forced out by you through your poor performance procedure within 24 months without delivering the results you set and agreed.

Part 5: How Do You Pick Winners?

The simple answer?

With great difficulty.

No recruitment process can guarantee successful candidates or guarantee fitting square pegs into square holes. So, at best, you need to take steps to satisfy yourself that you have made enough exhaustive explorations around a candidate's suitability for the job.

The starting point is to have a well-constructed and up-to-date Job Description that lists the skills and competencies as well as the experience required of the job holder. The Job Description should make clear if the role is an international sales management job accountable for delivering sales within defined costs or if it is a General Management (GM) role accountable for delivering Profit and Loss account (P&L). The latter job is much bigger with a greater impact on the business.

Titles are misleading. International Partnerships Manager/Director, Commercial Strategy Director/Manager for Emerging Markets; Manager/Director International Partner Markets; Director/Manager Partner Markets; Director Commercial Partnerships EMEA and I could go on. All these titles could be a simple or glorified Sales Manager or a serious P&L-holding General Manager role. You need to be clear about which one you want to attract to fulfil your role.

A P&L holder will be able to tell you his gross margin, his gross profit before tax, his sales revenue and costs and profit as a % of sales. They should be quoted at the Constant Exchange Rate of currency used for reporting by the company in an international setting so that changes in value reflect volume growth. A sales manager on the other hand will only know his costs and his sales revenue. Be clear. Be certain what you want in the role.

This is a particularly important distinction if you are to avoid attracting a swarm of non-qualifying candidates. International sales management is a smaller job and there are candidates for such a role in greater abundance than General Management roles. The latter can conduct the former's job. The former is unlikely to be able to immediately take on the latter role without the other skills and competencies required for the GM role.

As a line manager, you should decide the size and scope of the job. This is not an exercise to hand over to HR or a Talent Partner. The role will report to you and so you should be clear about what you want from the role and therefore the candidate for the role. Having done that, have it reviewed by HR for comments and suggestions. I do not recommend leaving this to HR for you to rubber-stamp. You know what you want from the job. They do not. They turn (or they should turn) your requirements for the ideal candidates into a Job Description with skills and competencies.

An area where I see frequent mistakes is not defining the key competencies or failure to define key competencies accurately. One HR mantra is that the strongest way to predict future performance is based on the candidate's past experiences. To explore these past experiences, we usually use behavioural event interviewing. In this approach, we explore a candidate's competency evaluation by asking them about a situation that involved using the competency and asking them to define a task or activity that required that competency. We then asked them to share what they did personally (not "we" or "they" or "the team" but focus on "I") – the candidate must always speak in the first person about what he or she did. An interviewer scores them on the behaviours associated with the competency.

That is a one-paragraph summary of Behavioural Event Interviewing (BEI). Its main advantage is that it (a) does not (or it should not) explore information that you already have in the candidate's job application and cover letter and (b) it does not ask the candidate what they would do in hypothetical situations or how to conduct a task – such as forecasting.

Instead, we focus on instances in that candidate's experience where they had to conduct those activities and play back what they did, how they went about it and what was the result. We focus on the candidate's actions. Asking someone to describe how to forecast is knowledge from a textbook. Asking them to describe a situation where a forecast was not delivered or struggled and asking them to define what went wrong, how they found out, what they did, and the result is far more powerful.

Competencies should be classified as 'Threshold' and 'Distinguishing'.

Threshold competencies are those required to deliver a satisfactory performance – to deliver the budget and metrics. There will typically be around five or six threshold competencies. These must be present for the candidate to deliver an acceptable result in the role.

Distinguishing competencies define superior performance. Thus, they tend to be an additional set of (fewer) competencies that are supplemental to threshold competencies. They represent what those who consistently deliver and achieve a superior result do to distinguish themselves from an 'acceptable' level of performance. Distinguishing competencies represent the difference between the mean level of performance on a Normal Gaussian Distribution curve (in the mid-point of the bell curve) and a candidate who is one or more standard deviations to the right of the curve.

Each competency must be defined in behavioural terms. This is another failure I frequently see and especially by HR of all people. They fail to define competencies in behavioural terms to anywhere near the level of granularity required to be able to score candidates on how strong they have demonstrated those competencies.

Why is it necessary to define each competency in behavioural terms? The reason is that when it is couched and defined in behavioural terms, you can identify if it is present and how strongly present it is. Let me illustrate this with an example.

Competency: Analytical Thinking.

Headline Definition: The ability to analyse a situation from multiple inputs and considerations to identify a strategy or address a business issue.

A more comprehensive definition might be to conduct cause and effect analysis on commercial, business, scientific, technological, and other information in a systematic, step-by-step manner. This includes identifying key issues, testing hypotheses, diagnosing problems and opportunities, making sound inferences from available information, and drawing logical conclusions. It includes applying deductive reasoning skills to problems often in a linear fashion making conclusions based on previously known facts.

These can be broken down into different levels that I have illustrated as a summary on the next page.

Behavioural Indicators help us to answer the question if a candidate has that competency, and how would I know it if I see it? If you see at least one or more of the following behavioural indicators at the different levels stratified, the higher the level of behaviours demonstrated, the stronger the competency:

So, a candidate that shows level 5 behaviours for analytical thinking in this example is stronger in that competency than a candidate that shows only level 2 behaviours.

You should also be aware that competency-based interviewing is quite alien in these developing export territories. That does not mean you should abandon it. Rather, if this is the case, put 50:50 emphasis on competency-based interviewing and traditional interviewing questions that focus on the candidate's experience and results.

When I recruited a Country Manager, candidates struggled to understand competency-based frameworks. So, I would also add traditional interviewing into the allotted time. And to compensate for the challenges posed by competency-based interviewing in such populations, I used case studies to explore each candidate – as I will explain on the next page.

The Behavioural Indicators in this Example (Analytical Thinking) are Summarised for Ease of Reference:

Behavioural Indicators – Analytical Thinking	Level 1	Level 2	Level 3	Level 4	Level 5
Definition	Breaks down straightforward problems into their constituent parts	Analyses relationships between concrete situations (the ability to see constellations of signs and symptoms)	Analyses multiple relationships involving difficult problems and situations.	Draws cause and effect inferences and solutions to address multi-faceted issues or situations	Applies advanced analytical strategies to complex events or situations
Indicators	Breaks down concrete problems into parts and organises information in a concise manner.	Identifies the cause-and-effect relationship between two aspects of a situation (A leads to B)	Defines the problem. Considers alternative solutions in coming up with a plan to resolve it	Identifies possible solutions and evaluates each one. Considers their implications (pros and cons)	Evaluates and interprets complex situations and integrates them into a complete response
	Recognizes pertinent facts and issues that make up a problem or issue	Weighs the relevant factors of a situation or problem and draws logical conclusions	Anticipates the risks or implications in a plan of action. Mitigates risks appropriately.	Analyses complex, evolving circumstances and takes corrective action to meet deadlines	Uses complex analytical techniques to integrate thinking into conceptual frameworks
	Uses robust judgment to determine what information is needed to assess a situation	Analyses the pros and cons of a solution and the risk in a given solution	Synthesizes complex ideas, issues and observations into a clear understanding	Compares and contrasts information from various sources in a sensitive and timely manner	Systematically evaluates alternative actions for implications before reaching a judgment
	Uses known models and methodologies to address a given problem or situation	Assesses the strengths and weaknesses of arguments to judge the merits of a case	Navigates ways around a wide range of guidelines; is an agile interpreter of guidelines	Identifies several potential causes of events or multiple-part consequences	Draws interpretative commentary from complex numerical or financial data
	Able to identify the key elements of a situation or problem through relevant questioning		Anticipates the risks in a suggested plan of action and devises strategies to mitigate their impact	Analyses multiple causal relationships among consequential parts of related problems	

Armed with an up-to-date and meaningful Job Description, let us move on to how I managed the recruitment process for this type of role for both a P&L holder as well as an International Sales Manager (that might bear the title "Country Manager" or "International Commercial Manager"). The differences I encountered meant that the latter roles were delivering sales within defined costs and the P&L role might have been a General Management role managing a cluster of markets or a geographic region.

First Stage: Eliminating the Impossible Candidates in the Responses to the Job Ad

How to identify candidates for interviews? They have sent a CV or Resume and an application cover letter. They may be an internal candidate that has submitted an intranet application on the job portal. Looking at those documents, how did I decide who to look at and who to reject?

This is where the CV is the document and the cover letter that gets a candidate to be put into the mix as opposed to straight rejection. CVs need to be clearly written by the candidate. I dislike professionally prepared CVs. I can spot them a mile away.

There is only one way to impress me in a CV. And that is to list results versus targets for the last three roles or a ten-year window – whichever is longer. I do not want to read a long list of job responsibilities. It tells me nothing about how well the applicant did the job. I am looking for a candidate that can deliver results, not boast about their responsibilities. Those results must include targets.

A candidate that states she delivered 8% growth year-on-year for five years says nothing about the standard of performance and the candidate's capabilities or results delivery. It might impress HR, but not me. Because when compared to the target I can see the calibre of the candidate. So, 8% growth versus a budget or target growth of 5% is good. But 8% growth versus a budget of 12% is sub-standard performance. Is that why the candidate is applying for my role? Is she on her way out at her present company and looking for a new nest in my company?

Those results must be available to be viewed at the interview if shortlisted – an invitation letter will ask the candidate to bring the results he achieved documented on a company letter-headed paper.

Next, I want to look at time-in-role. I am looking for sustained results delivery. No one-year or two-year wonder cowboys for me. I exclude people who have shown several moves in rapid succession. I want stability and consistent sustained results delivery because I am going to invest in that person's development and I want the benefit of that investment, not for it to go to another company.

Anyone who 'resigned' without a job to go to is always extremely suspicious. But I might shortlist to evaluate if I were light on candidates. When I have done so, and if their departure from their company has been confirmed to be suspicious at the interview, they never got to the next stage. But there could be a good candidate with plausible explanations for resignation without a job to go to. I know of some good examples. Fortunately, I was well connected and able to find out what really happened with such sudden departures despite how they explained 'conflict' or a new incoming boss setting impossible targets for everyone. Much of my enquiries were telephone calls to my contacts that had insights as to what really happened causing the candidates departure or impending departure.

Remember, you want this candidate, if appointed, to deliver a critical mass in five years. You do not want the candidate to interpret ambitious critical mass targets as "setting impossible demanding targets", do you?

My bosses always set me very demanding targets. Stretching? Yes. Difficult? Absolutely.

Impossible and unrealistic to achieve? Not likely. If I fail, my boss also fails. So, we have targets mutually agreed to be deliverables – but they are always stretching, demanding and difficult, never ever easy!

Some of them were so challenging and stretching, they could be described as

278

"To change the axis of rotation of the Earth three degrees to the left by the end of the year!"

Unless you set ambition, you will never achieve a critical mass in five years. Keep clearly focused on this sentence. If you have ambitions for progress, seniors want senior leaders who set ambitions and can go on to deliver them. Setting ambitions is the easy part. Delivering them is not.

If you do not set a stretching ambition and you do not strive for critical mass from the outset, you will have a mediocre, low-value business that grows little each year. You do not need such people that deem ambition as "setting impossible and demanding targets."

You need people with a history of achievement and delivery, which is sustained and stable over a period of time (no one- or two-year wonders).

The problem is that such people are happy in their present company. They are well paid to be retained in their current position so their motivation to leave is one or more of the following:

- Lack of career progression.
- Disillusioned because they may not have realised a promotion they applied for.
- Lack of personal development and limited career pathways for the future.

And such folk are not easy to find. So, it is your task to identify suitable candidates to invite for Stage 2. Because Stage 2 in my process costs money.

Stage 2 in my process involves paying for the use of Psychometric Tests. Do not waste it on those with the sort of holes in their CVs I have stated:

- Many roles in rapid succession.
- Lack of declaring results versus targets.

- Unexplained and suspicious resignation without a job to go to and many other red flags.

Neither should you ever shortlist the best of a bad bunch for Stage 2.

Readvertise, considering whether to change the channels and considering whether the job description needs to be downgraded. Recruiting the wrong people is a big mistake.

Do not do it out of desperation to fill a vacancy or recruit into a newly created role.

If they were asked to write a cover letter summarising how they fit the role and examples of what they have done to satisfy the job requirements, and they do not do that, do not take it any further. They have shown a disregard towards meeting your request in the cover letter. They have shown they cannot or will not do as asked. Do you want people like that?

Some folks in recruitment may disagree with me, and they are free to do that. But so often people recruit failures without knowing it and realise it too late. I see it all the time on social media. I know who they are where Africa is concerned. But I cannot mention names.

A serial job hunter who joins a company that fails abysmally and in two years is on the brink of being fired but manages to jump ship to another company before the axe falls only to go through the same process in two years again. But this time they're not so lucky. The next employer managed him out on poor performance or restructured and made his ineffective role redundant, so he now has no job and is unemployed for months. Or the guy who had a major compliance breach and was caught taking a member of the field force staff to a managers' conference; he put her up in his double bedroom only to be caught when the invoice was checked and there were charges for a double room and room service with two meals one evening at the same time. Believe me, it happens.

Now you have an idea of how to sort out the possibilities from the improbable, let us move on to Stage 2 of my process for those candidates who, based on their CV and cover letter application, you want to see in more depth.

Stage 2

I am an advocate of using Psychometric Tests in the selection process. But I do not recommend relying on HR to administer and interpret the tests. They are not doing the volume of testing needed to understand the accurate interpretation of test results, and they often struggle to put test results into context. They may be accredited to administer a certain test. But accreditation is not synonymous with competence and capability in interpretation of results.

For example, they cannot relate the candidate to the company norms or the manager's test results. I will develop this further as we go on and you will see what I mean.

Psychometric Tests

I am no expert on psychometric tests. There are folk who do this for a living, day in and day out. They know it all. But there is one thing that they do not know. "What is that?" you may ask.

They do not know what I am looking for in a candidate. They cannot know.

But if I share what I am looking for, they can devise tests that can help me find candidates with the <u>potential</u> to do the role that I am recruiting for. They can give me a broad view of the candidate. But this is not about if the job is good for this candidate. Tests do not pigeonhole candidates into jobs, as I was told by an expert in my corporate life.

So, for example, a test cannot define who can become a doctor or an airline pilot. They only can tell you if the basic ingredients for success are present or can be developed for such roles and how they may approach the job.

There are lots of tests available. I can only base my comments on the tests we used in my corporate life. That does not dismiss the validity or reliability of other tests. What is key is that you need to use tests that you or a tester have a high degree of understanding about, tests that are both valid and reliable for what you are seeking to assess.

Testing can help me in the selection process by telling me two crucial areas of information:

1. A candidate's cognitive bandwidth. How good, fast, and accurate they are with data and text. In other words, their ability to work with numbers and figures as well as written and verbal information. In loose terms, I might describe this as their 'aptitude', and I do not invite a forensic dissection of my analogy from a psychometric expert or a psychology expert.

2. A candidate's personality and, based on that personality, how the candidate might approach the tasks and deliverables in the role I am recruiting. They can also tell me what features in the job would make this candidate uncomfortable in the role and that, if this was a major part of the job, this might cause stress. They can give me a reasonably accurate picture of how the candidate might behave when under stress or pressure for results. And, of course, how emotionally stable (or unstable) a candidate is.

Based on this, I worked with a commercial former first-line sales manager and training manager who moved into psychometric testing as an internal consultant. We had recognised there was a gap between HR people being too generalist and not understanding the commercial pressures and environment. HR had a resource trained in the use of the tests I am going to share with you. But I did not use their 'service.'

The commercial guy, who was an internal consultant, sat in Sales Training and Management Development running the leadership development programmes and sales managers programmes. He could relate results and put them into context for three things:

a) Versus the managerial norms of a cross-section of middle and senior managers in the company – how I and others might find working with this person based on their results. To do this, we had profiled middle and senior managers across the company. Otherwise, an outside tester would compare the candidate to generic norms outside the company. Useful but not as powerful as against our own company middle and senior managers.

b) Versus the requirements in the Job Description – the competencies needed. Hopefully, you now see the essential requirement to have an up-to-date comprehensive Job Description before you even start to discuss recruiting for the role. A tester needs a reliable, accurate and up-to-date Job Description in order to interpret the test results and make meaningful remarks on that candidate's suitability for the role.

c) Cultural fit and style – that mystery factor that very few will admit but exists to cause staff to exit prematurely. We had a certain *"way we do things around here"* that some just could not work under. We were top quartile payers on basic pay as well as the total benefits package. That meant we demanded a high standard of results delivery and required velocity of results. Not everyone is fast to deliver results, but they are fast to take on an exceptional package and then be surprised when they are under pressure to deliver results! Unfortunately, that often leads to them having to be managed out of the company, which was a time-consuming, energy-zapping (and expensive) exercise for both of us.

I repeatedly used three tests, which became what I termed my standard three-battery tests that were recommended and administered by the internal consultant. There are folk out there with different tests based on personality, such as that based on Jungian Typology. But a drawback to so many of these tests is that they do not measure aptitude. They were cleverly marketed by companies with fancy-coloured wheels and graphs or charts. Beyond that, they were nowhere as comprehensive (in my opinion) as my standard "three battery tests", which comprised of products from a company specialising in this called Saville & Holdsworth®. There will be other tests from other providers that readers can explore too.

The three-battery tests are all administered online and are owned by Saville & Holdsworth®. They have accredited testers globally and can administer the test in different languages.

The tests I used were:

1. Numerical Critical Reasoning Test®.
2. Verbal Critical Reasoning Test®.
3. Occupational Profile Questionnaire – OPQ 32® – measures 32 dimensions of personality.

Tests 1 and 2 measure aptitude and help me see the cognitive bandwidth.

Test 3 measures personality on 32 dimensions. Tests 1 and 2 are timed online tests. Once the candidate starts, they must finish in the time allocated. They cannot start, pause, and resume later or another day. This is because they are measuring cognitive abilities with numbers as well as text. The time constraint puts pressure on a response.

Saville & Holdsworth® describes and explains these tests as follows:

> The numerical reasoning test measures the candidate's ability to interpret, analyse and draw logical conclusions based on numerical data presented in graphs and tables. It is not designed to measure the candidate's mathematical ability but his ability to use numerical data to make reasoned decisions and solve problems.
>
> The results of the numerical reasoning test reveals the extent to which a candidate is capable of:
>
> • Efficiently and effectively able to identify critical business-related issues and logically draw conclusions from numbers.
>
> • Efficiently monitoring performance and progress based on numbers presented as charts and tables.
>
> • Presenting and conveying business-related issues with clarity in the form of charts and tables.

There is no pass or fail result. The test score compares the candidate to similar persons in the same role generically across the industry, or against company norms.

We had company norms. I could compare the candidate to internal job holders in the company, or a peer group in the industry, on their relative strengths.

The test places the candidate's score into percentile bands. In brief, and as explained to me by my internal consultant, these bands place the candidate against similar or the same job holders. For example, a candidate for numerical critical reasoning might score 30 correct out of 40. This appears to be a strong result for the candidate. However, the candidate falls into the twentieth percentile. This is because similar job holders scored higher than this candidate.

As my test administrator explained to me, being in the twentieth percentile means that, if one hundred people in that job took the test, eighty would score higher than this candidate! For some of these positions, we already had established the percentiles that were needed to be considered for key roles such as these.

If the numerical reasoning test required the fifty-fifth percentile, then a candidate with the twentieth percentile falls far short of that aptitude and processing power needed for the role. It may not exclude being interviewed, but the candidate starts off with a serious handicap that will often be confirmed as the selection process continues.

One internal candidate for a Country Manager role scored eighth percentile for Numerical Critical Reasoning and twelfth percentile for Verbal Critical Reasoning. She was not shortlisted for the first interview. She argued vehemently that the test did not give her enough time and that, given more time, she would have had a much better result. She further argued that in the role she will develop this competency. The internal consultant revealed some shocking news when we looked at the scores deeper.

Candidate's scores for Numerical and Verbal Critical Reasoning place them not only into percentiles but also one of four possible quadrants on a two-by-two matrix:

Numerical Critical Reasoning Result Possibilities

Speed		High Accuracy	Low Accuracy
Slow		Acceptable Slow & Accurate	Unacceptable
Fast		Desirable Fast & Accurate	Clumsy

Imagine a candidate in that clumsy or unacceptable box and at the eighth percentile!

She has not got the cognitive bandwidth to be even considered for an interview! She persisted in remarking that, with practice, she could get better when on the job. My consultant said starkly that she could not and never would get better. He explained that this is an aptitude test that measures brain processing power. You may be able to improve scores marginally with practice – possibly from the eighth percentile up to the tenth percentile. But could never reach the fifty-fifth percentile that we had stipulated would be needed to be considered for an interview. To jump from the eighth to the fifty-fifth percentile would require a brain transplant. And unfortunately, those with that processing power are not prepared to offer theirs for transplant!

To put context into this result, the consultant told me that I could not rely on any figures or forecasts from this person if appointed to the role. They would likely be inaccurate. Secondly, she could not work to tight deadlines with accuracy. All of that was clear because she was in that low accuracy/slow speed box. The impact on me would be that I would have to do my job and hers – in which case, she would not be much use either way!

The Verbal Critical Reasoning Test® is described by Saville & Holdsworth® as:

This test includes reading passages of text and measures the ability to understand verbal information, think logically about written information, accurately draw logical conclusions, produce written reports, convey information to others in a clear manner, identify critical business-related issues and logically draw conclusions from business-related reading material, such as reports.

The Verbal Critical Reasoning Test® helps to understand the candidate's ability to:

- Produce written reports and documents with total clarity.
- Articulate business-related issues clearly and simply to me, their colleagues, other matrix managers, and their customers.

By now, I hope you can see the power of using these tests as a first sift to look at a first interview shortlist. The tests get under the person, and I can see behind that mask that every candidate portrays at the interview. These two tests give me a view of the candidate's brain processing power as my consultant used to say.

The third test looks at personality on 32 dimensions of personality. It is the Saville and Holdsworth® Occupational Personality Questionnaire® (SHL Personality Test). It is not timed.

Saville & Holdsworth® describes this test as follows:

- The OPQ® measures 32 different personality traits that are relevant to occupational settings. The test measures traits to determine a candidate's behavioural style at work. It can give a good view of how well the applicant fits the role for which they are applying.

The candidate is asked to make forced-choice responses (otherwise referred to as an ipsative approach). For instance, each question in the OPQ has four statements or adjectives, such as friendly, leader, team player and confident. The candidate is required to rate which best describes them (identifying the most and least like them out of the four statements/adjectives, rather than rating each individual statement or adjective on a scale). The 32 personality traits measured in the OPQ are grouped into categories, such as relationships, sociability (e.g., outgoing, socially confident), influence (e.g., persuasive, outspoken, independent-minded), empathy (e.g., democratic, caring), and thinking style (e.g., evaluative, rational). The OPQ also includes a social desirability measure to detect 'faking' responses.

- The multi-dimensional forced choice nature of the OPQ can be cognitively challenging for candidates taking this test. For instance, processing several items at the same time requires good reading skills and comprehension. Additionally, choosing which statement is most and least like the candidate requires the candidate to conduct several mental comparisons which can be stressful when under pressure and the stakes are high.

So, first sift is with the standard three-battery tests I have described. External firms can be commissioned to administer and interpret the test results and compile a report on each candidate. However, there is a lot of variability in interpretation and reporting. The key element is being able to put the results into context for the job, your company, and your staff in similar roles.

I am not a fan of using internal HR resources for this stage. They do not do enough of them to keep their interpretative skills honed and up to date. An external firm will likely be doing these tests each week, across several candidates and applying several internally trained and accredited resources. Interpretation of results and putting them into context for the organisation's staff is key.

Selection should not rely on tests. They are simply an adjunct to help evaluate a candidate in the selection process. Every candidate puts on a mask as to how they want you, the interviewer, to see them. It is easy to portray and hold that mask for an hour or two. But to get behind the mask, you need these psychometric tools to see what the candidate does not want you to see or become aware of until they are in the role where they cannot maintain that mask forever.

So, the second stage sift is my 'Standard Three Battery Test' using Saville & Holdsworth® Tests.

Some people may use these tests after the first interview or even after the second interview. There is no wrong or right time to introduce these tests. My personal preference is at the beginning of the process, adding to their CV and cover letter to help decide on the first interview list. I sometimes preceded the tests with a telephone screening phone call to clarify points that were not clear in their CV or cover letter before deciding whether to put the candidate through psychometric tests.

Stage 3

The next round in my process is the first interview. This was typically split into two parts:

1. A face-to-face interview against the competencies for the role. I always wrote to shortlisted candidates for first interview to explain that we use behavioural-based interviewing against competencies, stating the key competencies that we would be interviewing the candidate against. They were all advised to think of examples that could withstand the depth of interviewing and to prepare a backup example in case the first example was insufficient for us to assess the given competency. The time allocated for this face-to-face first interview was 45 - 60 minutes.

   I kept a scorecard against each of the competencies for the candidate's responses to the questioning (scoring them against the different levels for each competency).

   The scorecard formed the basis for providing feedback to unsuccessful candidates.

2. A case study devised by me. This followed the interview. The candidate was notified in the interview invitation letter that there would be a case study that would be provided at the interview, so there was no prior preparation needed. I created a case study based on fictional business issues that could be identified from the data and some information on the product portfolio positioning and platform. The candidate would be given the case study after the interview.

   The case study was printed material with a simple page asking them to:

a. Comment on the data.
b. Identify three business issues explaining what the issues are and how you arrived at them.
c. Propose three actions with metrics that can be used to correct the issues.

The timing for this was 30 minutes of preparation and analysis on their own with a flip chart to record their responses. That would be followed by 30 minutes to present the responses using the flip chart. This helped me to understand how they could present and articulate their analytical and critical thinking skills as well as their problem-solving skills. I already had their test results, so I could see in action how they fared against their test results.

I might call only four to six candidates for this interview. They had already been vetted using psychometrics prior to this interview.

Stage 4

The final stage would be to invite back two or three candidates from first interview for a second interview lasting 90 minutes. The candidate would be informed they were through to the next stage of the process and that they needed to prepare a presentation for 45 minutes with 15 minutes of questioning in a total one hour allocation.

In this presentation, we tested their ability to understand the specific challenges of our business – I would have sent them in the invitation pack for this final step, a short summary of our business in the territory, listing the therapy areas and sharing fictitious past P&L or sales and costs of the major therapy areas with five-year projections for P&L or sales and costs for the same therapy areas. I listed fictitious assumptions. This set the background for their presentation, which they needed to bring on a USB stick.

Their presentation would be on the theme of "Our business performance and challenge in this region" and they would be asked to define the three or four key issues for our business based on the data they had received and to list appropriate metrics to measure progress against those issues with an explanation of why these metrics would be critical to business success.

They would also be asked to list three or four critical actions to be taken for the business based on the data.

They needed to bring their own documented set of results, evidencing the delivery they had achieved, from their current and previous employers, making it clear that we wanted to see the results versus the targets set.

At the actual presentation, they would present with our own IT equipment and leave a copy of their presentation. As they were delivering it, I would state that there was breaking news – two of the assumptions are no longer valid and we had identified a high level of stocks (more than nine months of stock) at the distributor for the major brands on promotion. I asked them to comment and interpret the impact of their presentation and our business in the territory and identify any actions that were needed. This assessed their ability to think on the spot.

I would invite questions and describe the next steps and decision-making timelines to each of the candidates.

If we were not satisfied with any of the candidates, we did not recruit. I passionately believe that one should never take the best of a bad slate of candidates. I had to be satisfied beyond reasonable doubt that we had a candidate whom we could offer the job to that could deliver critical mass in five years, demonstrating his aptitude, and personality through the recruitment processes for these elements. We needed people that could demonstrate their ability through results – supported and validated by evidence. Results delivery was at the top of the list. But so was 'how' they were achieving those results. They needed to show an ability to work with and through people and to take people with them. They needed that blend of skills that put them in that minority box of being both good with people and good with things.

For ease of reference, I have summarised my approach to finding capable talent in the following diagram:

Schematic Summary of My Recruitment Process

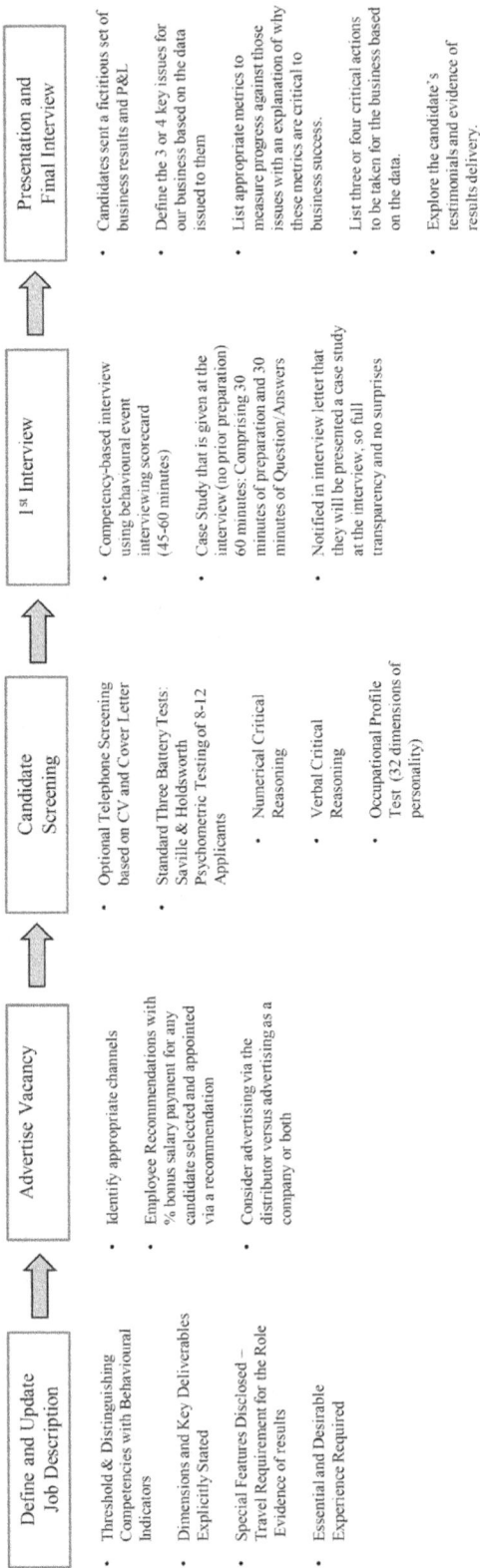

Define and Update Job Description	Advertise Vacancy	Candidate Screening	1st Interview	Presentation and Final Interview

- Threshold & Distinguishing Competencies with Behavioural Indicators
- Dimensions and Key Deliverables Explicitly Stated
- Special Features Disclosed – Travel Requirement for the Role Evidence of results
- Essential and Desirable Experience Required

- Identify appropriate channels
- Employee Recommendations with % bonus salary payment for any candidate selected and appointed via a recommendation
- Consider advertising via the distributor versus advertising as a company or both

- Optional Telephone Screening based on CV and Cover Letter
- Standard Three Battery Tests: Saville & Holdsworth Psychometric Testing of 8-12 Applicants
  - Numerical Critical Reasoning
  - Verbal Critical Reasoning
  - Occupational Profile Test (32 dimensions of personality)

- Competency-based interview using behavioural event interviewing scorecard (45-60 minutes)
- Case Study that is given at the interview (no prior preparation) 60 minutes: Comprising 30 minutes of preparation and 30 minutes of Question/Answers
- Notified in interview letter that they will be presented a case study at the interview, so full transparency and no surprises

- Candidates sent a fictitious set of business results and P&L
- Define the 3 or 4 key issues for our business based on the data issued to them
- List appropriate metrics to measure progress against those issues with an explanation of why these metrics are critical to business success.
- List three or four critical actions to be taken for the business based on the data.
- Explore the candidate's testimonials and evidence of results delivery.

Part 6: Location, Location, Location!

Thoughts on Location for the Job Holder

One of the questions I am asked with alarming regularity is "What are your thoughts on having the P&L role based in the region or the market? And aligned with this is the question of choosing a local or an ex-pat for this international scale-up.

To begin with location, the simple answer is it does not matter a jot where the role holder is located so long as:

1. You have a candidate with the talent, skills, and experience, and she can support her abilities with documented evidence of results-versus-targets on company-headed paper. This is where such candidates are extremely thin on the ground. The problem is more acute if you are recruiting (as in my experience) within Africa. I am sure there is a similar situation for other distributor markets in other regions.

2. The candidate has the coalface experience and actually has done the tasks and activities that you require to be done and supported those with real examples from past experience. This is related to (1) above but focuses on tasks and activities – for example "have you designed the go-to-market model, selected and negotiated the commercial agreements in markets X, Y and Z?" Test them! Try to ascertain if the candidate was the mule to a more senior staff member outside of the market or if the candidate had the authority for these activities and how well they did at them.

3. He is able and mobile to travel (up to 50% or more of the business year) into those markets. This is important. Because the job is out there in the market, not sitting in a nice office in a skyscraper in Dubai or Istanbul or South Africa or Singapore. This is relatively easy to find if you select a candidate of mature years, where their family has grown up or is in tertiary education and they have a stable domestic situation with a partner able to manage in his absence for a prolonged period of business trips. These market

visits are often in rapid succession. I would come back from a week in Kenya, and, within a week, I would fly out to Ghana or Lagos Nigeria. I had two passports, so when I was in Kenya with one passport, my PA would send the other passport off for a Nigerian visa ready for when I came back from Kenya.

ALL THREE conditions MUST be met. Location does not matter a jot if all three conditions are met.

I have yet to see an example of a company that reaped the benefits of changing the location of the job holder from outside Africa (as in my personal experience) and relocating it to Africa. One company produced a slogan: *"In Africa for Africa."*

It was dreamt up as part of another "coffee froth theme" – *"Getting Closer to Customers."* Both simply cut and paste statements from somewhere else. Irrelevant statements that mean absolutely nothing. That company had serial disasters moving the role location from outside Africa to inside Africa.

In more detail, the guy in this company example was outside Africa (the UK actually) and, as he was unwilling to relocate to South Africa, exited the company. That company appointed a local South African manager familiar with the South African model of healthcare to take over SSA. That South African manager brought the mindset of his local (wholesaler) model into SSA by dismantling the distributor models and replacing them with the South African wholesaler supply model. Remember that I mentioned earlier, trying to shoehorn a model from one market or region into another in SSA is a sure way to fail. And neither that Sales Manager nor his seniors knew the difference between a wholesaler and a distributor. This meant a disaster was looming and career derailment for several members was on the horizon.

That new manager in South Africa hardly spent time in the markets. Another BIG mistake! The flight time to reach Lagos from Johannesburg is around six/seven hours. From the UK it is around seven hours. But the business based *"in Africa for Africa"* spent extraordinarily little time in the markets of Sub-Saharan Africa.

Within two years of poor sales development and failing to meet his numbers he was out. In a ten-year period that company went through six Territory Directors for Africa. All because of failure to perform and deliver the numbers by each one of those six in turn.

Now tell me, what difference did it make *"getting closer to customers"* and being *"in Africa for Africa"*?

Why did being *"in Africa for Africa"* fail to deliver results and the numbers for the next decade (and beyond)?

The simple answer is that whoever dreamt up that idea was on some hallucinogenic drug. He broke the two cardinal features of the role I started to share with you:

1. Lacked the skills and capabilities with a demonstrated ability through results in SSA.

2. Did not (or could not?) spend the time in these markets.

The first casualty had little evidence of negotiating deals of high value and no distributor experience. Remember, South Africa is not a distributor market. It is a wholesaler market. This job holder could not understand the difference between a wholesaler and a distributor and therefore had a poor understanding of how to work distributor markets.

The leap from current experience in South Africa to Sub-Saharan Africa was a leap too far, flawed by an assumption that those skills from a career confined only to South Africa were transferable immediately into Sub-Saharan Africa. They were not.

That role holder was 'learning on the job' and within two years the flaws and cracks would be impossible to cover over. The numbers were an abject failure. A massive 'big bang' capital investment in rep numbers and vehicles in Nigeria broke the camel's back. The role holder believed that more noise would equate to more sales. This is simply not true in Africa and other emerging markets. Big bang expansions are usually the result of an arrogant senior with little appreciation of what it takes to succeed in partnership markets. Big bank expansions usually result in stepping on an Improvised Explosive Device and blowing the legs of that senior executive. Be warned!

Alongside Nigeria, Ghana went pear-shaped for that role holder. Kenya and East Africa followed as they alienated distributors by shifting to a wholesaler model across Sub-Saharan Africa. They probably thought distributors were just wholesalers and they could trade with more wholesalers to increase sales. But of course, by now, you know that this is a flawed approach. Because the only way to drive sales is by increasing demand, not adding more wholesalers. Remember, demand always precedes supply.

By the middle of year two, the scale of the disaster was a gaping huge hole on the side of the ship. This guy had steered the ship onto the iceberg and the ship began to list and take in more water. The senior team yelled *"All hands on deck."* But it wasn't going to rescue the situation. No, they merely rearranged the deck chairs on the ship while the orchestra played the 1970's hit single song "Dancing on the Ceiling".

Too late, the ship listed even more until her bow was pointing out of the water. The weight of the water broke the hull in two and she went down along with her crew. The captain never went down with the ship. He stayed on to repeat the exercise a few more time with successive incumbents.

Secondly, whatever it was, the guy appointed to run SSA did not spend the time in the market getting to know and understand the people that could bring him success - the owner distributors.

There followed a spate of six dead bodies over a ten-year period, all located *"in Africa for Africa."*

Did location matter? Not a jot.

You must recruit for demonstrable skills and experiences supported with evidence of results versus targets over a sustained period.

Then look for mobility to spend time in the market by examining the candidate's personal situation. If the guy does not have prior distributor experience, you need to look for the non-negotiable factors of a history of negotiating high value deals and a strong understanding of the financial side of running a business gained over several roles for several years in each role.

If you can find the skills and experience and staff that have actually done what you want to do in the market, then all is good. But there is a war for talent. It is even greater outside of the UK and the EU for people who have a documented set of results delivery in distributor markets. Your chance of finding real talent is considerably more challenging in Africa and many emerging markets, or as they are called "distributor markets "or "partner markets".

Anyone who has done what you want to have done – hired and fired distributors, set up new business and has the coalface experience that is absolutely vital – with demonstrable ability through results over five successive years or so, supported on letter-headed paper is not looking for a job. She is tied down to that company with golden chains around her feet. So, you end up advertising and who applies?

You guessed it. A large number of people (misfits) who are 'just looking' for better pay. Others are bluffers and there is a high likelihood that you will encounter candidates that were fired or pushed or resigned before being fired for non-performance. All of these are the sort of candidates you absolutely do not want to waste your time on. And there is a remarkable absence of the candidate you actually do want.

To prise these desirable and able guys out from their current employer, a different approach is required. But that costs money. Unwilling to invest in finding talent that can deliver results, you engage with a recruiter in Africa who sends you CVs of candidates she has probably never met and cannot vouch for. But chasing the placement fee is her driver, not your success with the right candidate every time.

We also have to turn to the vexed question of who would better lead your scale up, local staff or an ex-pat? I am also asked this with alarming regularity. The pharmaceutical and medical devices companies have blown hot and cold on this subject. Some have argued that it would be wisest to have an ex-pat located in the market or outside the market, others have suggested that having a local person based in the market to lead the scaleup would be preferable. Judging by the poor results with both types of appointments, neither camp got this right.

It does not matter a jot whether you choose a local guy in the market or an ex-pat in the market or located outside the market. Neither leads to success automatically based on this argument.

The reason is simple. As in the previous example, neither the local guy nor the ex-pat has the required skills, experience and capabilities supported by a documented record of evidence. Very often, neither candidate has the actual evidence and track record of having carried out successfully what you want them to do in this scaleup:

- Selecting and hiring distributors.

- Negotiating high-value commercial deals with distributors.

- Having terminated distributors as well as hiring replacement distributors and creating the cross-over plan moving from one to another distributor.

- Designing the best-fit commercial models.

- Having coalface evidence of having done these things and not having delegated all these to a team of staff that did it for them.

Being a local appointment without these qualities will not lead to success. In fact, very often the pool of local candidates has rarely carried P&L responsibility. They have been largely transactional task-focused sales managers working under close supervision and instruction from a senior in the corporate office. As an ambitious scaleup senior, you appoint such a local to set up a new business or to change the models and very quickly within 12-18 months you discover you appointed a lemon who has never done what you need to be done. She is seeking supervision from you; she has low operational velocity because she procrastinates (she actually does not know what she is doing) and is hiding her inadequacies from you.

You now find yourself doing her job and your job. And that means one of you is not needed.

A parallel argument holds for ex-pats also. I recall an example of a client that was a global European R&D innovator company in the top 20 global companies that recruited a candidate from Nigeria who was an ex-pat from a company outside Africa. This candidate was working for a small generics company which was not particularly successful in its Nigeria business that this candidate had headed up. Imagine recruiting a guy that was not successful for his employer? It happens. And more often than you can imagine. I have seen numerous misfits that were unsuccessful at delivering results jump ship to another company.

This client had carried out a deep dive into the SSA landscape from a big consulting company. The decision was taken to invest heavily in selected markets – Ghana, Nigeria, Kenya, and East Africa. The client recruited this ex-pat from Nigeria to head up East Africa with disastrous consequences. The reasons for such disastrous consequences were easily visible to me, but not that client.

Firstly, the client failed to understand that East and West Africa are like chalk and cheese. The market dynamics are completely different. The client had appointed an ex-pat from Nigeria (who had not been successful in Nigeria) to set up and establish a higher-ambition business in Kenya and East Africa. And the candidate was on an ex-pat European contract and, correspondingly, received higher remuneration than his previous generics company employer. His remuneration with this client included an expenses-paid package whereby his salary was banked in his country of domicile, and they gave him a generous "living expenses" allowance for rent and living costs in Kenya paid into Kenya!

But this gentleman was a complete and utter disaster and misfit:

- He had a generics (small company thinking) background and no sense of an R&D business's set of challenges or its business model.
- He had something akin to a market stall trader mentality – sell it cheap, pile it high.
- He appointed 'distributors' with this market stall trader and hawker mentalities that were actually wholesalers because the client had created a legal entity in Kenya and imported goods via an intermediary partner in a pre-wholesale consignment model operating out of South Africa to serve East Africa.
- He had no prior experience with East Africa and its dynamics across the markets of Kenya, Tanzania, and Uganda.
- He did not know the key clinical players or the government authority key staff.
- He lacked serious cognitive bandwidth on both a strategic as well as tactical and operational level.
- He was extremely poor with numbers and the financial understanding of a business.

I could go on, but you get the drift of an almighty cockup, and a dangerous implosion of the client's business is about to happen.

The client had recruited completely the wrong profile of the 'market-stall' trading model that could never ever achieve the higher ambitions to be delivered from that deep dive exercise.

The numbers were appalling and, even after more than two years in the post, they remained poor.

Embarrassingly, this gentleman conducted discussions with distributors and wholesalers with me in attendance with no prior preparation and consideration of the objectives and how they were going to be achieved.

His ad-lib approach and unstructured discussions outraged distributors who walked out of the meeting! He lacked a financial understanding of currencies and exchange rate risks and struggled to interpret stock and sales data supplied out of South Africa. There was a catalogue of disasters with his distributor interactions and his team that I had never witnessed before.

Not surprisingly, I had to report how I had found all this to his seniors. In a matter of months, those seniors took decisive actions, and he was no longer an ex-pat manager for the client and was dismissed. But the damage was already done. After he left the company, the fog cleared, and the landscape resembled Hiroshima the day after the nuclear bomb. Those same seniors then swung 180 degrees to appoint a local manager for East Africa. That too was equally disastrous for a different set of reasons.

The conclusion is not to get hung up on local versus ex-pat. At all times remain focused on the three key essentials I highlighted earlier:

Firstly, recruit for a demonstrable track record of skills and experience supported by evidence on company-headed paper citing performance versus the targets that were set. Look for tenure in roles. Several short-term stints do not indicate a strong performer. Find out why these were short stints.

Secondly, ensure that the candidate has the mobility to travel because the job needs a lot of time in the market.

Thirdly, make sure that the candidate has actually done what you need him to do with credible coalface experience. And try to verify what the candidate has claimed and presented to you through a network of contacts and connections.

This last part is difficult and often, HR or Talent Partners will stop you from doing it, but I had (and still have) a powerful network across Africa to be able to pick up a phone and ask, "What really happened to X or Y candidate?" and "Has he actually done X and Y, or did someone from corporate do X and Y?" so that I could establish the real reason for his leaving the company or his current standard of performance and assess if the candidate had done what I want him to do.

There are a lot of bluffers out there who will tell you, the recruiter, any rubbish that you might be gullible enough to believe. Remember, the person you want is not looking for a job.

Think about that. And reflect on it in the context of the applicant that you have in front of you.

How will you know who the guys you want are and how to approach them?

Time in the market for you is key. It develops contacts and connections. Through those contacts I know where the good guys are and how to make an approach. And that approach is not a recruiter sitting in the market or in South Africa that sends you CVs from a database of candidates they likely never met, let alone saw documented evidence of their results versus targets.

Be careful! There are a lot of bluffers out there that try it on. Do not let them succeed and fool you into taking them on.

Part 7: Recruitment Concluding Remarks

There are no guaranteed ways to pick winners for these roles. Finding good talented people to fill these positions that can deliver a critical mass in five years is particularly challenging for several reasons:

a) The people desired are happy in their role with their present company and not looking to move.

b) Those who may be looking to move would be for a narrow set of reasons, such as a lack of career opportunities or personal development, or they may have been unsuccessful with an internal promotion application.

c) They may not respond to a job ad but may be interested through a third-party executive search partner (a head-hunter).

Recruiting in a narrow talent pool carries significant risks. International sales and business development roles have a high staff churn. This is often attributed to a lack of performance. Those who perform tend to stay a considerable period in the role and are probably not looking for a new position.

Care must be taken to establish any candidate's past performance, which must be supported by company-headed letters confirming the results versus targets and budgets. This is especially important when examining a candidate with short 18- to 24-month tenures in several companies in succession over a five- or ten-year period.

Every company runs an annual appraisal scheme whereby the manager agrees an overall summary of his staff member's performance. I used to ask if the candidate would be comfortable sharing with me his manager's last two annual appraisal summaries.

Most stated they would not want to disclose them. I reminded them of the implications of that refusal and how it might be interpreted against their claims of the results portrayed.

Anyone who had a good strong set of results will have an annual appraisal summary confirming this. How do you interpret a refusal to share that summary with you as the recruiting manager?

There is a prevalence among candidates of poor understanding of distributor models and distributor markets and negotiating distributor agreements that can deliver a critical mass. Refer to my earlier sections around satisfying yourself that the local person, or otherwise, who is sitting in front of you has actually done what you want him to do in this role.

I always advocate being not only thorough but also ruthless when looking at applicant details.

Applicants are human. They can and they do lie! There are usually inaccuracies in every CV I have ever read. Prior to recruitment, an up-to-date Job Description, listing the threshold and distinguishing competencies for the role, is essential. These competencies must be defined with granularity at differing progressively deeper levels of behavioural indicators to gauge and assess how strongly a candidate displays a particular competency. In my example, I have illustrated this as Level 1 through to Level 5 for one competency.

It is essential to be clear and to always remember there is an immense difference between a role that requires delivery of sales within defined costs (a sales manager role) and a P&L General Manager role accountable for delivering sales, costs, margin, and profit targets.

The latter can do the former role. The former may not be able to do the latter role.

The latter role is a much bigger role that carries a higher remuneration package and has greater latitude and freedom to operate. However, it also carries a much higher financial risk to the business if targets are not delivered consistently year-on-year.

Any candidate can be a one- or two-year wonder. You need a candidate that can deliver consistently over five or more years and has a rounded blend of skills and experience across different roles that enables him/her to wear several hats interchangeably – such as sales manager, marketing manager, HR Manager, forecasting and logistics manager, for example.

Young pelvic thrusters are unlikely to have the complete and complex blend of skills and experience to deliver the critical mass over a five-year period. Consider the mature candidate in their forties for this blend of skills and experience.

I recommend that your recruitment process assesses for aptitude as well as personality using psychometric tests. There is merit in arbitrarily setting a percentile minimum that candidates need to satisfy for both numerical and verbal critical reasoning tests. Lack of cognitive bandwidth and brain 'processing power' leads to failure in so many candidates.

The recruitment process should also explore results delivery against targets and budgets.

Candidates that cannot produce their results versus targets but speak of 'growth' and 'launched three new products in five years' are usually a waste of time. This is because these examples do not show how well they performed. For example, 8% growth appears good at face value. But if the target was 12%, it is poor performance. And having launched three new products in five years is meaningless. They could all have been disastrous and failed to meet sales and market share targets.

A good recruitment process goes beyond the classic one-hour first interview and the 45-minute second interview where candidates can present a mask of what they want you to see. It is essential to get behind the mask they present using psychometric tests, interpreting them accurately and placing the results in context versus other similar roles and job holders in the company or the industry and building in practical case studies and presentations required of the candidates. Such a mix of elements in the process has a better chance of identifying a strong candidate – or identifying a mis-fit candidate to be avoided.

Never appoint or recruit *"the best of a bad bunch of inadequate candidates."* You will likely regret it very quickly and your credibility as a senior executive able to pick winners will go crashing through the floor.

CHAPTER 9
Conclusion and Reflections

In setting out to write this book, I was particularly keen to avoid textbook theories, focusing instead on sharing my real-life experience with examples from both a corporate life as a P&L holder in the role of Territory Director Africa at AstraZeneca and as a consultant through my own consulting company supporting global pharmaceutical companies in Africa to address their pain points and issues in these export markets. Some wanted help with how to set out on an international expansion journey. Others had suffered several years of pain, being unable to deliver their budget numbers and unable to attain a critical mass even after swallowing up all the costs of the investments made throughout that time.

I sincerely hope that readers will embrace the fact that the book has been liberally populated with practical examples, seeing their value, and allowing them to inform their own decision making. After all, my aim throughout all of this has been to give readers a high-quality awareness of how to deliver the numbers and attain a critical mass without making the mistakes I have seen being made, so often and by so many.

I had observed that for so many export sales and international scale-ups, clients faced one challenging issue that formed an Achilles Heel of international sales and scaleup.

That Achilles Heel is how to achieve a scalable critical mass within five years of investment for growth. I noticed that companies were particularly good at investing their monies into creating export sales across several clusters of countries. Some investment decisions were more hurried than others, and less well thought out. They failed to appreciate the complexities and risks to be managed versus the capabilities of the company.

When I examined these sales and business performances more closely, several things stood out:

1. None of them had defined and committed to delivering a critical mass within five years of investment and also after ten years of investment.

2. Forecasts were easily forgotten and rarely revisited for results versus the business case. Seniors were simply never held to account for those mediocre results versus the business case they had presented. This is a big mistake!

3. Very few had made reliable or accurate projections to evaluate the realisable size of the business opportunities before committing to regulatory submissions. Often these two activities were in parallel. This is wholly wrong and inappropriate.

4. Of those that had made an 'investment case', dictating that if they received 'x' funds over five years, they would deliver 'y' sales at 'z' profit, none of them went on to deliver those values. Instead, they consumed the investment monies (and more)!

The message was clear:

"Entering markets is easy. The difficulty is delivering the critical mass of business commensurate to the size of the opportunities versus the investment funds released by the senior Executive Board."

In other words, delivering the promises and the numbers made to the Executive Board eluded most job holders charged with and accountable for the international expansion and scaleup.

The typical picture of a senior international sales and business development role started to evolve in my mind as that of someone who could consume vast sums of investment cash and make lots of promises to his seniors about what will be delivered in terms of numbers but then go on consistently to fail to deliver those numbers for income and profit, time and time again.

Some of these seniors stayed on in the role, consistently under-performing and failing to deliver their promises, creating a bigger issue in the process. Their Executive Boards varied with respect to tolerance of such under-performance, with some removing such disasters very quickly while others allowed the under-performance to continue for several years.

Despite this varying degree of tolerance by senior Executive Boards, it was clearly expressed that what seniors required was a job holder that delivered successful results year-on-year over successive years. In other words, a consistent record of accomplishment and delivery of those numbers. Such a person became as scarce as finding hen's teeth!

So, I decided to share my experiences of what goes wrong, why it happens and what some of these solutions might look like. As you read my book, picture your current person and models, and compare and contrast them to the examples in this book. Learn to see where the gaps are between my success factors and your inability to deliver success and identify those factors that have proved repeatedly to disappoint you as a job holder or a senior Executive Board member.

So often, failure to achieve a critical mass can be attributed to two or all of the following:

1. Wrong model versus expectations.

2. Wrong partner that is a poor fit and will not deliver the expectations.

3. Wrong person in the job that lacks the skills and experience required to succeed.

In my experience, it was usually a combination of all three that led to a disappointing performance. Never one factor. Always two or all three factors.

Was it any wonder then that my mantra was born:

> *"The plains of Sub-Saharan Africa are littered with the corpses of corporate heroes who bravely went in declaring them to be lands*

of opportunity. They were excited to meet the challenges set by them, only to find that they needed to beat a hasty retreat within two years, admitting defeat with a career that was quickly derailing and leading towards an enforced exit from the company."

I will elaborate on those three attributes in failure to achieve a critical mass...

Wrong Model

The lowest order of entry is that of an agency model. An agency model may generate some sales for you but cannot achieve critical mass. This is because it is a passive model. You appoint an agent in a country who looks for customers for you and introduces you to those customers, for which he receives a success fee or commission based on the sales value to those customers. Those customers are your customers, not those of the agent. An agency model cannot achieve a critical mass because it is passive and, as you will have read in the chapter of go-to-market models and options, you have no control over the agent nor his efforts in the market.

Outside of an agency agreement, there are four distributor models and three legal affiliate models. The distributor models vary on costs to operate them and therefore the control you the principal will have over the efforts in the market. The models in order of increasing costs are:

- Hamburger
- Hamburger Plus
- Basic Scientific Office and
- Premium Scientific Office

Neither the Hamburger nor the Hamburger Plus model stands any chance of you achieving critical mass. Both these models are used by generics companies with tight margins and little available cost investment. As a model akin to a market trader model, both of these Hamburger models generate small value business for these companies at little cost.

The only model that stands a chance of achieving critical mass is the Premium Scientific Office Model, though very few principals will set up using this model. Instead, they will choose the Basic Scientific Office model as their preference, citing costs. This makes no sense to me, as I will explain.

The reason the Premium Scientific Model is the only one that stands a chance of achieving critical mass versus the Basic Model is that the Premium Model gives control over sales and marketing to you, the principal. In creating a Premium Scientific Model, you split out the distributor's supply-side roles of supply, distribution, logistics, regulatory and pharmacovigilance from the demand-creating sales and marketing and promotion activities.

In the basic model, you leave it all with the distributor, paying all the costs. In the premium model, you still pay all the costs, but you have control over the demand-creating activities that you do not have in the basic model. So why choose the Basic model, citing the costs?

Too often, companies make the mistake of being supply-focused. They want to push products for the distributor to buy. They try to appoint several distributors on whom they can 'push' an initial stockholding. This generates an invoiced sale. To understand this, you need to be aware that a sale is created when an invoice is raised, not when the cash is collected.

Whilst these distributors may take an initial stockholding, they will not order more if they do not sell the stock. This 'push' model is a recipe for failure and is flawed on several fronts.

Why is it flawed you ask?

The 'push' model is flawed because:

1. The model of starting with distributors (supply) does not address the demand side of the equation.

2. Having more distributors does not create more sales. It just means that whatever demand there is for your products is shared among several distributors.

3. Demand <u>always</u> precedes supply!

To achieve a critical mass, you need to first devise and then execute impeccably, a strategy that can create demand to deliver the value of that critical mass. Even if there is some form of coherent strategy, the execution is flawed on so many fronts. I can recall so many clients who would never dream of admitting they lacked such strategy. So, if the results were disappointing, then its execution must be flawed if they believed the strategy to be a coherent one.

In the case of pharmaceuticals, this demand-creation is to create prescriptions for your brands. Creating prescriptions is not easy. It means finding patients for your prescription drugs. And that is difficult and often rate-limiting for your market penetration. If your prices are affordable to a narrow group, your critical mass is dependent on the size of that group. I refer to this as 'the eligible population' within the country rather than the total population as I explain further on.

My clients had often made the mistake of massive expansion in headcount – both in head-office staff roles as well as field force sales reps. They passionately believed that "might is right" and that if we create more noise than the competition, we will truly succeed.

That idea is completely FALSE. More noise does not equate necessarily to more sales in distributor or partnership markets. It is not noise that succeeds. It is the ability to find and persuade customers to buy your products. Often, these customers are a fraction of the population size, as I will now explain.

The size of the customer group is dependent on price. The wealthy growth segment of the middle classes may be only 5-10% of the population. The poorer rest of the population would need a price drop of maybe 80% to bring them into your reach – but that price may be a loss-making price or not acceptable for the margin. These poorest customers are often described as "base of the pyramid" customers.

And therein lies a flaw in some clients – a strategy that straddles both the wealthy middle classes (perhaps 5-10% of the population) and the base of the pyramid customers. Be clear, that is not strategy. It is indecision. I describe such seniors and their Boards as *"they used to be indecisive, but now they are not so sure."*

Why is it important to define the patient segment with which you will actively work?

Because this choice of patient segment may dictate the channel you need to succeed in. For the wealthy 5-10% they will be private and self-funded or supported by private insurance. The base of the pyramid customers are served by Government through lowest cost tenders in Government Hospitals and Medical Centres. Such tenders are awarded to the cheapest generics from China and India in the pharmaceutical industry. Innovator R&D companies just struggle to compete due to their higher cost of goods. The quality argument in Government tenders is a publicity stunt. In reality, it is cost, and volume driven. The private out-of-pocket payment is high price/small volume whereas the Government channel is low price/high volume.

To create demand costs money. You need sales reps. They need cars (costly). They need a promotional marketing budget. Creating demand carries inherent risks. Risks such as you and/or your distributor lacking the skills and the time dedicated to creating demand. So, you consume cash from the investments but fail to deliver the sales budget because you failed to create demand to a level that can meet the critical mass target. And that leads to the career derailment of so many senior executives in international sales.

No senior Executive Board will tolerate a situation where you repeatedly consume the cash but fail to deliver the sales. They are even less tolerant if you are accountable for the P&L because, in a P&L, it is possible to deliver sales but fail to deliver the bottom-line profit.

Sometimes clients state that they were unable to deliver their numbers because of overstocks at the distributor(s). This resulted in them not ordering fresh stocks as they had remarkably high stockholding on their shelves already.

Any senior executive or Executive Board who accepts that argument for non-delivery is fooling himself and does not know this business well enough to be in charge of running it!

Why? Because there is no such thing as "overstocks".

EITHER

You failed to create the demand to forecast, leaving the distributor with stocks that he needed to use up before he would order more stock because of YOUR failure in the marketing of your products. My staff knew me well enough to learn that at business reviews, they could not recite "overstocks" because I would recite another mantra (which I will share a little later).

OR

You pushed abnormally high stocks onto the distributor to raise fake invoiced sales and then reversed them after the financial reporting was over. In this case, this is a serious compliance breach and artificial reporting of sales.

This is why another mantra was born with my teams and my clients:

"There is no such thing as overstocks, but there is a lack of demand to forecast and budget that you failed to create."

Bizarrely, some seniors will not pay a distributor for the marketing and sales costs to create demand. Or they may pay a negligible contribution to marketing expenses. To create the demand that is needed, they will ask the distributor to generate demand by employing reps funded out of his selling margin.

This model is prevalent among generic (copycat) manufactured products sold cheaply after patents have expired. Is it any wonder their sales are remarkably low in value versus the size of the opportunity? But their absence of costs likely makes these figures acceptable to these small generic's companies. Such companies probably do not set a critical mass target to be delivered within five years as many have a market trader mentally counting the day's takings and being satisfied with that each day.

In addition to four distributor models, there are three possible legal affiliate models. I never advise having a legal affiliate as a go-to-market model from the beginning. Some remarkable fools will tell you (as they have told me) that having a legal affiliate can *"move the needle"*.

Anyone who tells you this is revealing how little they understand international market models. Anyone who does take up this suggestion is too gullible for words. Hence another mantra: *"They don't know what they don't know."*

The only model that can *"move the needle"* is demand creation and that too has to be with a partner that can purchase and supply the volumes versus the demand opportunity. That partner must have the liquidity to pay you for such volumes.

Once critical mass has been achieved, the consideration for a legal affiliate is understandable but not always justified. At critical mass, you must be clear that, if you are considering whether to set up a legal affiliate, you must ensure you can define what a legal affiliate would give you that you do not have with your current model. And you must consider the risks and costs for such features that you identify as possible benefits over and above your current model that helped you to achieve critical mass.

If you look objectively at it, it might be possible that you will not see any gain by creating a legal affiliate but only additional risks and costs.

As a reader, you may be saying to yourself that I dislike and perhaps I am even against legal affiliates, instead being a very pro-distributor go-to-market model person. I must correct any such mutterings and thoughts. I am not averse to legal affiliates. However, I have seen so many clients that were advised (insanely) by consultants to use legal affiliates as their go-to-market model from the outset, or very early on in the expansion internationally, as well as a company that created legal affiliates all over Africa at critical mass that then never managed the prior trajectory of growth with the previous Premium Scientific Office Model in those markets.

So, I urge caution, and above all, please remember that a legal affiliate does not, and cannot *"move the needle"* as some fatally flawed seniors and consultants might tell you. If I was your consultant, please ensure that you never allow me to tell you *"You don't know what you don't know"* by proposing such a statement to me about *moving the needle*.

So, where do I see a place for a legal affiliate?

There are two situations where a legal affiliate is the best-fit model from the outset, and I urge companies to think carefully if they are considering a first-entry market model as a legal entity.

I have two simple rules to be answered if you want to create a legal entity:

1. Creating a legal entity must confer a significant advantage over a distributor model. Particularly a Premium Scientific Office Model where you have control of the staff and are in total control of demand creation, but you are not legally present in the market. In other words, it must give you something commercially for your P&L that a good distributor model does not give you. This is about answering what are the extra features you get over a distributor model and do they come with additional risks that are not present in the distributor model. Define that advantage, and those additional risks and articulate them in two sentences.

2. Alternatively, creating a legal entity must remove a restrictive element present in a distributor model, such as being able to hold your product licences and appoint multiple distributors. This is about answering what a legal affiliate removes from a scientific office or distributor model and the advantage thus gained. Define that restrictive element and the benefits and articulate it in two sentences.

If you can define either or both, a legal entity is the preferred mode of market entry.

There are three basic legal affiliate models. They differ only in how the supply side of the demand/supply equation is managed. The first legal affiliate model has its own distribution and logistics operations. This is rare. To own your logistics, warehousing and distribution operation in a new market is investing in your suicide!

The most common legal affiliate model is where the affiliate contracts with an intermediary third-party warehousing and distribution logistics partner to warehouse its stocks and to supply its customers, which are primarily wholesalers. Such a logistics partner is sometimes referred to as a *'box-shifter'*. Any go-to-market model that involves the use of an 'intermediary' partner or box-shifter is adding costs and risks to your business that are entirely avoidable with a direct-to-distributor export model from your manufacturing site. This deployment of an 'intermediary' partner or 'box-shifter' is a model that I do not recommend for exports into new markets.

The model I do recommend for a legal affiliate is to partner with a distributor that manages the supply by buying your products from the manufacturing sites and selling them to his customers to meet the demand created by you in the legal affiliate. In practice, this model is not prevalent – at least across SSA where the business is run out of South Africa. The local seniors seem to prefer the 'box-shifter' model for exports into SSA out of South Africa in a model based on *"custody of supply"* but in real terms this is a Pre-Wholesale Consignment Model. I can explain why this is not a good fit model.

A wrong model is a go-to-market model trading through wholesalers, not distributors. This is often associated with a legal affiliate and using the services of a an intermediary third-party 'box-shifter' distribution and logistics partner in a Pre-Wholesale Consignment Model. This model may be appropriate for a large domestic market for a legal affiliate such as South Africa but extending it to an export model into new markets is (in my experience and my considered view) completely unnecessary and it is the wrong model that will not allow you to attain a critical mass. Your business will drown in the costs and risks arising from this model as I have explained in the section earlier in the book.

The deployment of a pre-wholesale consignment export model is often associated with a copy-and-paste model, typically from South Africa (where it is used successfully by many pharma companies for the South African market) to export markets into Sub-Saharan Africa (SSA) where it is wholly inappropriate, costly, and risky.

That brings me to the subject of wholesalers. Any go-to-market model that engages a principal (you) in directly invoicing sales to wholesalers is a recipe for disaster. Wholesalers are not distributors. But all distributors are wholesalers. In a trading model where you, as principal, supply wholesalers directly, you are the distributor. This is because you import products and engage a 'box-shifter' to provide warehousing, supply, and distribution services. In a large market (for example South Africa) many legal affiliate pharmaceutical companies use this as the trading model. It is likely to be less expensive than having one's own warehousing distribution and logistics company with a fleet of trucks and drivers. This warehousing and distribution is not a core business for a pharmaceutical company unless it has a massive business of many hundreds of millions of dollars of business to justify such a costly investment in infrastructure. The logistics partner is a "box-shifter" supplying those customers (wholesalers and clinics) that you nominate.

Hence, I say that South Africa is not a distributor market. It is a wholesaler market! Trying to expand a wholesaler market model into distributor export markets is a non-starter. This is why I say the preferred option should always be simple and direct supply to a carefully chosen distributor in each market with four to six orders placed directly with the manufacturing site. The products for export are made-to-order to avoid wastage and eliminate inventory and working capital. For international scale-up expansion and entry, my preferred supply model and the supply route are always therefore a direct distribution model every time.

Wrong Partner

Finding the right partner appears to elude so many companies. Part of the explanation may be down to the way they went about finding a distributor. Selecting partners that you met at a trade fair or congress, or symposium is not a good way to find a partner. This is because you know extraordinarily little about them, and you may be taken in by their overpowering persuasiveness that they can work wonders with your products and get you in the market in record time. However, you know nothing about who else they represent and how well they are doing in the marketplace.

Equally bad is using free or low-cost Government bodies for export trade that offer subsidised flights and introductions to distributors. Free advice is rarely good value for money. Expertise in the territories that you want to expand internationally may be poor or out-of-date, from some former senior executive who retired years ago but found a role as a freelance advisor for some government body earning some easy pocket money to top up his pension.

The free or subsidised flights take you to a market to meet an in-market advisor who will tell you very little about what you need to know and a lot about the things you do not need to know. Much of it will be general information that you could glean for yourself through internet search engines about that country. The distributors they introduce you to are likely to have come from a Yellow Pages directory or a list provided by the regulatory authorities. The latter does not recommend any one distributor over another. They state it is up to you to do your due diligence when picking a distributor to represent you in the market.

Before you think about a distributor to partner with, you must first be clear on what you want in a distributor, what you want him to do, and which model you want him to work to. This could be a Non-Exclusive Agreement only – a Basic Scientific Office where he pays for selling costs and staff out of his sales margin or you pay the staff costs and marketing costs, but he manages them or a Premium Scientific Office where you meet all those costs and the staff are under your direct control and command – or perhaps at the other end of the scale, a Hamburger Model.

So, to begin with, you need to define what your ideal distributor looks like. And for each of the criteria, you need to express how important they are in your decision-making by assigning a weight out of 100. The total of weightings across your ideal distributor criteria must total 100.

Armed with this, you need to explore each distributor and assign a score out of 5 for each criterion. The higher the score the greater the match with that criterion. Multiply the score by the weight to arrive at a total score. Pick your top 4 or maybe 5 distributors for further exploratory talks.

Factors to consider in your list of criteria might be:

- Non-competing interests are essential.
- Liquidity – can he pay you? How is he financially?
- Stockholding level. Can he and is he willing to commit to holding 12 weeks stocks, excluding goods on order?
- Is he able to work to four orders per annum or a maximum of six orders per annum in your just-in-time manufacturing operations that make goods to forecasted orders?
- Market intelligence. How well does he understand the market for your customers and the market opportunities?
- Willingness to share risks with you – for example, will he contribute to launch costs for new products or pay the initial probationary period staff costs for three months?
- Admin support. Does he have payroll and admin staff? Finance function, HR support to employ and terminate staff in compliance with local laws.
- Regulatory support and pharmacovigilance.
- Will he and can he work to your preferred go-to-market model?
- Will he work to a Non-Exclusive Agreement?
- Will he accept split product lists if any brands compete with his other principal's products, and you give competing brands to another distributor?

- How prepared is he to roll up his sleeves to get your business established or does he simply want you to do all the hard work whilst he skims a nice 25% margin from fulfilling sales orders for your brands that you generated with your investment?
- Will he work with your pricing model for in-market sales to his customers?
- How does he come across? Can you work with him and his staff?

Where clients have made a sound decision to use a distributor go-to-market model, they go on to make a big mistake with how they choose and implement such a go-to-market model in choosing the wrong partner. Some make an even bigger mistake by signing up a single distributor that is present across several countries on the basis that *"it gives us one single point of contact with the distributor instead of having to deal with several countries."*

This is an argument of no value or relevance and is a sign of gullible seniors because *"they don't know what they don't know."* You cannot deal with a single point of contact. You will HAVE to manage each on a market-by-market basis with their Head of Market multiplied by the number of markets you signed up under that one distributor basis. This leads to the same burden and challenges as if you had picked a different distributor in each market. Do not be fooled. Dealing with a pan-African or pan-Regional or pan-geographic distributor does not reduce your burden of work. It also carries severe risks and drawbacks.

A regional distributor present in several markets is never strong across all those markets he is present in, no matter how much he tries to convince you! Placing your precious brands into such a guy is akin to placing all your eggs in one basket only to find that none of them will ever hatch.

Never fall for this sleight of hand trick and bluff. You are not picking the strongest distributor against your ideal distributor criteria across all the markets where he is present. I once had an exploratory discussion with a client wanting to set up in Africa – west Africa, east Africa, and the Southern Africa cluster (Angola, Zambia, Zimbabwe), excluding South Africa. He explained that he was talking to a distributor that was present across 90% of his markets. I advised him against this selection on several fronts:

- The distributor was known to me. It was European and focused for many years on French-speaking Africa (Francophone SSA) and had expanded into Anglophone SSA. They lacked some of the understanding of Anglophone Markets versus the much greater understanding of French markets. Anglophone SSA is a much bigger opportunity and completely different to Francophone SSA.
- The move into anglophone by that French distributor was by acquisitions. The acquired distributors were not the strongest players in those markets.
- The distributor decided and proposed (sold) the market entry model and persuaded the prospect this was the best model.
- That French distributor's sales from combined Portuguese-speaking (Lusophone) and English-speaking (Anglophone) SSA was small, at around 12% of their total business over several years, meaning that they are not growing their share of the anglophone business. This suggests that they are not actually strong in these areas of Africa!
- The prospect was new to SSA and so was the distributor. That is akin to the blind leading the blind.
- I knew there were other, better, stronger-fit distributors across his markets than this pan-African distributor.

The prospect explained they were close to signing the Agreement. I told him they would regret making such a bad decision. Two years later, the Head of Africa was shown the door. I know their sales were abysmal and the choice of distributor was a major factor in that failure.

That prospect never deployed a structured approach to selecting distributors. How did they even start talking to such an outfit? It was likely that the word got out that he was wanting to expand into Africa and some of these distributors started to tout for the business. Never reveal your hand so easily. Good distributors do not need to indulge in such touting and pressure tactics to get principals to sign them up in a legal agreement.

I always advise never to explore a pan-African or pan-regional deal with a single distributor present across different markets. You are not picking the strongest player across all the markets by putting all your eggs in one basket.

Instead, I advise a structured approach with a clear list of ideal distributor criteria each given their own weightings and scores. If a pan-African or pan-Regional player scores enough to be included <u>for that one market</u>, then evaluate further and if they are the best fit, then proceed to sign them up as your distributor for that ONE market, not pan-regional or pan-Africa.

The message of these reflections for distributors is to ALWAYS choose a distributor on a market-by-market basis AFTER you decide the market and the go-to-market model for each market or country. When you know the model that you want to work with, disregard anyone that tries to persuade you to use a different model and only talk to those prepared to work with your model – never the other way around! Take the lead. Be clear about what it is that you want from your cognitive processes and company preparedness for risks.

Choosing the wrong partner is a very costly mistake. Signing up a distributor is quick and easy in comparison to terminating a distributor. Terminating a distributor is a costly, messy affair that can be drawn out over such a prolonged period that many businesses will never recover from this experience. I know of companies that terminated a distributor, settled with heavy payments to the terminated distributor, appointed another distributor and STILL had no better results in the country with the next distributor!

I must state explicitly that you should be clear if you are dealing with a 'real distributor' or an 'intermediary' box-shifter. These intermediary partners may label themselves as a "Master Distributor" or a "Regional Hub Distributor". On the other hand, they may avoid the label of 'distributor' altogether, describing themselves as:

- Supply chain management experts offering distribution services to your customers.

- A distribution service that allows you flexibility in setting your stockholding practices, pricing, credit and returns policies.
- End-to-end freight management and distribution services.

If they do not buy your goods and sell to their customers in the market, they are NOT a distributor. They are an 'intermediary', a 'middleman' between you and your customers.

In acting as an intermediary, they may unravel a "custody of supply" model in front of your eyes as the panacea for all your ills that you faced with the prior use of real distributors. Those ills? Running out of stocks at the distributor. But the solution to that is not to hold stocks locally on consignment.

A dangerous proposal is being made in front of your eyes that you may not realise.

In a custody of supply model, you own the stock on consignment. That means you pay (internally) within your company to be supplied stocks from your manufacturing sites. You own the stock until it is sold. You lay them up in a warehouse provided by the intermediary partner. You now carry risks of stock expiring or becoming short dated and having to be destroyed. The charges are expensive for their services and including all the different elements of charges could reach up to 20% of your invoiced value of stocks.

This box-shifter supplies wholesalers and clinics and hospitals that you specify. The invoicing may be carried out by them and maybe also the cash collection (all chargeable services). But you take the risks of those customers that were supplied defaulting on payment. The box shifter has no risks.

Far too many pharmaceuticals have not understood this model until I have come along on a client engagement and unravelled it for them. They did not know what they did not know.

When I have shown them how all these costs and charges are completely avoidable in a direct-export-to-distributor model into the market, they have had their eyes opened and wondered how on Earth they were taken in by such an intermediary model.

Beware! Intermediary models cost a lot and transfer many risks to you. Don't do it unless you can see the benefits of needlessly burning money and like to take a lot of risks.

Strange as it may sound, there are plenty of fools running these international markets.

Do not be one of them!

Wrong Person

Some companies make a recruitment mistake that just does not work out. Turns out the guy was just not up to it to deliver the ambitions and the expected critical mass. Leaving aside the critical mass (that is a destination a few years down the road), the guy could not deliver the small five annual steps of delivering the budgets!

To rub salt into the wounds, those seniors replaced the guy that did not work out with another *"impressively qualified guy"* that repeats the mistakes of the prior guy. And this can go on for several years in succession.

It seems recruiting the wrong person into the role is easier than recruiting the right person.

So why the mismatch?

My view is that there are several flawed thoughts or assumptions when seniors think about recruiting a person for international business development in these markets that are usually described as "distributor", "partner" or "partnership" markets.

Some of these flawed thoughts or assumptions might be:

- Thinking that these markets are a stepping stone along the way to developing a young pelvic thruster for a serious role in a large developed market. This young pelvic thruster could be a sales manager in a larger market needing to develop financial P&L experience or a candidate that has shown good results in an affiliate in a senior or mid-senior commercial role and needs to be assessed for potential for a GM role elsewhere in the business.

- Thinking that a candidate can learn vital skills on-the-job, such as negotiating skills, designing commercial and supply agreements, setting pricing and margin for products, understanding basic contracts for product bundled deals, such as block & volume contracts, and developing ambassador skills for the company with Government Health Ministries.

- Appointing a guy with some distributor market experience in another region in the mistaken belief that he can set up a new business in a new geography or deliver a critical mass in a new geography where a predecessor failed. Furthermore, this candidate highly likely never set this business up in another region (such as Latin America or the SE Asia markets of Cambodia, Laos, and Vietnam). Asking such a candidate to set up a new business would be a foolish mistake.

- Appointing a candidate with a poor understanding of the financial side of running a business into a P&L or General Management role in the mistaken belief that a local finance guy at the regional hub will take care of the financial side of things. That finance guy should be supporting the candidate. He does not do the financial side of the business for him as well as his other regional financial reporting duties.

In my personal view and experience, all of the above point to a candidate ill-prepared for such a responsible and accountable role. One feature of these markets is that, until they can attain a critical mass within five or more years, the cost allocated to their success is low versus the ambition of sales projections. Senior Executive Boards are quick to demand high sales growth, but they are prudent and frugal in allocating a cost level that makes this sales growth easy. They will ensure the level is set low enough to make staying inside the cost budget tight and make sure there is no surplus of cash each year.

And to compound that, the sales growth per annum very significantly exceeds cost growth. For example, my cost growth, Compound Annual Growth Rate (CAGR) over five years was set at 7% per annum. But my sales growth was set at 11% per annum and my profit growth per annum was set up at 17% to be delivered with only a cost growth of 7%!

I delivered 3% cost growth versus a budget of 7%, 18% sales growth versus a budget of 11% and 35% profit growth versus a budget of 17% per annum on my way towards achieving critical mass across my major markets.

The implication of taking a candidate to deliver impressive sales growth over five years with prudent cost growth is that there is little or no headroom to take on expensive headcounts in these markets. That implies that, if you are to stand a chance of success, if you do not have the costs to be able to recruit lots of headcounts, then the job holder needs to multi-task and be able to carry out those roles. Namely, the roles of marketing director, sales director, sales training manager, HR recruitment and selection, key account manager, pricing and market access manager, business negotiations, forecasting manager and compliance and risk-mitigation manager and so on.

So, I make the case for a more experienced senior mature candidate who will be a better fit for these roles over a young pelvic-thruster.

Thirty years or so earlier back in the 1990s, companies would deploy staff into these distributor markets that were small value business to 'get them out of the way' if for example, they were not delivering numbers as first or second line sales manager or a marketer that made an absolute disaster of a new product launch. The idea being to retain them inside the company but in roles where the potential for them to inflict damage through non-delivery was contained and manageable. Corporate seniors had remarkably less ambition for these distributor markets. They were focused on North America, Japan, and Europe which were all growing with low double-digit growth. Finding the successive waves of talent for these major markets preoccupied seniors.

Today, corporate seniors are realising that instead of these distributor markets becoming diversion routes, they are now mainstream business with cash investments and results that have to be realised and delivered. So, there is a case for suggesting that seniors now need to consider their more mature candidates that offer the blend of skills to succeed. In other words, they must consider appointing some of their most talented experienced guys into these roles rather than sending a young pelvic thruster to these markets like a lamb to slaughter.

Corporate seniors have made numerous rounds of investments only to be disappointed with the lack of delivery on results. One feature that I noticed with client work where these clients failed to achieve a critical mass was that they were 'top-heavy' in their costly office-based headcount that directly consumed funds but 'light' on customer-facing headcount that generated revenue. These top-heavy office-based staff typically consumed a huge slice of the prudent cost budget but added little or no value. The value is in customer-facing roles that directly generate demand, for which they had too few staff.

Try to consider headcount as falling into two main camps. Camp 1 is for those that consume cash but directly generate income for the company and Camp 2 is for those that consume cash and indirectly bring income and support the direct income generators. Such indirect contribution is difficult to measure and allocate to those roles.

Choose camp 2 occupiers very carefully. This is where there may be non-value adding roles that must be taken out if critical mass has not been reached.

Focus on demand-generating roles that interact with customers. Critical mass being achieved is dependent on demand creation. Think carefully about roles where the demand generation contributions are blurred or difficult to see. Let me explain with another real example.

A client has four sales reps and one field-based manager and an office-based sales manager. Sales per annum? Around $200,000! Bizarre you say? Yes. But true. In this example, either a sales manager or a field-based manager but not both was better value. And going one better, my recommendation was to have no field manager nor an office sales manager. The four reps report directly to the Country Manager, who has four reps, and the Country Manager is also the field sales manager, and his time is 80% in the field directly selling to customers and accompanying reps on sales calls and developing their selling skills and coaching them.

This equates to spending around 18 out of 22 working days per month in the field with customers and selling as well as developing the selling skills of his reps and being an ambassador for the company with Government authorities etc.

Set sales per capita targets for your sales reps. Sales per capita start low in Year 1 but each year they rise almost exponentially as your sales ambition towards critical mass rises. If you increase reps during that five-year term, the sales per capita will drop. Make sure that you set it appropriately for the new higher headcount. As an example, a prospect entered Africa with around $300k in sales from four reps and one field manager/supervisor. That meant sales per capita of $75k for the reps and, if I include the sales supervisor, it fell to $60k per capita.

I set a minimum of $500k per capita for the reps and it had to be achieved within three years. So, if I had six reps, they should generate $3m in ex-factory invoiced sales by Year 3. If I added two reps, the sales per capita fell to $375k. So, the following year or a maximum of two years, the figures needed to get to $4m to arrive back at $500k sales per capita.

Bizarre as it sounds, there are clients that do not raise sales per capita targets when they increase their sales reps. None of my managers could raise their sales rep numbers without an uplift in sales per capita to fund those extra reps.

There HAS to be a trade-off. Let's say we agree a sales target of $3m from four reps (sales per capita $750k), with gross margin of 80% ($2.4m) with a cost budget of $1.05m (35% of sales). If that manager wants two extra reps (total 6) the sales per capita drops to $500k. The new target with that sales per capita at $750k must be $4.5m by year 3 to get back to where he was prior to the two additional reps. Year 4 the sales per capita should be set at $900k meaning sales target in year 4 of $5.4m and in year 5 it must be set at $1m per capita meaning the sales target in year 5 must be set at $6m.

Now tell me, these examples are basics of sales force excellence or commercial excellence.

So why do very few set such targets and allow mediocre targets with large headcounts?

Truly baffles me. If that client has a salesforce effectiveness person or persons or maybe commercial excellence, what are they doing? Anyone with such a function that is failing to deliver results and numbers does not have salesforce or commercial excellence. So why are you keeping this non-value-adding function? Can it be downsized or removed altogether?

I had some markets where the sales per capita were $900k per rep by Year 5 from a baseline of $200k per rep. And it was delivered! Massive exponential rise in productivity per rep.

I was the commercial excellence manager, and it was built-into my role. No separate headcount. I had to do it alongside my P&L accountability. And present progress at each quarterly review.

Without such metrics, your ambitions are highly likely doomed as is your career trajectory if it is not delivered. Ambition goes hand-in-glove with critical mass. Fail to set ambition and you fail to deliver a critical mass.

To find a senior international sales and business development manager candidate that can do all of the roles and wear the many hats that are required to be worn due to not having the capacity within the budget for a high headcount, the candidate needs to have been in multiple roles for several years in each role. As I stated earlier, that usually rules out a young mid-to-late 30s pelvic thruster on a rising 'career trajectory' destined for the Board.

There is no magic age. You need to be guided by experience across several roles. At an approximation, such a candidate is unlikely to be below the early-40s in age, possibly mid-to-late 40s onwards. But of course, we cannot dictate age requirements, HR would not be happy. So, focus on time in roles across key roles that you need the candidate to have a track record of success in. There should be no candidates who have one-year-wonder stints in any roles!

Putting all these thoughts together, I think there is a case for considering the appointment of a candidate at the tail-end of a career that can be in the role for at least five or maybe even ten years (so long as he or she can deliver the budgets each year) from which they can spend a stint at a small legal affiliate elsewhere (outside of the top markets of Western Europe's five big markets, North America, Japan, and China). I call such a candidate a 'terminal appointment', whereby they finish their career with this role or spend their final few years in a small legal affiliate before taking early retirement in their late 50s or entering into their early 60s.

But the vexed question is "How do you pick a winner?" Not every mature candidate would be a good fit for these roles. There are plenty of dud mature candidates put out to grass. Believe me, I have seen plenty. Problems that a company has not been able to offload but kept alive in non-descript roles. The walking dead or career zombies.

So, "How do you pick a winner?"

I get asked this question with alarming regularity even though I am not in recruitment. But I did spend a period in HR when I was a sales training manager, and the role was moved out of the sales department to the HR department. So, I learnt quite a bit about broader general training across the company and from an HR function I learnt recruitment, selection, and how to identify talent for senior roles. I became familiar with assessment centres and developed a basic understanding of the use of psychometrics. I became a Cap-Gemini-trained facilitator and Change Agent. Those facilitation skills have come in handy more times than I can remember, designing the processes, ensuring the inclusion of all participants, and helping the group achieve consensus and agreement.

Back to that vexed question: "How do you pick a winner?"

Answer: "With great difficulty."

No one (including myself) can predict or guarantee a candidate's success in the role being recruited. There is only one guaranteed prediction in life – it has a predictability score of 1 (a score of 1 means a certain event). That event? Death!

The only way to predict a candidate's likely success in a role is <u>after</u> the candidate is appointed, by which time it is too late if you picked a bad candidate.

But when I looked at how I went about recruiting winners, I noticed how superficially companies went about the same task and then they wondered why they got it so wrong and picked a square peg for a round hole.

What do I mean by a superficial approach? Some examples to illustrate:

- No up-to-date Job Description. Often a cut and paste for a similar job in South Africa would be used for a Country Manager job in Kenya. These two jobs are chalk and cheese.
- No clarity on required competencies split out by threshold (essential to do the job) and distinguishing (competencies that define a superior performance).
- Lack of granularity in the behavioural indicators for each competency making it impossible to assess the level of competency in a candidate's responses at interview.
- Recruiting manager fails to define the job role and leaves it to HR. This is simply lazy. Only you know what you want in the job and the sort of person that you want in terms of skills and experience. You cannot let HR define these qualities. But you can expect a healthy challenge from HR on your demands and specifications. That challenge is always welcomed and indeed I had it numerous times. Sometimes we agreed on some points, and sometimes we disagreed. But I, as the senior line manager, always had the casting vote to decide the final candidate irrespective of the challenges from HR, which I always welcomed. It is a necessary challenge if nothing else to test my cognition.
- Lack of a real structured approach to test and discover candidates that best fit the profile for the job. There was a lot of reliance on a simple interview with HR and then a second interview with the recruiting line manager, with or without the HR manager. In my estimation, this approach is outdated and no longer valid for such senior roles with the business

333

challenges and risks that are to be navigated by the job holder that you are going to appoint.

So, you ask, "What did I do differently to get a better chance of picking a winner?"

I designed and adopted a process where I was at the centre, not HR. Surprised? Remember, I spent a period in the HR department. I was involved in a re-grading of my job at that time, so I learnt about writing job descriptions. What is key in the job description is that, apart from defining the responsibilities of the role and the competencies and the key results areas to be delivered, it was important to position the job from its dimensions.

How big was the job? How many people? What was the value or aspiration of the business to be achieved in five years? How much was the job determined by rules and procedures versus freedom to operate and set your work rate over having it set for you by others, and how strong a weighting was there on outputs and deliverables? In other words, determining to what extent the job was input or output focused. Business Development roles are output-focused (results delivery with hard numbers as measures and metrics) with relative freedom to operate to prospect, identify opportunities, sell, and close deals.

The more senior the role, the greater the freedom to operate rather than be bound by rules and procedures. Seniority in roles shifts the emphasis from doing to thinking. And so on. So critical thinking skills are essential in a senior international P&L role.

Therefore, with this prior HR department experience, I was uniquely placed to do this job description writing it myself and fly it past HR, who always gave me a big "agreed" reply. But if you cannot do this, you need to give all these full considerations BEFORE involving HR so that you have an adult discussion to reach an agreement for HR to translate these into the job description that they are going to write for you.

What does it take for a candidate to succeed? In my personal experience, the following are particularly important factors:

- **Coalface experience** – having done things attributable to one's efforts and results. Not the results of those under you. The last person you want is a blue-sky gazer or a belly-button gazer who spends his time picking the fluff out of his belly button. This is a candidate who did nothing and took all the credit from the work of his staff. In these roles, he is unlikely to have those staff under him until at least critical mass is achieved. He cannot operate at the coalface!

- **Problem-solving and Critical-thinking skills** – identifying the real problem and not going by how the problem appears. Getting to the root factors behind the problem. This is addressing the cause, not the symptoms and being able to identify those root factors that often are disparate and unrelated.

- **Analytical thinking** – the ability to identify the data, draw accurate conclusions and rule out assumptions based on data. The ability to challenge numbers through numerical dexterity and data.

- **Negotiation skills and experience at the coalface** – not that which was done by others in the team or the department. As an example, the candidate MUST have demonstrable examples of having negotiated high-value contracts or setting up a brand-new business from scratch. In other words, (again) demonstrable coalface experience.

- **Concern with impact** – being able to couch your words and decisions in language, choice of words, style, tone, and voice that demonstrates concern for how those messages may impact on the listeners. This is about HOW you communicate over WHAT you communicate.

- **Strong clear critical reasoning skills** – the ability to be able to understand written and spoken text for what it says and, more importantly, what it is not saying. Candidates high on this can make valid assumptions, they can rule out invalid assumptions

335

and deduce reasonable conclusions from the replies. The candidate needs a high score on critical reasoning skills to be able to author accurate reports, assimilate emails and legal documents quickly but precisely and accurately. He needs to respond through a careful choice of words that must be watertight if legally challenged by a distributor or customer or a member of staff.

- **Financial skills and numeracy.** Employing a candidate into a P&L role without sound financial understanding is a sure-fire recipe for failure. Managing a P&L is extremely demanding. Understand that from the outset. For many a sales manager, this can be a chasm too far to be traversed and they risk falling into that "Valley of Death".

Managing sales within costs (a sales manager or a marketing manager) is amazingly easy in comparison. I know because I have done both jobs – Sales Management as well as P&L holder (third-line management level). A P&L holder has additional metrics that can mean delivering sales within costs may still result in missed profit and margin targets.

If you are to pick winners, your process must be structured in such a way that you can explore these factors in each candidate. Judging by the high failure rate in recruiting candidates into these roles, my guess is that exploration of these factors was not built into the process or only superficially at best.

The process I used was very thorough and structured:

I. First sift based on CV and cover letter. Instant rejection, those candidates who:

   a. Did not do as asked. If they were asked to write a one-page summary explaining why they can move the needle and how they match the job requirement, but they did not do that, they would go no further. They had shown disregard for what was asked of them before even becoming employees. Do I want people who do not do as they are asked?

b. Fail to list their achievements across the last three roles with numbers versus targets or budgets. I am looking for a candidate with a consistent record of results delivery versus targets. I do not want to hear 12% growth. It tells me nothing about how good the candidate is. If the target was 10% then it was above target growth. But if the target growth was set at 18% it was a serious under-performance. People who talk about 'growth' in the business usually (not always) turn out to be the biggest bluffers and buffoons and are best avoided.

c. A telephone screen with borderline candidates where it looks interesting but needs further clarity before deciding whether to take it further. An example might be to clarify the 'sales growth' or launch of new products to assess how well those launches actually went.

2. The first shortlist of candidates would be around 8-12, based on their CVs and in the reply to the job ad. These first shortlisted candidates take Psychometric tests. I used Savile & Holdsworth® tests:

i. Numerical Critical Reasoning®. (Test of aptitude).
ii. Verbal Critical Reasoning®. (Test of aptitude).
iii. The Occupational Profile Questionnaire (OPQ 32)® measures personality.

We used minimum threshold norms for consideration of certain roles. For instance, we might want the fifty-fifth percentile or greater for Numerical and Verbal critical reasoning. Candidates that are a small amount under (for example at fifty-second percentile or fiftieth percentile) may not automatically be excluded. But candidates that are way under (say tenth percentile) would go no further.

3. First interview might be for 6-8 candidates. This is a one-hour behavioural-based (competency-based) interview. The candidates were informed which competencies we would be exploring with a basic definition of each competency to prepare examples and to bring their documented results and their last annual appraisal for inspection only (nothing will be retained

by us). This interview is then followed by a case study given to them at the interview. They were notified that at the interview, they will be given a case study to examine and comment on. I designed this case study to test their aptitude with data and ability to analyse complex problems, their ability to identify key issues from data and make sound reasoned deductions from the information given to them.

4. The second interview might be three or a maximum of four candidates but could be just two candidates. These candidates are given a brief to prepare and told that the next stage will not cover anything in the interview that they have had. The candidate would be informed the next stage of the process is to prepare a presentation of a total of 60 minutes including questioning. Enclosed in the invitation letter I would include a (fictitious) summary of our business in the territory listing the therapy areas and sharing fictitious past P&L or sales and costs of the major therapy areas with forward five-year projections for P&L or sales and costs for the same therapy areas. I listed fictitious assumptions. Their presentation would be on the theme of "Our business performance and challenge in this region" and they would be asked to define the three or four key issues for our business, based on the data they had received, and to list appropriate metrics to measure progress against those issues with an explanation of why these metrics are critical to business success. They would also be asked to list three or four critical actions to be taken for the business based on the data.

This second interview with its presentation tested their ability to understand their thinking and analytical/problem-solving processes specific to the challenges of our business.

They would be asked to bring the documented set of results delivery from their current and previous employers, making it clear that we wanted to see the results versus the targets set. If they had presented it at the first interview, we would want to see it again. If they failed to bring it to the first interview, but we were sufficiently interested in the candidate as a possibility, we would now confirm that they needed to bring these results as a key part of the selection process. We would make it clear that a decision could go against them without the documentary evidence, meaning we may not make an offer, or it might impact heavily on the candidate if we made an offer.

What did I mean about how the absence of data might impact or go against them? We would prefer to offer a candidate the job with the results they provided on their company-headed paper. So, such a candidate would lose out, with all other things being equal (which they rarely are).

But what if the shortlisted candidate did not or was unable to produce documentary evidence but we were impressed with the rest of the process? I would negotiate a job offer at a greatly reduced rate because we had no documentary proof of the results. I would make an offer with a promise to review and (based on performance meeting expectations and targets) uplift the package at six months and again at 12 months, based on continued sustained performance in the role (the second half of the year would have a higher growth figure set as target).

So, in the first year, they could have two uplifts on the package and thereafter fall into line with everyone else with an annual review. Sometimes a candidate would accept on this basis, sometimes they would refuse. If they refused, it conveyed some messages about the candidate's confidence and ability to deliver the results claimed in past employment.

As a reader, you must be asking if the candidate without documentary proof turned out to be a good choice. Well, yes and no. We usually found negative aspects of the candidate's performance at six and twelve months that meant they did not get the uplift they were expecting. Their performance was 'average' or even one standard deviation to the left in a normal or Gaussian Distribution curve. At the end of 18 months, they usually left out of their own choice to seek a better package by selling their recent big pharma experience to a smaller gullible company.

Ideally, we wanted a selected candidate to be at the right-hand side of the Gaussian Distribution curve, not the left of the modal value. With the right structure, focus and process, it became more likely we came across these 'superior performers' and tied them down with packages that any other company would bust their pay bands if they tried to poach or recruit them. Once on the corporate treadmill, I managed them in a tight but flexible sympathetic coaching manner to drive a higher performance so that they never became complacent.

Very few left me to better the package of the role they held with me. Some left because they struggled to maintain that consistent results delivery I demanded. They wanted an easier ride and were prepared to accept a similar (lesser) package for that privilege.

If we were not satisfied with any of the candidates, we did not recruit.

I passionately believe that one should never take the best of a bad slate of candidates. I had to be satisfied beyond reasonable doubt that we had a candidate whom we could offer the job to that could deliver critical mass in five years, demonstrating his aptitude, and personality through the recruitment processes for these elements. Remember, my results depended on the sum of the staff under me to deliver their share of results. I could not afford to carry a poor performer in such critical roles.

We needed people who could demonstrate their ability through results – supported and validated by evidence. Results delivery was at the top of the list. But so was 'how' they were achieving those results. They needed to show an ability to work with and through people and to take people with them. They needed that blend of skills that put them in that minority box of being good with both people and being good with things.

Too many mistakes happen in recruitment and selection when there is a lack of such a structured approach. But, again, I stress that, even with the rigour of the approach, there are no guarantees. But you reduce your risk significantly with such a joined-up, structured approach.

On the vexed question of local versus ex-pat and location (in the market or outside the market), it really does not matter a jot. Recruit for skills, experience, and demonstrable track record of results versus targets supported by company-headed documents. Recruit candidates with mobility that can spend time in the market. And above all, ensure that the candidate has actually done the things that you need him to do and has actually worked at that coalface himself and not relied on others doing it for him.

This final chapter has tried to condense the entire book into a few pages. As a reader, you should be aware that the challenge, as always with such a task, is deciding what to focus on and what to exclude without subtracting too much value. This final chapter is merely my thoughts recited as conclusions and reflections on having authored the book to give you a sense of a headline top-level view of the contents of the book. In attempting such a top-level view, it has been necessary to omit great swathes of details that you should not lose. Therefore, a full read is always advised and recommended if you want to get the most from this book.

All that remains for me is to give you, the reader, my best wishes for your future success. Take on board the learnings and commit to action. Without action, nothing will happen. It is down to you to make it happen. There is no luck. Just a structured, reasoned approach as to how you should go about it and a reminder that you should stick to the process. Mistakes happen when you disregard the learnings that I have shared, and when you deviate from the story into untested approaches and methodologies. Stay on the right path painted by this book and success will follow.

On the next and final page, I share my learnings and the lessons I impressed on my clients for you to remind yourself as you go about this international business.

If you want to share your successes as a result of reading this book, or you simply want to explore how I can work to support and help you as an advisor or consultant, or you want to share your success stories, please reach out to me at amit@samkoman.com.

It would be wonderful to read your success stories.

And I Leave You with These Closing Thoughts

1. People you meet will convince you everything <u>and</u> anything is possible!

2. <u>Nothing</u> is as easy as it first appears.

3. People will promise you the Earth and deliver nothing.

4. A distributor's promise (should you fall for it) can be your door to an early exit from the company.

5. Nothing happens fast in distributor markets. It always takes more time to enter the market than originally thought.

6. Regulatory activities <u>always</u> take more time than claimed.

7. Very few staff, including seniors, really understand distributor markets and their complexity – *"they simply do not know what they do not know."*

8. The casualty and fall-out rate of seniors in international distributor markets is often unusually high! *The plains of Sub-Saharan Africa are littered with the corpses of seniors.*

9. Set realistic timelines and expectations with seniors.

10. Beware anyone who uses the phrase: *"All you have to do is…"*

11. The models with the greatest chance of delivering a critical mass are based on strategies formulated on an in-depth understanding on a market-by-market basis and being in control of demand-creation activities.

12. Start with a blank sheet of paper. Transplanting a model from a different market or region is flawed. The dynamics vary. Understand the market-by-market dynamics.

13. Keep it lean and light up to critical mass. Invest in sales roles and define sales per capita that equate to your critical mass. Set and manage ambitious sales productivity and delivery.

14. Begin with the demand side in the demand/supply equation. Never the other way around.

15. Demand always precedes supply. Demand creates critical mass. Get the demand right, and sales follow – but only if the distributor has the liquidity to pay you.

16. Pan-regional or pan-continental and multiple distributors <u>do not</u> drive sales.

17. Wholesalers are not distributors, but all distributors are wholesalers.

18. Your go-to-market model should be a distributor model, not a wholesaler model through the use of an intermediary partner or box-shifter in a custody of supply (consignment) model.

19. When you feel optimism; think of Rule 2!

20. When you feel pessimism; think of Rule 1!